SMOKE JUMPER, MOON PILOT

MOON PILOT

The Remarkable Life of
Apollo 14 Astronaut
Stuart Roosa

SMOKE JUMPER, MOON PILOT

The Remarkable Life of
Apollo 14 Astronaut
Stuart Roosa

Willie G. Moseley

Foreword by Apollo 16 Moonwalker Charlie Duke

Acclaim Press
MORLEY, MISSOURI

Acclaim Press
— Your Next Great Book —
P.O. Box 238
Morley, MO 63767
(573) 472-9800
www.acclaimpress.com

Book and Cover Design: Tiffany Glastetter

Library of Congress has catalogued the hardcover edition as:

Moseley, Willie G.
Smoke Jumper, Moon Pilot: The Remarkable Life of Apollo 14 Astronaut Stuart A. Roosa / by Willie G. Moseley.
    p. cm.
  Includes bibliographical references and index.
  ISBN-13: 978-1-935001-76-8 (alk. paper)
  ISBN-10: 1-935001-76-0 (alk. paper)
  1. Roosa, Stuart A. (Stuart Allen), 1933-1994. 2. Astronauts--United States--Biography. I. Title.
  TL789.85.A4M67 2011
  629.450092--dc23
  [B]
                                        2011017000

_____

First Paperback Edition, Printed 2021
ISBN: 978-956027-07-5 | 1-956027-07-6

Printed in the United States of America
10 9 8 7 6 5 4 3 2 1

CONTENTS

This is for the Missus.

FOREWORD

This book is about the life of one of the most outstanding men of my generation. This is the story of Stu Roosa, and he was my best friend.

I first met Stu in the summer of 1964 at Edwards Air Force Base, California. We had both been selected to enter what was then called the USAF Aerospace Research Pilot School (ARPS), in the class of 64C. Stu arrived with his wife, Joan, and his four children while I was there with my wife, Dotty. Our Southern traditions began to bond us together very quickly.

We had arrived about a month before our class was to start, so Stu and I volunteered to work in Base Operations flying courier missions and other duties. During our flights together, we were able to get to know one another, and it became evident to me that we would become very close friends. Stu was one of the most likable guys I had ever met. It was also apparent that Stu was a very sharp pilot.

As the year progressed, Stu and I became even closer. Stu was easier to get to know than just about anyone I had ever met. He had a good sense of humor, and we both loved the outdoors. I was fascinated with Stu's smoke jumping stories.

It also became obvious to me that Stu would be one of our top graduates, if not the top. With his engineering degree, he easily mastered the academic side of ARPS. His flying skills were superb. He was very focused as a pilot, as he was thorough in planning a flight, and superior in execution.

I loved to compete with Stu. I learned a lot from him over our year together at ARPS, and even though we were competing, he was always ready to help out a fellow classmate.

During the year at Edwards, the Roosa and Duke families also became very close. That friendship strengthened over the years, as we served together as astronauts, and after NASA, when we moved on to other careers.

Stu had a deep love for Joan and his children. Though we worked hard, Stu was a devoted husband and father. The Roosa family was one of the closest families that we have ever known. What an example they gave everyone. To them, there was nothing more important than the love of family and of country. They were all patriots.

Shortly after we graduated from ARPS, we both volunteered for the NASA astronaut program. We were selected, and started our training in 1966. Stu and I called ourselves the "Dynamic Duo" of the Astronaut Office. When Stu was selected to be the Command Module Pilot on Apollo 14, I was very pleased. NASA had made a good choice. Stu was as focused as ever on his job, and he had continued to hone his flying skills so the Command Module was in capable hands. We cheered as we welcomed them home.

We each left NASA after more than ten years as astronauts, and started our business careers. Stu took his talents as a pilot and used them to develop a very successful business. His ability to focus, his attention to detail, his work ethic, and his love of people insured such success.

When he died unexpectedly, I lost a best friend. As Stu Roosa inspired me, may he inspire you to reach for the Moon!

Charlie Duke
Lunar Module Pilot
Apollo 16

SMOKE JUMPER, MOON PILOT

The Remarkable Life of
Apollo 14 Astronaut
Stuart Roosa

CHILDHOOD, CLAREMORE

The Earliest Days

A Roosa family legend recounts that around 1914, after Dewey Roosa became a young man capable of making his own decisions, he left a New York mill town located in an area of the state where family members had lived for over 200 years, pedaling as fast as he could on a bicycle.

The Roosa name and heritage is Dutch. The earliest Roosas to come to America had done so in 1660, settling into the upstate New York area, where Dewey was born on November 24, 1898. Apparently, Dewey decided he did not want to live, work and die in the same small town as previous generations had done.

He headed west.

In 1917, Dewey was living in Ohio, and joined the Army. While he did not participate in combat during World War I, he served in the Army of Occupation in Germany following the signing of the armistice.

It was while he was in the Army that Roosa learned the skills that he would utilize in his post-service career as a surveyor in the Army Corps of Engineers in the 1920s and 1930s. In those days, the lack of sophisticated equipment meant that such a job had a very migratory lifestyle, and Dewey's travels took him all across the country.

In the late Twenties, he was assigned to survey the new dam at the Oologah Lake project, located on the Verdigris River in northeast Oklahoma. A small town with the same name as the lake was located nearby. Town, lake and dam were all named for a Cherokee Indian chief, and the English translation of the moniker is "Dark Cloud."

Most of Oologah Lake's 49 square miles of surface area is located in Rogers County, and its county seat, Claremore, is located on historic U.S. Highway Route 66 about ten miles southwest of Oologah. Oklahoma's second-largest city, Tulsa, is approximately 28 miles southeast of Claremore.

American humorist Will Rogers had been born on a ranch just east of Oologah, but he would claim Claremore as his hometown, and Claremore would reciprocate with the same claim.

Dewey resided at a boarding house in Claremore while working on the Oologah Dam survey project. He met a petite and pretty young woman of French heritage named Lorine DeLozier, who was working at the house for her aunt, who was the proprietor.

Dewey was 30 when he met Lorine, who was 19, having been born on June 3, 1909. He was smitten, and she was also apparently immediately entranced by the handsome, square-jawed surveyor, because a romance quickly developed, and the couple eloped just a few weeks after they had met, marrying on March 27, 1929. Once they were husband and wife, Lorine traveled with Dewey in his transient occupation. Dewey was described as the quieter and more thoughtful of the couple, while Lorine was more gregarious.

Their first son, Daniel Dewey Roosa, was born on September 28, 1931, in Casper, Wyoming. He would be known by his nickname, Danny.

The family was residing in Durango, Colorado when their second son, Stuart Allen Roosa, was born on August 16, 1933. The red hair that distinguished Dewey and Lorine's sons came from her side of the family. The younger boy's nickname was Stu.

It was said that the family remained in Durango only for the duration of Lorine's recuperation from childbirth before they relocated elsewhere on yet another surveying job. Danny and Stuart lived in numerous locales during their first years, and if Lorine accompanied Dewey into the woods on one of his surveying trips into a remote area, she would often tether her toddlers to a tree, as the woods were so thick that the youngsters might never be found if they wandered off.

At one point, Dewey even surveyed part of Highway 1 in Alaska, and Lorine and the two boys accompanied him on the rugged assignment. While there, they lived in primitive structures that were a type of adobe hut, migrating from one to another. On one occasion, one of the huts in which the family was residing began to collapse; Lorine grabbed both children and rushed outside as it was coming down.

Ultimately, Lorine and Dewey agreed that a family "base" would be needed when the boys reached school age, and they moved to the Claremore area in the early Forties to put down roots. Dewey would still travel extensively, but the Roosas now had a permanent home, and the boys would have what would hopefully prove to be a normal childhood.

The Roosas started up a chicken farm just outside of Claremore. Dewey had visions of developing chicken farms on a large basis, and a large sign that said "Roosa Poultry Farm" was installed by the road in front of the family's residence.

Dewey's background motivated him to build a tornado shelter (with proper drainage) in the rural location. The shelter was large enough to accommodate the family and several neighbors. That facility may have figured into the naming of "Cyclone," a pet donkey that Stu acquired.

The Roosas did not have indoor plumbing until the family moved into Claremore when Stu was in high school. When they were living in the country, a washtub would be filled in the kitchen for baths. Being the youngest, Stu had to bathe last.

The boys began attending grade school at the Justus School, located east of Claremore on State Highway 20 (and within walking distance of the Roosa home). Danny and Stu were tough, independent kids, possibly because of the unique lifestyle they had experienced before the Roosas settled into the Claremore area.

———

Roosa's longtime friend, Jimmie Dollard, doesn't consider Claremore to originally have been a town in the "greater Tulsa area," but admits that in modern times, his hometown would probably be considered a "commuter community" for residents who drive to work each weekday in the Sooner State's second largest city.

"I was born there during the Depression," the retired technical engineer recounted. "It was just a dinky little country town, and it was a poor town, but its claim to fame is that it was the home of Will Rogers. He wrote for *The Claremore Progress*, the local paper, for years."

Another longtime friend of Stu's was Clarence Wheatley, who recalled, "I was attending second grade school at Justus—a little country three-room schoolhouse, when Stuart arrived after the start of the school year. The teacher was Mrs. Thomas, and I was somewhat of the teacher's pet…(so she) assigned me the duty of introducing Stuart and showing him around. From that day forward, we became the best of friends."

Stu's academic prowess was obvious even at that young age, as Wheatley noted, "We all noticed that Stuart could read much faster than anyone else in our class."

Justus School records indicate that Stuart had a perfect 4.0 grade average. Former classmates such as Harley Swan recalled playing softball games with Roosa on Sunday afternoons. Stu had also begun to take a serious interest in hunting, which had been originally nurtured by the times he had spent outdoors while his family traveled on surveying trips.

Lorine would eventually work at Montgomery Ward's in Claremore, as would Danny, when he became old enough to handle employment.

———

World War II didn't reach into Claremore and the surrounding area all that much, but the town contributed its share of volunteers.

And Stuart Roosa's "epiphany" regarding flying happened shortly after the war had ended. He was out in a field near his house, when suddenly, several P-38 "Lightning" fighter planes roared overhead. The unique twin-engine, twin-tailed aircraft had become a frontline fighter during the war, and their noisy promenade fascinated the twelve-year old boy.

Later, Stu spotted the pilots of the P-38s in downtown Claremore. They were wearing leather flight jackets and had a confident countenance that was almost a swagger.

The sight and sound of that flyover, as well as spotting the pilots in public, was a personally encaustic experience for Stu. In addition to his hunting activities, he also began to develop an interest in aircraft. He bought inexpensive models and assembled them, suspending them on strings from the ceiling of his bedroom.

High School Times

Jimmie Dollard met Stu Roosa in junior high school.

"We got together because of quail hunting, oddly enough," Dollard recalled. "We both found it fascinating, and we continued to hunt through high school—it was his after-school passion, and he would take along his Cocker Spaniel, Skippy, which he taught to retrieve. His reflexes were incredible, and I think his coordination and reaction time foretold his future as a hot jet pilot. He was the quickest shot I ever saw. Believe it or not, he used a bolt-action 20-gauge (shotgun), and he usually had a 'double' down before I got off a single shot with my pump (-action shotgun)!"

Corroboration of Roosa's abilities came from Wheatley:

"Stuart had allergies, and always carried a handkerchief in his left front pocket, but he had excellent hand-eye coordination. There was a punching bag that he could really make 'sing,' and he was a good shot when he was bird hunting."

———

Dollard, Roosa and Wheatley had a mutual friend named Tommy Towne. The four boys were all in the same class at Claremore High School, and would ultimately become almost inseparable throughout their time in the small town.

In addition to hunting together, Roosa and Dollard double-dated as well. While they went out with girls often, and Roosa had girlfriends at times, there was never a relationship for him that evolved into a serious romance that included allusions to a possible permanent commitment.

16

Roosa, Dollard, Wheatley and Towne would pal around for the duration of their high school years, passing the time like standard American teenagers of that era. The quartet would cruise up and down the main street of Claremore (sometimes until the early morning hours), whenever one of the foursome was able to borrow a parent's car or could afford to buy a near-junker, as cars were not particularly common in that locale and in such times. One gag that the boys would pull more than once was to shine a spotlight on cars sitting in parks, trying to make the couples therein think the pranksters were actually the police.

Still, Dollard said that what the group had in common was a "straight arrow" attitude. The foursome was fun-loving, but sensible:

"You know that old saying that goes 'We don't smoke, we don't chew, and we don't go with girls that do'? Well, that pretty much described us. I don't think any of the four of us ever took a drink while we were in high school...and as far as I know, Stuart never smoked."

While he was in good physical shape, and fared well in "pickup" games of basketball and volleyball, Roosa did not participate in the high school's organized sports programs.

He did, however, become a member of the Civil Air Patrol (CAP), further nurturing his interest in flying. Dollard, also a CAP member, estimated that one-fourth of their class joined the auxiliary flying organization.

"We'd go out to the local airport," said Dollard. "The highlight, of course, was when we would go on flights. There were a couple of old World War II planes out there as well—a B-17 and a trainer; I believe it was a T-32. Stuart loved to get in those, and even though he didn't fly them himself, those planes succeeded in motivating him even more regarding engineering and flying."

Dollard recalled that during their senior year, he and Roosa took their first airplane rides in a single-engine, Stinson L-5 trainer that the government had donated to the local CAP group. Moreover, Roosa enjoyed fantasizing about flying while sitting in a non-working Link trainer, which was a primitive, airplane-shaped "simulator," although that term wasn't applied to the Link trainer. There was also a North American T-6 "Texan" trainer that was on display at the Claremore airport, and Stu would sit in its cockpit as well.

Wheatley added that while in high school, Roosa "...read a series of books about a World War II fighter pilot...I can't remember the series, but they were small, pocket-type books, at least ten or fifteen of them."

—⁓—

Dollard recalled that Stu had a "burning desire" to be an engineer as far back as eighth grade, and talked about his aspirations often. The CAP experiences simply motivated Roosa to excel even more in math and science.

The greatest academic influence on Roosa was mathematics teacher Miss Esther Gassett, who, according to Dollard, "…insisted on straight A's, and groomed us for math contests at state colleges. Stuart led some of the math and physics teams."

Miss Gassett's expectation was that Claremore's teams could and should win as many awards in such competitions as the other schools in the state *combined*, and such goals were usually attained.

Former Claremore High School classmate Donna Lantow Fettig recalled a geometry class taught by the legendary mathematics teacher:

"It amazed me when Stuart asked Miss Esther Gassett for additional problems, because he was enjoying them. He loved to learn, obviously. Claremore High School was very fortunate to have such an outstanding math teacher. This undoubtedly helped Stuart immensely."

"She was a mentor like none other," Dollard said of Gassett. "An absolute disciplinarian; I think she was of German heritage. She took good students under her wing; she would take us to her house after school or at night, and drill us in math, to prepare for the competitions at (the University of) Oklahoma and Oklahoma A&M. She would work us very, very hard, to the point that we pretty much knew in advance what we could expect. Both of those schools would have 'meets' in the spring, and were trying to attract good students."

Roosa's scholastic efforts garnered praise from another teacher, Dorothy McKeever, whose husband was principal of Claremore High School. Mrs. McKeever taught Stuart eleventh grade English, and recounted, "He was a terrific student; very quiet, but clever. A real joy to work with."

On a field trip during their senior year to tour the dam at Grand Lake O' the Cherokees, another large lake east of Oologah Lake, Roosa emphasized his engineering goals by telling Dollard, "Someday I want my name to be on a dam like this."

Another talent in which both Roosa boys excelled was woodworking. Danny won a state championship, and Stu, who loved working with a lathe, won the same championship the next two years in a row. The younger boy would kid his older sibling about having won the event twice.

—–∿∿–—

As he matured as a teenager, Stu developed a love for what was marketed as country music in such times, particularly songs that conjured up images of the wide-open spaces of the West. He did not play a musical instrument, and was not a particularly good singer ("He was one of the few I knew who would sing worse than I did, and I was awful," Dollard chuckled).

Most music fans in the Claremore area, including Roosa and friends, garnered most of their musical entertainment from the radio. The record business was in a period of transition, as fragile 78 rpm discs surrendered the market to 45 rpm "singles" and 33 1/3 rpm albums, but the Roosas didn't own a record player.

The Roosas did own a radio, however, and Stu would often sit in the living room on Saturday nights, pulling cockleburs from Skippy's fur while listening to the Grand Ole Opry in Nashville, broadcast by the powerful WSM radio station.

Whenever Roosa, Dollard, Wheatley, and Towne were cruising in a car, Stu made sure the radio was tuned to a country station. He preferred songs with lyrics instead of instrumentals, and liked some of Hank Williams' material.

His favorite song of all time was a 1950 hit called "Cry of the Wild Goose," written by Terry Gilkyson, and popularized by Frankie Laine. The lyrics allude to the freedom of a migratory bird beckoning as a kindred spirit to a human male, and there was also the implication of not settling down in a permanent relationship with a female. Most likely, Roosa felt like it referred to his own personal spirit, including exploring new frontiers. He loved to sing along with the song, albeit not particularly well, in an amateurish-but-sincere vocal competition with the golden-voiced Laine.

More than one radio station in Tulsa featured country music, and oftentimes, live music by such area stars as Leon McAuliffe and Johnnie Lee Wills could be heard.

Roosa also enjoyed funny or whimsical tunes, and would hum or sing along with those types of songs. He liked to listen to "country gospel" or powerful Christian hymns such as "Battle Hymn of the Republic" or "Onward Christian Soldiers."

Certain "pop" music hits of the day appealed to Stuart, but he did not actively seek out such music since he could not relate to it as well as certain country songs. He liked some of the recordings by Patti Page, who also had Claremore roots, and Kay Starr.

—◦◦◦—

Traditional Christianity was interesting to Roosa, and although his family did not attend church regularly, Stu began to develop a spiritual life on his own volition, and attended Claremont Baptist Church and First Christian Church. It should be noted, however, that a girl that Roosa had dated often was also a member of the latter church.

Dollard confirmed that Roosa wasn't outgoing about his personal faith, but did have religious convictions, and attended one church or the other on a regular basis.

Wheatley recalls that Roosa attended a Billy Graham "preaching event" in the seventh grade and became a follower of the famous evangelist.

———~~~———

Excelling in academics, Roosa made state honor rolls on more than one occasion. He participated in plays, including Rodgers and Hammerstein's *Oklahoma* and a three-act comedy, *Beauty and the Beef*, both staged in Roosa's senior year. He was on the staff of the school newspaper, the *Tatler*, and in his senior year, was class Vice-President; Towne was class President. Stuart was also editor of the school yearbook, the *Zebra*.

On the senior class trip to a nearby lake, Roosa and several cohorts pulled off a harmless prank, "commandeering" the excursion boat on which the students were riding. Wearing eye patches and brandishing wooden swords, the pseudo-pirates hoisted a Jolly Roger flag. Roosa would be seen wearing an eye patch in another memorable image two decades later.

The Claremore High School Class of 1951 had 51 graduates. In the senior Who's Who, Stuart Roosa was cited for his "brains."

Jimmie Dollard summed up his recollection of his school days in Claremore with Roosa by noting: "If I could use only one word to describe Stuart, it would be 'focused'—he was extremely focused on his goal of becoming an engineer, which meant he was extremely focused on his studies…but the engineering goal would shift to becoming a jet pilot once we got into college. He was even 'focused' when we were quail hunting!"

Dollard had also been motivated by a possible engineering career, and both boys determined they would attend Oklahoma A&M College, which would become Oklahoma State University in 1957. However, their mutual passion for the Western outdoors would first take them all the way to the forests near Bovil, Idaho to share a tent as U.S. Forest Service employees during the summer after they graduated, and that experience would lead to other adventures in the woods of the Pacific Northwest for the two members of Claremore High School's Class of 1951.

SMOKE JUMPER

Summer 1951, Freshman Year

"Somehow, the allure of the mountains and the forests seemed to be overwhelming for both of us," Jimmie Dollard said of his mutual decision with Roosa to work in the forests of Idaho the summer after they graduated from high school, and Dollard emphasized Roosa's enthusiasm about the outdoors from earlier years:

"Stuart's family would take a typical summer vacation, where they'd get in the car and drive out west, and he would come back all 'pumped up,' telling me about places like the Garden of the Gods, the Royal Gorge (both in Colorado), and the Grand Canyon."

Roosa loved evergreen trees, and Claremore had few to none. He told Dollard of his determination to work in the pristine woods someday.

The twosome began to seek employment in the great American outdoors, and writing to the U.S. Forest Service garnered them summer jobs at Blister Rust Control (BRC) Camp 52 in the St. Joe Forest in central Idaho. The camp was located on Feather Creek, about five miles northeast of a small community called Bovil.

Blister rust is a disease that is devastating to white/five-needle pines, and is caused by a fungus (*Cronartium ribicola*). Curiously, it cannot spread from pine tree to pine tree, but utilizes alternate host plants collectively called "ribes," exemplified by gooseberry plants and currants. An eradication program designed to eliminate such alternate hosts was in effect from 1916 to 1967.

The Civilian Conservation Corps, one of the new agencies created by President Franklin Roosevelt during the Great Depression, was also involved with blister rust control. Ultimately, the ambitious plan to annihilate ribes was unsuccessful, and government agencies later switched to a strategy of cultivating and planting hardier white pines that were blister rust-resistant.

However, it was the eradication program that brought Dollard and Roosa to the Idaho woods soon after they had graduated from high school.

Camps were set out in white pine forests in an effort to systematically eliminate ribes, which many of the workers referred to as simply "weeds." Such camps also had fire control training as part of their duties.

The temporary establishments usually had a population around 40, and workers lived in foursomes in tents. Some workers soon quit because of the isolation. At BRC Camp 52, Stu and Jimmie shared a tent with two other workers, Bob Gonia, a student at the University of Minnesota, and Dave Finney from Chicago, who was not a college student.

Nearby beaver ponds offered great trout fishing. The camp had four showers with hot water, and Dollard described the two cooks as "grandmotherly…we were their boys, and I've never had better food than that."

There were no cars at the camp where the two Oklahoma teenagers were assigned, and the last two miles of "road" to the camp were suitable for four-wheel-drive vehicles or trucks only. The camp itself had one large truck in which the workers rode to their assignments across mountain trails.

There was also no electricity at BRC Camp 52, so Roosa was unable to listen to country music on a radio. Moreover, the location was so isolated that most radio signals would have been difficult to pick up.

———ᴧᴧᴧ———

The job description of most of the BRC Camp 52 workers could be termed as manual weed control on a large scale, as areas about forty yards wide would first be marked out with strings, and were designated as "lanes." Men would pull "drag lines," about ten yards apart, between such string borders, and would then search between the drag lines, pulling out any ribe they spotted. They would then drag the lower line up 10 yards and repeat the process.

The five work days per week were eight hours long, with 30 minutes allowed for lunch, and ten-minute breaks in the morning and afternoon. A minimum of one to three acres per day were expected to be cleaned, depending on the terrain, as well as the tree and brush cover. Days that were rained out were made up on weekends.

"We walked all day, everyday," Dollard said succinctly. "I was the 'stringer' who put the string down, using a map and fixed compass readings. I had a large ball of string, like you'd find at old-fashioned hardware stores. That kind of work was preferable."

Workers had only one quart-sized canteen of water per day. Each worker packed his own lunch sack from the dining tent table for such treks. The typical daily contents of such sacks consisted of four oranges, two apples, two large sandwiches (stuffed with meat, cheese, tomatoes, lettuce, etc.), a bag of carrots and celery, two boiled eggs, and a bag of cookies or perhaps some cake. The oranges are noteworthy, as they helped overcome thirst.

Such work was tedious and boring, but Stu loved the solitude, and the opportunity to experience nature. He also loved the trout fishing near the camp.

According to the 2000 census, Bovil has a population of 305, but it was even smaller when BRC Camp 52 was stationed several miles away. The community had been a boom town during the glory days of white pine logging several decades earlier, but by the middle of the century, its large loggers' dorm was boarded up, as was another building that was reported to have been a brothel.

"All of the white pine was logged out," Dollard says of Bovil's history, "leaving only fir, spruce, and mature larch trees, which were less desirable. Then the blister rust killed all of the new white pine, so the town died."

By 1951, Bovil had only a filling station, a sundries/ice cream store, and a bar. On more than one Saturday afternoon, Roosa and Dollard would walk five miles to Bovil, buy a milkshake, and then walk back to camp.

The twosome would also walk to Bovil on Sunday mornings to attend church. Dollard admitted that while he and Stu were practitioners of the traditional-values lifestyle—and "traditional values" didn't exist as a term in such times—the primary reasons for their treks to Bovil on Sundays were to meet girls, "...and there was nothing to do in camp anyway."

—⁓—

The Oklahomans also had to participate in firefighting as well as blister rust control. They were in a "fire crew," which usually consisted of 20 to 40 men who trained together to fight forest fires when called.

Tools for fire crew members included a combination axe/mattock called a pulaski, named after Ed Pulaski, an early 1900s forest ranger who is credited with "re-inventing"/re-introducing the tool, which had originally been introduced in 1876. Fire crews also used crosscut saws and shovels, and in certain terrains, a McCloud tool (a large combination of a hoe and rake) was used.

The basic job of the crews was to dig a fire line—a trail against a fire—in order to separate the blaze from its fuel sources. They would also attempt to extinguish the fire by shoveling dirt on it. Most forest fires burn from the ground up, so stopping it at ground level will usually extinguish any higher portions of it.

The exception is the dreaded conflagration known as a "crown fire," where a blaze that is driven by high winds can quickly move from tree top to tree top. In such a scenario, firefighters on the ground were helpless, and had to wait for the wind to die down.

Fire crew members did have specialized assignments; i.e., crews were like organized sports teams—specific individuals had specific duties.

The leader marked the trail to be followed with ax marks on trees, and each crew member followed down the line, making his own nicks. Sawyers brought up the rear, removing large logs. A good crew could build a fire line in such a manner through rough terrain at nearly the pace of walking.

—m—

The first fire Roosa and Dollard fought was in July of 1951, and for all of their later firefighting experiences, that blaze was the biggest they ever battled. The crew was called out to fight a fire at a logging area; the initial fire had started other fires, and the total number of firefighters—including many crews, as well as loggers and volunteers—was estimated at approximately 1,000.

The BRC Camp 52 rode in trucks to the fire site, arriving around midnight. Working alongside more experienced firefighters in 16-hour shifts, the crew would be gone from camp ten days, without a change of clothes, and only sleeping bags for rest.

The logging operation was located at the top of a hill, and the raging fire was consuming large logs in huge piles known as "cold decks." Initial approach to the fire was deemed unsafe due to the cold deck inferno, so the firefighters watched, fascinated, as the cold decks came apart, and blazing logs rolled or tumbled end-over-end downhill.

Neophytes Dollard and Roosa figured that the huge fire might be a standard example of what they would be facing as firefighters, but their foreman quickly informed them that it was the most spectacular blaze he had seen in 30 years.

The fire crews ultimately started a fire line, working all night. They would continue working 16-hour shifts, through the nights, and would attempt to sleep in daytime, although heat and insect pests made such rest unpleasant.

One morning, Stu, Jimmie, and others had to wait while another crew felled a burning "snag" (dead tree). As it fell, the snag unexpectedly "jackknifed"—its top broke off and fell the opposite direction from the trunk, striking and killing a crew member that had worked on bringing it down.

Neither Roosa nor Dollard saw the victim, who was not from their camp. However, the incident made an indelible impression on the two teenagers about the dangers that accompany any adventures in fighting forest fires.

The fire had been basically put out in five or six days, but the crew in which Dollard and Roosa were members was assigned to mop up, which involved extinguishing any source of smoke, and going through ashes with bare hands to find "hot spots" (potential sources for re-ignition), which were opened and cooled. Such work was dirty, but a fire was not considered to be officially extinguished until mop up was completed.

About two days before their deployment to the fire was completed, the workers spied a nearby "spot fire" that had popped up across a small canyon near their location, having been generated by flying embers from the blaze they had been fighting. A plane roared overhead, and men in parachutes jumped from the plane, disappearing into the thick woods.

"We all watched that, and said 'Boy, that's really cool'," Dollard recalled.

—⁓—

Two days later, the BRC Camp 52 firefighters shipped out, tired and filthy after ten straight days of putting down a massive fire. They stopped by a Forest Ranger station to get a shower and perhaps sleep in an actual bed, but as it turned out, the "smoke jumpers" that the BRC camp workers had seen bailing out of the airplane earlier were at the same station. The aerial firefighters had used up all of the hot water, and had commandeered all of the beds.

"The 'spot fire' had been inaccessible to us because of the small canyon," Dollard recalled. "That's why the smoke jumpers had been called."

Roosa and Dollard were impressed by these rugged individuals, and determined that such duty might be a better deal if the perks included such priority luxuries as bedding and hot water. The twosome got applications to become smoke jumpers, but Dollard recalls that Roosa was somewhat reluctant.

—⁓—

Returning to the Sooner State, the Claremore graduates began their freshman year as roommates at Oklahoma A&M College in Stillwater.

Stu studied civil engineering, while Jimmie worked in general engineering. They both struggled, but made good grades. Dollard and Roosa shared some classes, so they studied together for those particular courses. Both boys also took ROTC training as part of their curriculum.

The twosome rented a room in a rooming house near the campus, and ate their meals at a boarding house down the street. Their room had a bunk bed, two desks with chairs, and a small closet. Laundry machines were located in the rooming house basement.

Perhaps not surprisingly, Roosa studied with the radio tuned to a country music station.

Neither student had a car, and seldom dated on campus, due to the intensity of their studies. They would hitchhike home to Claremore approximately every other weekend, and would date local girls.

Clarence Wheatley also attended Oklahoma A&M, and also hitch-hiked home on numerous weekends. When Roosa's parents moved to Tucson, Arizona in the middle of his freshman year, Stu often stayed at Wheatley's house on weekends he returned to Claremore after his parents' relocation to the Grand Canyon State.

—∧∧∧—

As had been the case in Claremore, Dollard and Roosa attended Baptist churches in Stillwater, as well as First Christian Church, and participated in the student organizations that churches offered.

Freshman year also provided what Dollard recalls as "…the only time Stuart ever got really mad at me, and probably for good reason."

Both students had a freshman chemistry class in a huge lecture hall at seven in the morning. The lecturer was described by Dollard as "… awful; his basic approach was to stand at a lectern and read the book to his young charges, but he got furious if anyone fell asleep. He did not take roll, and did not give pop quizzes, so I stayed in the rooming house, read the book, and did the homework during that hour. Stuart dutifully went to class."

Tests were machine-graded, and were multiple-choice. There were usually five or six possible answers for each question, containing one or two correct responses.

On the first test of the semester, Dollard noticed a statement at the top that read: "Grades will be based on right minus wrong/3." He quickly realized that when in doubt, a question should still be answered instead of being left blank, as the value of a wrong answer would be divided by three.

The test was long, and many students did not finish, but Dollard sailed through, marking answers he knew to be correct, and choosing some answer for questions where he was unsure.

Overall, the test grades were quite low, but Jimmie had garnered an A, while Stu had made a C, and most of their friends had scored even lower.

As is sometimes the case regarding scholastic examinations, many, if not most, class members had dived right into the test without paying enough attention to the details of the instructions. Dollard realized he had discovered the system, but because of his competitive nature, coupled with concern that the system would be discontinued by the instructor if too many other students found out about such a discovery, Dollard shared his secret with no one—not even Roosa.

There were four more similar tests, including the final, and all of them had a similar grading system. Once Jimmie figured out the system, he stopped attending chemistry class, and concentrated on other courses. Yet he continued to get A's—easily—while Roosa attended class and worked hard to attain decent results.

When the final exam was looming, a conscientious Dollard revealed the key to his success to Roosa, who managed to do well enough on the final to pull his final grade up. However, he stayed mad at Dollard for several days for not telling him about the secret earlier.

—◦◦◦—

Dollard would graduate from Oklahoma A&M in 1955 with a degree in Engineering.

However, he recalls his own days in Stillwater as "...an unpleasant blur to me. I had to work almost full-time, and carried a full Engineering (curriculum) load, trying to stay on the Dean's list. I had not one spare moment, from 5:30 a.m. to 1:00 a.m. I was either working or studying, and I have no vivid memories—either good or bad—of those years."

As for Roosa, his career goals began to undergo a profound change during his freshman year, as his passion for flying had steadily grown, and would ultimately overtake his passion for engineering.

Toward the end of their first year of college, the two freshmen had numerous discussions about plans for the summer to earn money for the next school year.

Roosa would have been required to attend a summer surveying camp for civil engineers in 1952 as part of the Oklahoma A&M curriculum, and he was torn between the love of the Northwest that he had experienced the previous summer, and the impending surveying camp requirement.

Dollard believes that the mandatory attendance at the camp was also an important factor in Roosa's enthusiasm for engineering ultimately being sublimated to a desire to fly, and wasn't particularly surprised when Roosa declined to sign up for surveying camp. Stu was fully aware that his chances for getting an engineering degree from Oklahoma A&M would be damaged, perhaps irreparably.

Moreover, in the back of his mind, Stu also wondered if, and how, any experience with a smoke jumping crew might also enhance his chances at a flying career.

Summer 1952

Around the same time Roosa decided to refrain from attending the summer surveying camp for engineering students, Dollard applied to the Forest Service to become a smoke jumper. Roosa didn't apply, and actually chastised Dollard for doing such.

Dollard's application was accepted, and he was directed to report to McCall, Idaho when school was out.

However, Dollard's mother had to be rushed to the hospital for an emergency operation the day before he was to leave for Idaho. He stayed in Claremore until she was out of danger, and was ultimately unable to attend smoke jumper rookie training. Now without a summer job, he contacted Roosa through Stu's parents, who were now living in Tucson.

Roosa had taken a job as a surveying helper in Sandpoint, Idaho, about 30 miles north of Coeur d'Alene, on the border with Washington State, working out of the Priest River Ranger Station. Dollard quickly joined Roosa, and got similar employment.

The basic job guidelines for Roosa and Dollard were cutting brush and holding the rod for their surveyor boss, who turned out to be an obnoxious tyrant, and had little respect or use for the "college boys" that were part of his crew. Even though they loved being back in the woods of the Northwest, Roosa and Dollard were miserable.

However, while at the Priest River Station, they both made friends with a South Dakota native named Jim Oleson, with whom they would share later alternate adventures.

Around the end of June, Roosa informed Dollard he planned to quit, observing that life was too short to work under such oppressive conditions, and the job would not advance his career. Dollard decided to quit as well, for the same reasons.

Both students were apprehensive about the future, as no income meant no college the next year, which would most likely result in their being drafted into the service due to their college deferment being discontinued.

"We hitchhiked to Missoula (Montana)," Dollard recalled, "stayed overnight with the guy we caught a ride with, and pondered our fate."

Dollard would find employment at Missoula White Pine and Sash, a local lumber mill, working the midnight shift. Roosa was determined to find some kind of job related to engineering, if possible, so the two friends parted company.

Stu would quickly land a job with the Bureau of Land Management in eastern Montana, working with a road surveying crew. He wasn't scheduled to report to work until July 9th, so he returned to Missoula the first weekend of July, to go sightseeing with Dollard. The two Oklahomans were still enamored with the West, and were determined to absorb as much of its raw beauty as possible.

Dollard recalled with a chuckle that "Hitchhiking was our standard mode of transportation; in those days, the risk to rider and driver was not like today."

That Saturday, they were picked up by an elderly Missoula couple that was going to visit the Grand Coulee Dam, an engineering and construction marvel, located on the Columbia River in Washington. The hydroelectric dam is the largest concrete structure in the United States, and the largest electricity-producing facility in the country. The two Oklahomans spent a fascinating day at the dam, then rode back to Missoula with the same couple.

On Sunday, Roosa and Dollard had an extensive discussion about what their respective futures might hold.

Dollard's future prospects would abruptly change, as the next day he received a telegram notifying him that a second smoke jumpers' class was about to start up at the Cave Junction, Oregon base, which was located at the Illinois Valley airport. Cave Junction is a small community in the southwest corner of Oregon, approximately ten miles above the California state line. Several trainees in the first class had washed out, and he was invited to join this unexpected supplemental effort. The Oklahoman quit his mill job that same day, before his shift started, and prepared to hitchhike to his new venture.

Dollard was slated to report for training at Cave Junction on July 9th, the same day Stu was due to report to the Land Management job, so he and Roosa decided to visit Clarence Wheatley and Tommy Towne, who were working for the Forest Service in southwest Washington, which Dollard described as "...generally on the way to CJ." (The initials of Cave Junction served as its nickname for the smoke jumpers.)

The two called the work site where Towne and Wheatley were assigned, but the fire dispatcher advised that the other Oklahomans had checked out until after the Fourth of July holiday.

Almost 60 years after the fact, Dollard recalled in detail that Roosa then assumed the role of detective in their effort to locate their two Claremore friends:

"Stuart and I had no idea where Tom and Clarence had gone, but Stuart decided that wherever they were, it was west of where we were, so Tuesday morning, we set out hitchhiking towards southwest Washington, making phone calls along the way. One call was to Tommy's dad, who had no idea where they were, but he told us that Tommy had a girlfriend from OBU (Oklahoma Baptist University) somewhere in Oregon. 'Bingo!' we thought, 'but where?'"

"As we hitchhiked through Coeur d'Alene, Spokane, Pasco, then down the Columbia River, we continued making calls from pay phones. A second call to their dispatcher at their job site revealed that they had checked out to Dallas, Oregon, but had left no phone number or address. We kept on hitchhiking towards Dallas, and put up for the night at some cheap hotel near there. We got to that small, sleepy town, which is just west of Salem, around noon on July 4th. But how were we going to find Tommy and Clarence, even if they were here?"

"Stuart reasoned that if someone from Dallas, Oregon went all the way to Oklahoma to attend OBU, she would probably be a dedicated Baptist, so we found the number for the pastor of the First Baptist Church in the phone book, called him, and introduced ourselves. We asked if he had a young lady in his church attending OBU, and 'Bingo' again—her family was one of the pillars of the church, and he gave us her name and number. We called, and when the young lady's mother answered, we asked if she knew Tommy Towne. She said, 'Why, yes; he's right here. Do you want to talk to him?'"

"Tommy was stunned to find out we were only a few blocks away. We were picked up and taken to his girlfriend's house, where plans were underway for a picnic and evening fireworks display at the local park. Tommy's girlfriend already had arranged a date for Clarence, and she hurriedly got dates for Stuart and me. Our dates were young and very forgettable, but we enjoyed the picnic and their fireworks."

Roosa's intuition and methodical tenacity had put the four friends from Claremore together for a memorable reunion during the summer holiday.

The following day, Roosa and Dollard went their separate ways again. Jimmie proceeded to Cave Junction, and Stuart headed back to Montana. The two former roommates would not see each other again until Dollard visited Roosa in Tucson, Arizona during semester break the next college school year.

However, Roosa and Dollard quickly began corresponding by post card. Roosa ended up being disappointed with his surveying job in eastern Montana, and was intrigued by Dollard's accounts of smoke jumper training, as well as the ensuing firefighting adventures for which Dollard had trained.

—⁓—

Dollard is of the opinion that this particular time was also critical in Roosa's decision to seek a flying career instead of an engineering career. Roosa had become aware that a would-be pilot could sign up with the Air Force's aviation cadet program, which only required two years of college instead of a degree.

Since Lorine and Dewey Roosa had moved to Tucson during his freshman year at Oklahoma A&M, Stu made a firm decision in the summer of 1952 to transfer to the University of Arizona in that same city for his sophomore year, in order to get the requisite two years of college for the cadet flight school program offered by the Air Force.

One weekend in August, Roosa showed up unexpectedly at Cave Junction. Dollard was gone on an excursion to climb Mount Shasta, some 100 miles away in Siskiyou County, California, with other smoke jumper recruits. Although Mount Shasta, with an elevation of 14,179 feet, is in the Cascade Range, it stands out as an individual landmark, as it is a stratovolcano. Such volcanoes are solitary and conical, and historically, have been known to have explosive eruptions (Krakatoa being perhaps the ultimate example). On a clear day, Mount Shasta was actually visible from Cave Junction.

Stu waited at the camp, but left before Dollard and the other CJ jumpers returned from Mount Shasta. The crew members who had conversed with Roosa during his visit told Dollard that Stu had checked out the facilities and the airplane (a single-engine Noorduyn Norseman), and had picked up a smoke jumper application before he left.

Roosa informed Dollard via correspondence that he had liked the CJ guys, liked what he had seen, and was confident that he would be a smoke jumper in 1953.

Any earlier private thoughts the redheaded Oklahoman may have had about how being a smoke jumper might be a "plus" regarding future career (flying) goals were now obvious, and Roosa also let Dollard know that he thought such an experience would help him get into flight school with the Air Force.

—⁓—

During his second year of college, Stu resided with his parents in Tucson, and commuted to classes at the University of Arizona, excelling in his studies. When he completed his sophomore year, he immediately set his sights on Cave Junction, and was already planning on applying for the aviation cadet program, following a solitary summer as a smoke jumper.

Curiously, Dollard attempted to join the Army in January of 1953, but was classified 4-F when he took his physical, due to a lack of eardrums (he would have tympanic membranes constructed later in his life).

Dollard's 4-F designation makes for more than one "what if"-type of speculation regarding his relationship to Roosa. Dollard recalled that had he passed the Army's physical, he would have been assigned to the Army's 45th Division, which had a large number of troops that were killed or wounded in the Korean conflict. In addition, Dollard states that had he gone to Korea, he would obviously not be able to jump in the summer of 1953, and he wonders if Roosa would have gone through as a rookie that year.

CJ-53

"Smoke jumper."

The very term conjures up the image of world-class bravado and adventure, even before the details of such a job and lifestyle are imparted. Obviously, the notion of jumping into thick woods—or preferably, a nearby field or meadow—by parachute to fight forest fires implies that only hardy individuals need apply.

The basic concept of smoke jumping is to get firefighters to isolated forest fires in an expeditious manner, before a blaze has a chance to expand. The idea of using airplanes as observer craft to look for forest fires and/or monitor the direction of fires dates back to the World War I era, and experiments regarding parachuting firefighters into remote areas began in the mid-1930s.

In 1939, smoke jumping became an official facet of the U.S. Forest Service, with the first jumps being made in July of 1940, and such dangerous work has continued to present day.

Moreover, the Bureau of Land Management (BLM) also instituted smoke jumping, and presently has such contingents in Fairbanks, Alaska and Boise, Idaho.

Perhaps not unexpectedly, smoke jumping was introduced in the erstwhile Soviet Union in the mid-Thirties, and Russian smoke jumpers, who are just as tough as their American counterparts, often associate with their U.S. brethren to share firefighting tips and recount their experiences. It's a bond that is probably understood best by the smoke jumpers themselves.

Since the first official firefighting jumps in 1940, approximately 5,000 individuals in the United States have earned this unique designation. Bases have been expanded, of course, and training is more extensive, as is the technology, than what Stuart Roosa would have encountered in 1953. Over the decades, there have also been numerous changes in the length of training, length of on-duty shifts, parachute design, jump equipment, communications gear, and aircraft that are utilized, but the basic mission is still the same.

In the early Fifties, there were five bases to which smoke jumpers (and trainees) were assigned. From the times of their opening, they were:

Winthrop, Washington (also known as the North Cascade base)—1940, 1945-present day
Missoula, Montana—1940-present day
McCall, Idaho—1943-present day
Cave Junction, Oregon—1943-1981
Idaho City, Idaho—1948-1969

A base at Redmond, Oregon opened in 1964, is still open, and took over some of the territory covered by the Cave Junction base. Another base at Redding, California opened in 1957, is still open, and also covers a portion of the territory formerly covered by Cave Junction.

The selection process for smoke jumpers was, and still is, extremely competitive. Accordingly, the dropout/washout rate among actual smoke jumper trainees who were selected was very low.

After submitting an application, Roosa garnered a slot as a trainee at Cave Junction, and he and Dollard reported to Pacific Northwest forest jobs for the third summer in a row—Dollard as a certified veteran smoke jumper, Roosa as a neophyte.

The same day Roosa and Dollard arrived at Cave Junction, Jim Oleson, their friend from the Priest River Station the previous summer, walked in, having also been accepted as a trainee.

The standard personnel lineup at Cave Junction included 24 jumpers, four squad leaders, a jump plane pilot, two cooks, and a clerk. Squad leaders were responsible for training the new recruits.

Obvious inquiries could be made about the similarities between basic military training and training for rookie smoke jumpers. Both experiences are very structured, but the mission is different—smoke jumpers were trained for an alternate type of "combat."

Jimmie Dollard agrees with the notion that the training and subsequent service were important and positive facets of a smoke jumper's life that would follow him for the rest of his days.

"You can't overemphasize the importance of smoke jumping," he said. "You'd show up as an insecure teenager, and you'd leave as a confident young man. And I know that smoke jumping had a profound impact on shaping Stu's character. He was a good athlete, and very goal-oriented. His increasing confidence became more evident as the season went on. There was never any doubt in anyone's mind that he would make it, and I never saw him get discouraged."

In the 1950s, smoke jumper training lasted four weeks. Classroom work lasted four hours each morning. Physical training was held for four hours each afternoon. Like trainees *and* veterans, Roosa complained about the five-mile runs, as well as long training hikes, which required trainees to carry a 100-pound backpack.

Trainees began their practice jumps during the fourth week, and made seven practice jumps during the training period. Their first jumps were into fields, and the seventh was an appropriately-named "timber jump" into woods, which was also referred to as a "graduation jump," as it figured into a smoker jumper's certification. Returning veterans were required to make two "refresher" jumps.

The aircraft at some smoke jumper stations often consisted of venerable Ford Tri-Motors (the "Tin Goose") or Douglas DC-3s. Those planes could carry 14 or more jumpers and their gear. However, in 1953, CJ only had the aforementioned smaller, single-engine Noorduyn Norseman, piloted by Ed Scholz. The Norseman was a high-wing, fabric-covered airplane with a large and powerful radial engine, and was often seen with floats on its undercarriage instead of landing gear, as it was popular as a workhorse plane in the back country of Canada and Alaska. Its cruising speed was approximately 160 miles per hour. It had a large side door, which made for an easier egress by the jumpers.

The side door itself was left off the fuselage during fire flights, which meant that the occupants had to contend with a deafening roar from the engine, air turbulence from the slip stream, and exhaust fumes blowing into the interior. Conversation among the jumpers was almost impossible, and Dollard recounted that airsickness, when it happened, was usually caused by rough air, fumes, and/or what he cryptically termed "the prior night's activities."

The Norseman was capable of carrying four jumpers and their gear, a "spotter" (who was also a squad leader), and the pilot. The spotter would occupy the co-pilot's seat, and would work with the pilot to determine flight paths, wind direction, and wind speed. Yelling as best as possible over the drone of the engine, the spotter would brief the jumpers on the fire, the jump spot, the equipment drop spot, the route out of the area, and where the jumpers would meet ground contact personnel.

"There were no seats on the plane," said Dollard. "The low ceiling did not allow you to stand up, and the suit and harness were uncomfortable, forcing you into a crouching position. With four suited jumpers and all the gear, it was quite crowded."

Standard procedure meant that when the plane reached its target, the spotter would leave the co-pilot seat to direct the jumpers out of the door, communicating with the pilot by using hand signals.

The two-piece, heavily-padded outfit worn by smoke jumpers in the middle of the 20th Century was bulky, but well-suited for such a dangerous occupation. The jacket had a high collar to protect the neck, and the jump pants had large pockets in the legs for the letdown rope, in case a jumper landed in a tree. Leg pockets also contained yellow strips of cloth called signal streamers. A football helmet with a mesh face mask completed the outfit.

The actual bailout was preceded by several runs by the Norseman over the proposed drop area, as the spotter dropped streamers out of the door to check the wind. When the spotter signaled "final run," the first jumper would crouch in the doorway, with the second jumper close behind. Both would confirm that their static lines had been hooked up by the spotter.

When the airplane was over the exit point, the pilot would cut the propeller, and the spotter would slap the first jumper on the shoulder, a command to exit. The second jumper would exit as quickly as possible in an effort to place the twosome close to each other upon landing.

Jumpers would exit the airplane carrying two parachutes, a harness, map case, and a small amount of personal gear, which totaled around 90 pounds. Standard altitude for bailout was 1,500 feet. When smoke jumpers bailed out, they would fall twelve feet before the fully-extended static line jerked the cover off of the main parachute and held the apex of the parachute with a break cord until the silk and lines were fully extended, at which point the static line broke free. The time frame from the leap to the snap-off of the static line was approximately two seconds. The reserve chute was manually operated, if needed, by a D-handle rip cord.

If there was a four-man crew jumping, the first two had to be on the ground and were required to signal that they were okay before the final two bailed out.

A nearby area would be selected from the plane as the spot for the "fire packs" (one for each jumper) to be dropped by cargo parachute following the bailout of the jumpers.

No radios accompanied the smoke jumpers. When the leader got on the ground, he would lay out an "L" with two signal streamers to let the pilot know he was safe on terra firma, and when he confirmed all jumpers were down, a second "L" would be laid out.

Smoke jumpers would then proceed to the designated drop area for the fire packs. Inside each fire pack were hand tools, including a pulaski, shovel, and file. The supply packet also included food for three days, and a canteen of water.

Planes would then be signaled for any additional tools that were needed, such as a saw or climbing spurs, the latter of which would be used to retrieve supply parachutes that had caught in trees. Climbing spurs could also be utilized in retrieving jumper parachutes that had been left in trees, but that action occurred after the fire had been extinguished, as part of the mopping up process.

—⁓—

Roosa made his first training jump on July 7th, and his "timber/ graduation jump" was made on July 15th.

Once training was completed, and certification tests had been passed, there was usually no award ceremony for the new smoke jumpers, who were now known as "rookies," but a good-sized beer party was often held at the nearby swimming hole. New jumpers received a set of wings, but these items were usually just passed out, albeit not necessarily at the beer party, and not as part of any ceremony.

Veteran smoke jumpers refer to themselves by the initials of the base where they were trained, and the year they were certified. Jimmie Dollard's designation was CJ-52; Roosa's was to be CJ-53.

—⁓—

The foreman of the Cave Junction base who monitored the initial training of the 1953 trainees was Cliff Marshall, who, like numerous other early smoke jumpers, had been a paratrooper in World War II. Marshall was with the fabled 82nd Airborne Division in that conflict, and made combat jumps in Sicily, Normandy, and Holland. He became a smoke jumper in 1946, training in Montana, and took over the reins of the Cave Junction base in 1947.

At the end of June 1953, however, Marshall resigned, having been hired for a position at a national parachute test facility located in El Centro, California.

The regional office of the Forest Service, located in Portland, Oregon, assigned another former World War II paratrooper, Jim Allen, to the top position at Cave Junction. Roosa quickly grew to respect Allen's leadership qualities, and considered him a mentor.

Allen's personal history regarding his earlier paratrooper and smoke jumper days is also intriguing. When World War II erupted, he signed up as a paratrooper, even though he had never even been aloft in a plane.

As a member of another legendary outfit, the 101st Airborne Division, Allen made his first combat drop in Holland in September, 1944. The 101st Airborne, the 82nd Airborne, and the British 6th Airborne Division all went into Dutch territory together, and were on the front lines for two months, Allen recalls.

That particular military action, known as Operation Market Garden, has been pronounced as the largest airborne assault of all time, and was the subject of a 1974 book written by Cornelius Ryan, and a 1977 movie, both titled *A Bridge Too Far.*

On December 20th, Allen was wounded at Bastogne, Belgium during the Battle of the Bulge, Germany's final offensive push. Surgeons operated on his leg in a school house, and he and other wounded troops were evacuated shortly before the Germans surrounded the city. General Anthony McAuliffe's terse one-word reply to a German demand for surrender, "Nuts," was one of the shorter and more-memorable phrases of World War II history.

"I went to Paris by train, and was then flown to London," Allen recalled. "I was in a DC-3 airplane that was equipped with litters for the trip. It happened to be the first time I ever *landed* in an airplane. I had made twelve jumps out of airplanes before then without making a landing!"

Allen still has shrapnel in his thigh from his wound at Bastogne.

Following the war, Allen returned to Camas, Washington, where he had been raised, to work in the paper mill, but quickly responded to a newspaper article that stated that the Forest Service was looking for ex-paratroopers to be smoke jumpers. Upon being certified in 1946, Allen served at the Winthrop base during fire season. The foreman was Francis B. Lufkin, a legend among smoke jumpers as one of its earliest pioneers; Lufkin had begun jumping in 1940. Allen was promoted to squad leader, and Lufkin eventually got Allen a full-time civil service job that enabled his younger charge to quit his job at the paper mill.

It's not surprising that in 1953, Roosa considered Allen to be a role model.

Allen took over as foreman at Cave Junction on July 4th. In that era, only the foreman, pilot, and a single squad leader, Orv Looper, were employed year-round.

"I recall being impressed with Stuart Roosa during that period," Allen remembered. "He stood out, with several others, with their above-average intelligence and work ethics."

37

Allen also had high praise for the squad leaders at CJ, pronouncing them to have been "the backbone of the unit." He recalled that while Dollard was not a squad leader, "...he was well qualified to be one. (Vacancies) for those positions just did not open up while he was there."

The "foreman" position soon garnered the loftier-sounding title of "Project Air Officer," and Orv Looper became known as Smoke Jumper Foreman. Allen would continue to do practice jumps, and functioned as a spotter when a squad leader wasn't available, but he was also the spotter for trainees on their first jumps onto a practice field. Ultimately, and perhaps not surprisingly, his position became more of a full-time desk job.

—⁓—

The Cave Junction base was headquartered at the Illinois Valley airport, but in the summer of 1953, the runway at that facility had to be resurfaced, so the unit temporarily stationed the plane and a rotating crew living in temporary quarters near the airport in Medford, Oregon, about 50 miles east of the CJ base. Requests for jumpers that came into Cave Junction would be quickly forwarded to the squad leader at Medford.

If only two jumpers flew out of Medford on an emergency call, two replacement jumpers would be flown to Medford from a private airport in Cave Junction; the base had made arrangements with the owner to ferry two jumpers and their gear to Medford under such circumstances. Replacing all four jumpers at Medford meant two trips for the private pilot.

The private pilot would also ferry used parachutes back to Cave Junction from Medford. The parachutes would be repaired and repacked by two female parachute riggers at the Cave Junction paraloft, and would then be returned to Medford.

While the basic scenario for a summer at the CJ base normally saw two dozen jumpers stationed at the facility, the government required that a minimum of four jumpers had to be on the grounds and on call at all times. Jumpers were given room and board at the base, and their camaraderie and gung-ho attitude ensured that plenty of personnel were always available for a fire call.

By comparison, Missoula had 150 jumpers, McCall had 60, and both Winthrop and Idaho City were about the same size as the Cave Junction station.

Once "trainees" were certified, and became "rookies," two jump lists were compiled—one list was made up of veteran smoke jumpers, the other listed rookies, and the order of each was determined by drawing names.

Following a jump, the names would rotate to the bottom of each list, and after rookies had made a jump or two, their names would be moved over to the veterans' list. The top names on each of the two lists would be in line for the next jump, and such front-runners had to be on base and on call when their names were in such a position.

"It was our goal to get the plane in the air within fifteen minutes after the request was received," Allen detailed, "so it was necessary that the ones on the top (of the lists) be available."

Due to the smaller size of CJ, jumpers at from that station often went out two at a time instead of four. If a request was received for four or more jumpers, a squad leader would assume command of the group.

"In many cases, maybe we should have dropped more jumpers to do the job right," CJ veteran Chuck Sheley recalled. "There was always the option of returning to base and bringing back more jumpers, but that seldom happened."

Another tendency of the CJ operation was to drop the jumpers as close to fires as possible. Such a plan meant that some firefighters would land in some of the tallest trees in the United States, and Sheley has 20/20 hindsight about the dangers of landing in tall timber:

"It seemed like a great strategy at the time, but with the wisdom of age, if I was doing it again I would drop the jumper in the closest open spot, or at a place where he had a better chance of getting to the ground. There was a higher chance of injury created by landing in timber that was 150 to 200 feet tall...in many cases, a person could jump a mile away from the fire and walk to it in sufficient time. Getting out of a high tree takes a lot of time, and an injured jumper creates a whole new and difficult situation."

When jumpers had extinguished a fire, they would retrieve any personnel parachutes that were hung up in trees, assemble their packs, and take the best route to the nearest road; jump leaders had a map case with a compass, map, and note pad. Maps were marked prior to takeoff by CJ office personnel, coordinating with the Ranger station nearest the fire, which was usually been the station that had initially spotted the blaze. The maps included notations of the route to the road, and an estimated time that the jumpers would be picked up. Sometimes the vehicles would return the jumpers to CJ, and sometimes they were driven to the nearest Ranger station.

As for the gear that the jumpers had taken to the ground or that had been dropped in, they were allowed to leave pulaskis and shovels but were required to return saws and climbing spurs.

A stereotypical route out meant hiking a few miles cross country, then more miles by trail; an average of about ten miles total.

In the early Fifties, helicopters were not used to extract jumpers, due to the expense of their operation plus poor performance at high altitude. However, some helicopters were on standby in the Pacific Northwest in case a medical evacuation was needed.

Occasionally, "pack strings" of mules, led by a "packer" on a horse, picked up jumpers. An extra horse was available for each jumper, and Dollard recalls riding a horse in a pack string for 42 miles after fighting one extremely isolated fire.

—⁓—

Members of the crew of the Cave Junction base were assigned to various forest improvement projects while waiting for an alarm, but had to be ready to move as soon as they were notified.

"You hear a bell ring, you jump in an airplane, and take off," Dollard summarized. "You don't know what state you're going to, but they give you a map. When you land, you've got to face that fire and put it out as quickly as possible. You have to assume a lot of responsibility for yourself."

The CJ-52 veteran also recalled that other than the firefighter who was killed by the jackknifing snag in 1951, he and Roosa never came near any other fatality in their time with the Forest Service. However, all smoke jumpers were mindful of the legendary tragedy that had occurred in 1949 at Mann Gulch, in Montana.

On August 5th of that year, 15 smoke jumpers from the Missoula base had parachuted from a C-47 to fight a rapidly-spreading inferno that had been started by lightning. The wind contributed to an almost-explosive spread of the fire, turning the blaze into a literal "firestorm," and soon after landing, ten of the jumpers had perished. Two died of burns the next day, and a firefighter on the ground also died. It was the first incident in the smoke jumpers' history with such a catastrophic loss of life, and was a sobering reminder of the abrupt and inherent dangers that were part of such an occupation.

The Mann Gulch incident would inspire a 1952 movie, *Red Skies of Montana*, starring Richard Widmark, as well as Norman Maclean's best-selling 1993 book, *Young Men and Fire*. When the real smoke jumpers saw the movie in the early Fifties, they considered its plot to be ludicrous, as it included segments where smoke jumpers used dynamite and a motorized trail machine. In reality, smoke jumpers never used such items.

—⁓—

As it turned out, all of the 1953 fires were jumped from Medford. Roosa, Dollard, and Oleson were in the first crew, and slept in the warehouse of the Forest Service division headquartered in that town. After a crew worked a fire out of Medford, they would return to Cave Junction, at the bottom of rotation list.

Dollard was the lead jumper on Roosa's first on-duty fire jump on August 3rd, which was located near Toad Lake in the nearby Umpqua National Forest. A contingent of three jumpers was dispatched; the third was another rookie from the same class as Roosa. Dollard recalled that he and Roosa managed to land in a meadow, but the other rookie happened to float into a huge snag. He fell to the ground, breaking lots of dead limbs on the way, but was uninjured. The fire was ultimately found and rapidly extinguished.

"I would like to tell you that we fought a roaring inferno," Dollard said of the experience, "but it was a cakewalk. We met a relief ground crew near the fire; they had hiked all night, and the Forest Service had lost track of them. The five of us cleared and trenched a small area with pulaskis, and dropped the burning snag with a crosscut saw, putting it out with shovels of dirt. We left the ground crew to mop up while we went to retrieve our gear. We spent the night, and the next morning, walked uphill a couple of thousand feet, and about three miles, to a lookout post, where we were picked up, taken to the nearest airfield, and flown back to Medford."

Curiously, that was the only time Dollard and Roosa made an actual fire call jump together.

Allen, a meticulous records-keeper, stated that Roosa's fire jumps in 1953 were made in the Klamath Forest in northern California, the Umpqua Forest in southwest Oregon, and the Six Rivers Forest in northern California. Roosa performed his duties well at all fires, according his files.

And while it might make for a more robust or more impressive recollection to note that Roosa and his associates had jumped into the wilderness to successfully battle rampaging walls of flame against overwhelming odds, as a smoke jumper he never had the same type of experience with a huge forest fire like the one that he and Dollard fought in July of 1951. The primary purpose of a smoke jumper crew is to react quickly, and to contain a forest fire before it becomes unmanageable— therefore much more dangerous for smoke jumpers and regular forest fire fighters—and Roosa's jumps accomplished exactly that.

—ww—

Roosa had a car, and Dollard and Oleson didn't. Stu had acquired a nearly-new 1952 Ford sedan in Arizona, so he usually had the say-so regarding what activities the threesome would pursue during off-time, since he had the "wheels." When not on call, they would spend weekends at Crater Lake, located some 50 miles northeast of Medford, or would climb Mount Thielsen, another extinct stratovolcano in the Cascade Range, located just north of Crater Lake.

They also went to the Oregon Shakespeare Festival in Ashland, just southeast of Medford, not so much for any personal cultural enrichment, but because a bevy of attractive females attended stage productions presented there.

—⁓—

Rumors have swirled for decades about to what extent the U.S government's Central Intelligence Agency (CIA) and other government agencies may have "recruited" individual smoke jumpers for clandestine operations. Such recruits would, of course, have had appropriate training and a sense of derring-do that would also be requisite for such classified work.

It's a subject that is still discussed by retired smoke jumpers over a half-century after they were active with the Forest Service, and it's still intriguing, but the fact that one of their own ultimately went to the Moon is also discussed among such retirees.

—⁓—

Jim Allen retired in 1976, having accumulated a total of 33 years of government service (three in the army, seven at the Winthrop smoke jumper base, thirteen at Cave Junction, and ten as the manager of the Redmond, Oregon, Air Center).

Veteran smoke jumper Charley Moseley put in a number of years at the Cave Junction base. He is an unofficial historian for that facility, and his duties include keeping former jumpers in touch with each other. He has an interesting perspective about smoke jumpers who served only one year instead of several seasons:

"While most jumpers jumped more than one year, I have found over the years that those who were only able to jump one year have kept an amazing recall of nearly everything that happened during that particular summer," Moseley said, "and can recall the names and faces of just about every person there. The experience seems to have been so profound, it is just 'stamped' into their brains."

A group photo of the CJ contingent for 1953 shows Roosa, Dollard, Allen, and the rest of the group posing in front of the Noorduyn Norseman, wearing their jump suits. The huge circular protective collar and the helmets that many smoke jumpers, including Roosa, are holding make them look like they're attired in primitive space suits, a la Flash Gordon or Buck Rogers.

The summer of 1953 would indeed turn out to be the only season that Stuart Roosa served as a smoke jumper for the U.S. Forest Service.

Years later, however, he would ultimately honor his compatriots in that very unique occupation in a very unique way.

∧IR FORCE

Training

His solitary summer as a smoke jumper complete, Stu applied for the Air Force aviation cadet program.

Roosa would later inform Dollard that when he was interviewed for pilot training with the Air Force, he was quizzed by a recruiter about his potential for flight. Many applicants were interviewed for approximately two hours, and some were eliminated at that point.

However, when Roosa was interviewed, the Air Force recruiter examined his records and noted that the applicant had been a smoke jumper, asking for details.

After a brief explanation of his hazardous duties with the Forest Service, Roosa was accepted into the cadet program, validating his earlier belief that service as a smoke jumper would enhance his chances to become a pilot.

The recruiter reportedly commented that if Roosa had gotten through smoke jumper training and service, he should make it through flight training easily.

―∧∧―

In modern times, the usual path to a cockpit for an Air Force commissioned officer is via Reserve Officers' Training Corps (ROTC) programs at selected colleges and universities, the Air Force Academy in Colorado Springs, Colorado, or that branch of service's Officer Training School (OTS). Soon after being commissioned, new second lieutenants who are would-be pilots proceed to flight schools at various bases across the U.S.

A fourth commissioning (and flying) option once existed, however.

Aviation cadet programs had an intriguing, if not permanent, place in the chronology of the U.S. military. Their intermittent history extended from 1917 until 1965, and they were most active in times of national emergency.

Usually, such circumstances were imminent or outright warfare, when the Air Force and its predecessors such as the Army Air Corps experienced abrupt increases in demands for pilots and other airmen.

During the program's history, criteria varied regarding how a student would ultimately be commissioned as a military officer. In the middle of the Twentieth Century, a would-be pilot who successfully completed the aviation cadet program was awarded a commission as a second lieutenant as well as his wings at the same time.

Among the famous military aviators who won their wings in cadet programs were Jimmy Doolittle, who led the fabled bombing of Tokyo by Air Corps B-25s in early 1942, and General Curtis LeMay, who formulated strategies for the Air Force after it became a separate branch of service following World War II, and entered both the jet age and the atomic age.

The cadet program's two-years-of-college requirement that Roosa encountered had not always been in effect, and at various points in its history, some individuals signed up right out of high school.

When Roosa joined the cadets in late 1953, two years of college had also been waived for enlisted personnel who had already served 18 months in the Air Force, provided they qualified as cadets, but the scholastic requirement *was* still in effect for *new* recruits. The Air Force aviation cadet program was part of the Air Training Command, and was still going strong in that annum, thanks to the Korean conflict.

Apollo 16 moonwalker Charlie Duke, who would be chosen as an astronaut at the same time as Roosa, recalled that he and Roosa once compared their respective paths to an Apollo spacecraft.

"Stu and I discussed that a little bit," Duke said. "I recall that he selected the aviation cadet program because that was the quickest way to get into a cockpit, which was his goal—to be an Air Force pilot. He was *that* motivated."

—⁓—

Roosa reported to Lackland Air Force Base in San Antonio, Texas for pre-flight training.

The Lackland facility had actually been established in 1942 as an adjunct to Kelly Field, and was originally known as the San Antonio Aviation Cadet Center; it was named after Brigadier General Frank Lackland in 1947. General Lackland had been the individual to originate the idea of a separate aviation cadet reception and training center for Kelly Field.

Lackland would later become the sole basic training facility for the Air Force's enlisted personnel, and such is the case to this day.

And the introduction and indoctrination to the Air Force for aviation cadets did not differ much from basic training for enlisted personnel. Inductees were abruptly introduced to a tightly-structured and disciplined lifestyle—which included a requisite skinhead haircut. Their first weeks in the Air Force were directed by gruff training instructors (TIs) wearing "Smokey Bear hats." Squadrons of young men marched everywhere they went, learned Air Force customs and courtesies, underwent mandatory physical fitness programs, and were tested constantly regarding their intellectual and physical abilities.

When Roosa arrived, a new cadet program regimen that had been instituted the previous year meant that pre-flight Lackland training had been lengthened to twelve weeks.

Aviation cadets at Lackland *were* taken aloft on indoctrination flights, usually in the Air Force's reliable (and usually-yellow-and-blue-colored) North American T-6G "Texan" trainer.

After Roosa completed his cadet orientation ride in a T-6, he quickly disengaged his harness when the plane stopped, jumped out of the cockpit, and threw up on the tarmac.

—∿∿—

After Lackland, Roosa and the other aviation cadet candidates began undergraduate pilot training (UPT), and were integrated into a class along with other pilot trainees who were already commissioned officers from service academies or ROTC programs, as well as Air Force officers who had already been flying as navigators or bombardiers, but were now seeking to upgrade to pilot status. Some of the candidates already had pilots' licenses, and some had even earned the right to fly as teenagers, but they still had to go through the Air Force's required training.

UPT consisted of two facets, "Primary" and "Basic," with classes for each part being conducted at separate facilities.

Aviation classes were designated by a year in which they were supposed to complete training, with a letter that indicated the alphabetical and chronological order of the class in that particular annum. Roosa's class was designated as 55K.

Roosa and other 55K class members reported to Spence Air Base, which had been established in 1941 near Moultrie, Georgia. Their Primary training experience at the Peach State facility would last slightly over six months.

Built in former tobacco and cotton fields of southwest Georgia just prior to the entry of the U.S. into World War II, the base was named for a World War I pilot, Thomas Lewis Spence, of nearby Thomasville, Georgia, who had been killed in a plane crash in France.

During the Second World War, the Georgia facility had served as an "Advanced" single-engine training base, i.e., specialized training beyond UPT, and almost 6,000 pilots had trained there.

The status of Spence AB had been changed to a Basic flight site in February of 1945, but the base closed in November of the same year.

Spence was reactivated as a Primary flight training base in 1951, when the Korean conflict increased the demand for pilots. The facility had to undergo major renovations, and this time around, Spence was actually run by a civilian contractor, Hawthorne Flying Service of Charleston, South Carolina, operating as Hawthorne School of Aeronautics. Other private companies also ran other Primary flight schools at air bases around the country.

The designation for Spence in its new incarnation was as a "Contract Primary Flying Training" base. A total of nine such bases were created or were reactivated during the Korean War.

The Hawthorne company had also operated contract schools during World War II. The civilian contractor provided personnel to instruct and support student pilots, and was also responsible for housing the students in barracks, and feeding them as well.

The Air Force still was still in charge at Spence, however. The student pilots were members of 3302nd Pilot Training Squadron, and its upper command was responsible for all military activities of all military personnel. The 3302nd's Military Check Pilots would periodically spot-check students as well as Hawthorne instructors to ascertain that all personnel on the base were conforming to Air Force standards.

Moreover, a mobile Air Force standardization team would sometimes visit the base to conduct unannounced performance inspections.

Classes varied in size, with most instructor pilots assigned to four students each. The instructor/ratio could vary, however, and flight commanders and assistant flight commanders might handle only one or two students.

Previous Spence trainees had included future X-15 pilot Mike Adams (52C), and Gemini/Apollo astronaut Jim McDivitt (52G).

Charlie Duke was an example of a commissioned officer who went through Primary flight training at Spence in the Fifties. He had graduated from the U.S. Naval Academy at Annapolis, Maryland, but had gone on active duty with the Air Force. Duke was a student at Spence in class 59B.

Students from numerous foreign countries also trained at Spence.

Rotation of classes occurred every six weeks, with the graduating members of one class reporting for duty at other bases for Basic training as a new flight reported for duty at Spence.

Records indicate that class 55K began training at that facility in the southwest portion of the Peach State on April 8, 1954. The class began with 141 students. Like all classes, 55K was divided into two flights. Each flight had its own name and insignia, and such monikers and emblems carried over from graduating classes to incoming classes. The two 55K flights were named Bearcat and Tiger.

One flight from a class would fly in the morning, while the other flight was doing classroom work and Link training. The assignments were reversed in the afternoon.

All students—commissioned officers or cadets—went through the same training syllabus, and received the same instruction and treatment by instructors. Officers and cadets would also march together in parades, and Duke was of the opinion that since most of the officers had come out of service academies, they knew how to march better than new cadets.

However, commissioned officers were housed in separate quarters, and had separate dining facilities and recreational facilities. Hawthorne instructor pilots had access to most of the officers' facilities.

Moreover, the dangers and/or possibilities of washing out were applicable to all trainees, and even some young officers who had graduated high in their classes at service academies were eliminated.

President Harry Truman had ordered the U.S. military to be integrated in the late 1940s, but beyond the perimeter of Spence Air Base in the early Fifties, the state of Georgia still practiced segregation. Black student pilots would participate fully in training, but on rare occasions, the local environment outside the base wasn't hospitable.

"We had a few black students," recalled former Hawthorne instructor Bruce Watson, "probably one to three in most classes. On the flight line, they were 'just one of the boys', and from everything I saw, that's exactly the way they were treated by their fellow students. I heard discussions about a couple of minor incidents off-base that indicated some of the local citizens were still having a little problem adjusting, but it wasn't anything significant."

Most Moultrie area citizens exhibited stereotypical Southern hospitality for the transient would-be pilots, and numerous Southern belles kept company with the future flyboys.

"I do know that some of the cadets were at least somewhat involved with some of the local girls," said Bob McKinley, who was a member of class 55N, some months after Roosa's time at Spence, "but typically, when we had a three-day pass, we would head down to Florida for some beach time, or maybe we'd go to Albany or Tallahassee."

—✐✐✐—

The primary training aircraft at Spence was the redoubtable T-6G Texan, but the Piper PA-18 "Super Cub" was also used. A new trainer, the North

American T-28 "Trojan," was being phased in at Spence at the time Roosa was there, but records indicate that Class 55K did not train in the new model.

Students first trained in the Piper PA-18 for what was known as Primary—Phase I, and normally soloed in that aircraft after eight to ten hours of "dual" flying (with an instructor), then continued with solo and dual flights until they reached 20 hours.

Transitioning to the larger and more complex T-6G for Primary—Phase II, students would have to do a larger number of dual hours before soloing in the Texan. The total of 120 hours in the bigger trainer was usually split as approximately 70 hours of dual flying and 50 hours solo, and meticulous flight records were kept for each candidate that documented dual flight time, solo flight time, and number of landings in both aircraft models.

And it was with the T-6G that training became diversified, as students would be schooled in flight procedures that included "hooded" flight time, which simulated instrument flying (with a interior hood covering the view from the canopy; 25 hours), navigation (cross country; 12 hours), night flying (eight hours), and aerobatics (ten hours). Aerobatics included such classic maneuvers as slow rolls, barrel rolls, aileron rolls, loops, clover leafs, Cuban eights, and Immelmann turns. Navigation, night flying, and aerobatics included dual and solo flying.

Of course, there also was plenty of ground work in the classroom, as well as in Link trainers.

Two nearby "auxiliary" fields affiliated with the Spence operation were located at Tifton and Thomasville, and a third, Sunset Field, was situated in a rural area south of Moultrie.

"The auxiliary fields were used to take the load off of the 'home' field," Watson explained. "There were simply too many planes in the air on a typical day for everyone to operate off of one field. This was especially true if one or more flights were shooting landing stages. It was common for an entire flight to take off from Spence, go to one of the auxiliary fields, and operate from there for their entire (daily) training period, then return to Spence on their last flight of the day."

Accidents could and did occur, but only three minor accidents happened at Spence while 55K was training there. None of the accidents resulted in any injuries, and none involved a 55K student.

Moreover, Spence received Air Force commendations citing its standardization and safety records on more than one occasion. The base reportedly had the best safety record of the nine contract flight schools.

As training at Spence began to wind down for a particular class, students were allowed to apply for "Basic" flight training that they felt would orient them towards either single-engine fighter aircraft or multi-engine aircraft.

Roosa went for fighters, and was selected to attend at Williams Air Force Base in Arizona.

On September 17th, 117 members of class 55K graduated from Primary training at Spence Air Base. Twenty students had been eliminated for flying deficiencies, one for academic deficiency, two for fear of flying, and four for "other" reasons. Six students were held over until a later class. The washout rate for 55K was considered typical for Spence classes.

Spence Air Base would close again in 1961. During its second go-round as a flight training facility, its impressive totals would include over a million hours flown, 2.5 million takeoffs and landings, and over 6400 graduates, including pilots from over 30 countries.

In addition to Charlie Duke, another later trainee who went through the Spence Air Base program and would end up with NASA was future Apollo flight director Gene Kranz (61F).

—⁓—

Next stop for Roosa was Williams Air Force Base in Mesa, Arizona, about 30 miles southeast of Phoenix; i.e., about a hundred miles from his parents' home in Tucson. The base had been named for Arizona native Lt. Charles Linton Williams (1898-1927), who had been killed in a plane crash in Hawaii.

Williams had also opened in 1941, and over a 52-year history, some 26,500 pilots would win their wings at the facility. At one point, Williams was supplying some 25 percent of the Air Force's pilots.

The main difference between Spence Air Base and Williams Air Force Base was that Basic flight training was being conducted at a fully-operational Air Force facility; i.e., a fully-operational military environment, and the instructors were veteran Air Force pilots instead of contracted civilians. On-base facilities such as the Base Exchange (BX) and Officers' Club were also much nicer at an "Air Force Base" than at an "Air Base"... but the aviation cadets in 55K had yet to become officers.

Training at "Willie" (as it was nicknamed by Air Force personnel) was, of course, more intense, but the airplanes flew faster. Formation flying techniques that had not been part of the Primary flight curriculum were also interpolated.

Additional facets of the curriculum during Basic included more intentionally-stressful physiological regimens, such as training in altitude chambers, ejection seats, partial pressure suits, and night vision.

The 55K members began by flying the aforementioned T-28 Trojan in Basic Phase I, and their airborne training routines, including aerobatics and formation flying, grew more complicated, as did their classroom work. Washouts could and did occur in Basic flight training as well; i.e., just because a pilot had graduated from Primary flight training wasn't any guarantee that he would make it through Basic. Of course, aircraft accidents also occurred in this second phase of training.

Perhaps the most eagerly anticipated step up for pilot trainees was Basic Phase II, the transition to a jet aircraft. For 55K members and thousands of other military student pilots, their first jet ride took place in the venerable Lockheed T-33 "Shooting Star," a trainer version of the F-80, which had been the Air Force's first operational jet fighter.

Jet aircraft were still fairly new in the mid-Fifties, having only been viable for around a decade. However, technology was rapidly developing, as were the speed capabilities of jets, and the sensation of being "pushed" by a jet engine instead of being "pulled" by a piston engine-powered propeller was enthralling for most would-be pilots. The T-33 would ultimately acquire the same reputation for reliability as a jet trainer as the T-6G had for propeller-driven trainers.

Hours spent in the T-28 totaled approximately 40 dual, 20 solo, 20 hooded, and two hours each of dual and solo night flight.

Hours spent in the T-33 totaled approximately 35 dual, 35 solo, 15 hooded, five hours of dual night flight, and three hours of solo night flight.

Roosa and his classmates were presented with their pilot's wings on March 13, 1955, and those who had been aviation cadets were commissioned as second lieutenants in the United States Air Force. They also received their first Instrument Certificate cards, validating that they were flight school graduates.

In spite of its history of training thousands of pilots, Williams Air Force Base would close in 1993, as a result of the 1991 decision-making by the national Base Realignment and Closure (BRAC) Commission.

—∿∿—

After winning his wings, Roosa was officially assigned to become a fighter pilot, having been able to choose his direction by finishing high in the 55K class rankings. Now he would be getting into aircraft that were top models for the Air Force.

Subsequent fighter training for Roosa took place at gunnery school in Del Rio, Texas (later Laughlin Air Force Base), and Luke Air Force Base in Arizona, located some 15 miles west of Phoenix. Luke had been named for Frank Luke, Jr., a World War I pilot who had been killed in action, and was the first American aviator to receive the Congressional Medal of Honor.

Roosa continued to prove to be a proficient pilot, impressing his instructors at the fighter schools. Techniques included chasing after airborne targets, and ground strafing.

Stu's first assignment following advanced fighter training would take him to the East Coast, where he would meet his life partner.

Langley Air Force Base

Now a fully-qualified fighter pilot, Roosa reported to the fabled 510th Fighter Squadron, then stationed at Langley Air Force Base in the Tidewater area of Virginia. The "Nickel-Dime" Squadron, a.k.a. the Buzzards, had a proud history that included their participation in D-Day, flying P-47 Thunderbolts.

When Roosa arrived at Langley in late 1955, the 510th was flying the Republic F-84F Thunderstreak. The swept-wing, single-engine turbojet fighter was an improvement over the straight-wing F-84 Thunderjet on which it was based.

The F-84F had been operational since May of 1954, and had also been the model recently flown by the Air Force's Thunderbirds flight demonstration team (which began its history with the F-84 Thunderjet). Its top speed was 695 miles per hour at sea level, or Mach 0.91, just shy of the speed of sound. It had a normal range of 860 miles but was capable of being refueled in mid-air from a tanker aircraft. The Thunderstreak's armament consisted of six .50 caliber machine guns, and it could carry up to three tons of externally-mounted rockets or bombs.

Roosa was now in a frontline Air Force squadron, flying a frontline jet fighter.

In the earlier days of the Cold War, jet aircraft—bombers and fighters—were responsible for delivering nuclear weapons to targets, before the advent of intercontinental ballistic missiles. Many F-84F squadrons, including the 510th, were responsible for escorting huge bombers such as the B-36 "Peacemaker" on bombing missions over enemy territory.

However, the F-84F had the capability of delivering a single nuclear weapon itself. One bizarre experiment conducted by the Air Force involved strapping a Thunderstreak underneath a B-36 in a cradle-like device. Such a configuration for the fighter was known as a "parasite" mode. The Peacemaker would use its range and altitude to cover a long distance, whereupon the F-84F would be detached, and would deliver the nuclear device to the target. Afterwards, the Thunderstreak would rendezvous with the B-36, and would re-connect to the cradle for the journey home.

While that idea got no further than the experimental stage, the 510th squadron would practice standard flight nuclear warhead delivery missions domestically as well as overseas (usually in West Germany, which was still a hot spot in the Cold War). The logo on the 510th squadron patch included a three-orbit atom to signify its mission.

One method for an F-84F to "drop" a nuclear bomb on its target was radically different from a standard gravity drop, as seen with most bombers. What's more, the tactic, known as "Over The Shoulder," also now seems almost as strange as the "parasite fighter" concept as a strategy for combat aircraft, but in its time, the maneuver was a bona fide flight plan that was practiced extensively by Thunderstreak pilots.

To perform the "Over The Shoulder" maneuver, the pilot of an F-84F would approach a target, but would actually fly *over and beyond* it. The aircraft would then be put into an abrupt vertical climb. Pulling backwards slightly from straight vertical, the pilot would release the weapon at the same time. Upon release, the airplane would immediately execute a tight loop backwards, rolling over back to horizontal.

Ideally, the nuclear bomb would continue its upward path, and would then loop over in a much larger arc than the tight loop that the Thunderstreak had just done. The weapon would head back to earth, detonating at its target. The F-84F was supposed to be out of danger when the explosion occurred.

Roosa would practice this maneuver many times, even while the 510th was deployed in Europe.

"My father used to describe this maneuver quite a bit," says Jack Roosa, who became an Air Force fighter pilot himself. "He never told me what his target was in Russia, but he did tell me that he would not have enough gas to make it back. It was a one-way mission."

—∿∿—

Around the same time Roosa reported to Langley, the Air Force's Thunderbirds team was in the process of transitioning to the North American F-100 Super Sabre, and the new fighter would also be acquired by the 510th during Roosa's tenure.

The F-100 was the world's first production supersonic fighter, and was somewhat of a beast for pilots who had been used to flying jets that were sub-sonic, i.e., planes that could not fly faster than the speed of sound. The earliest test versions of this first plane in the Air Force's "century series" had a terrible accident rate, and the initial versions of the plane were grounded. The vertical stabilizer would end up being reconfigured on subsequent models of the F-100.

The 510th went through a transition period to the F-100D model from September 1956 through May 1957. More F-100 "D" models were built than any other type, and it was considered the most improved and dependable version of the Super Sabre.

The F-100 was touted as being able break the "sound barrier" in level flight, but many pilots insisted that it actually had to be in a slightly-nose-down flight path to burst through the sonic wall. Top speed for the F-100 was 864 miles per hour at 35,000 feet (Mach 1.3), and its armament consisted of M-39E cannons. It also had six "hardpoints" under its wings, to which rockets or bombs could be attached.

The 510th was, of course, nuclear-capable in the F-100 as well, and still utilized the "Over The Shoulder" maneuver with the Super Sabre.

And as it turned out, the new aircraft also figured into Roosa meeting the woman he would marry.

———

One memorable evening in October of 1956, representatives of North American Aircraft sponsored a party at the Langley Officers' Club on base, celebrating the acquisition of the F-100D. The soirée was held in a separate room from the main section of the "O Club," but the folding partition was eventually pushed out of the way, and members of the 510th, who were drinking a concoction of champagne and beer that they had mixed together, mingled with other persons at the club.

Stuart spotted an attractive brunette among a group of females. She had a round, open face, and eyes that would probably impress an observer as reflecting intelligence.

A family legend recounts that Roosa turned to the bartender and said "See that woman right there? I'm going to marry her."

———

Tupelo, Mississippi is perhaps most famous as the birthplace of Elvis Presley, and while Joan Barrett had indeed attended elementary school with the future musical icon, she was a traditional Southern belle who was the daughter of that town's leading veterinarian, John "Doc" Barrett, and his wife Mary Ethel. The affluent family resided in a large house, and even had servants.

Joan's parents were members of Tupelo society, and she carried herself with the type of poise expected from ladies who had grown up in prominent families of the Deep South. She was a graduate of Mississippi State College for Women, where she had garnered a degree in History, with the intent of becoming a teacher.

She was among several Mississippi women, all teachers, who had recently moved to the Tidewater area in a collective and determined effort to further their lives outside of the Magnolia State, although one of them had just broken off an engagement. Reportedly, when they were trying to decide where to relocate, one of Joan's friends threw a dart at a map of the United States, and it landed on Norfolk, Virginia, so the women opted to apply for teaching jobs in that area.

Some of the Deep South transplants, including Joan, were living in a rented beach house. She was teaching at a school in Hampton.

One of the other teachers' cousins was stationed at Langley, and that evening, the group was attending a birthday party at the Officers' Club.

Stu approached Joan, and his first words to her were: "Have you ever had champagne and beer?"

Startled, her initial reaction was one of disgust, but she tried a bit of the mixture, and decided she liked it. The couple would re-enact their first encounter more than once during their married life.

Roosa asked for Joan's phone number, and she complied, but when she didn't hear from him for a couple of weeks, she decided he would probably never call her. As it turned out, Stu had a short temporary duty assignment, known as a TDY in military parlance, and he called her soon after he returned.

One of their first get-togethers revolved around Thanksgiving dinner for Roosa and some of his peers. Stu had gotten a turkey—he might have even shot it, as he still hunted when he was able to do so, but the details have been lost over the decades. Joan, whose passion was cooking, prepared the bird for the holiday, and Roosa was impressed by her culinary expertise.

In spite of his pragmatic personality, and any lingering identification with the independent spirit he attributed to Frankie Laine's "Cry of the Wild Goose," Roosa was quickly smitten, just as his father had reacted when the elder Roosa had met Lorine DeLozier.

—◈—

Joan was "playing the field," dating other men, but wasn't serious with anyone, primarily because she'd had a steady beau in Tupelo, and the Barretts' peers assumed that Joan and the local man would eventually marry. When Joan relocated to Virginia, however, the twosome agreed to date other people.

Undaunted by any other competitors he might have in Virginia or Mississippi, Roosa applied his usual focused and determined method to his courtship of the teacher from the Deep South. Stu was fascinated by the gracious Southern lady who was a socialite, and who had manners. Not surprisingly, Joan was quickly able to determine Stu's intentions.

Roosa's local "competition" would call Joan, asking her for dates on Friday or Saturday, and in a unique "tactic," Stu, recognizing that Joan was a practicing Catholic, began escorting her to Mass on Sundays. Roosa himself was relatively unfamiliar with the Catholic Church and its doctrine.

It was after Mass one Sunday that Stu drove Joan to a hangar at Langley, showing her his personal F-100, and she was impressed by the supersonic machine and the fact that Roosa was its pilot.

He actually asked her to marry him on their third date, but Joan turned him down.

Stu also apparently had a jealous streak, and would later exhibit it in an unusual manner, utilizing his F-100.

Roosa had already acquired a reputation for being proficient at "buzzing"—swooping out of the sky to skim horizontally at blinding speed just above the ground or a tree line, or just over a particular landmark. He found out that Joan was slated to attend a cocktail party at another home on the beach with another pilot she had been seeing on occasion. Stu happened to have a night mission in an F-100 at the time the party would be taking place, and he managed to confirm where the house was located.

The Super Sabre had a built-in booster known as an "afterburner" for its engine. The afterburners on F-100s and other early supersonic fighters were more "explosive" when they were touched off, whereas modern fighters have a more efficient "staged afterburner."

An afterburner is basically a mechanism where raw fuel is dumped in behind a turbine engine. The fuel ignites in the jetstream, instead of inside the engine to power the turbine blades. A staged afterburner in a present-day fighter offers a smooth transition, whereas the afterburner in an F-100, the original supersonic fighter, had one setting—100%, full-on (also referred to as a "hard light" characteristic). There was no metering of the fuel, which was simply dumped in all at once, resulting in one solid ignition of the gas—nothing less than a contained explosion in the tailpipe of a jet. Whenever the flame hit, the entire load of fuel that had been introduced behind the turbine would ignite with a huge concussion.

Accordingly, while lighting off an afterburner wasn't the same as breaking Mach, it could produce a similar sound.

Roosa had completed his night-flying assignment, and was returning to Langley. A check of his gauges indicated that he had enough fuel to light off the afterburner.

With the F-100, there was approximately a one and a half second delay from the time the afterburner was selected and the time it lit.

Stu spotted the house where the party was being held, and the Super Sabre swooped down to treetop level.

He hit the afterburner switch some distance from his "target," wondering—for a second and a half—if he had calculated correctly.

BOOM!

A huge concussion shook the entire house, and many of the party-goers actually hit the floor.

Roosa had timed his unique-and-somewhat-complicated prank perfectly.

—⁓—

Staying honest with her Mississippi beau, Joan wrote that she had been on several dates with Stuart Roosa, a pilot at nearby Langley Air Force Base. The "steady" in Tupelo must have sensed that something was up, as he wrote her back quickly, informing Joan that he didn't want her to go out with Roosa anymore.

She was torn about her long-term intentions, because she had begun to develop feelings for the red-headed pilot from Oklahoma. Such reciprocal indications only strengthened Roosa's resolve, and he even took out short-term loans to be able to afford to buy fancy dinners on dates with Joan.

Joan and Stuart began to get more serious in their relationship, recognizing qualities in each other that indicated they were thinking about spending the rest of their lives together, and Stu began a clandestine educational effort that would surprise and delight Joan (and later, her family)—he began to take lessons on converting to Catholicism.

Roosa saw such an education and conversion as part of his mission of commitment to Joan, who was a "committed" Catholic, thanks to her parents. Her father was Irish-Catholic, and Mary Ethel had been Southern Baptist before becoming a Catholic after marrying Doc. As for his own evolution regarding Christianity, Stu had been put off at times by some of the "fire-and-brimstone"/"burn-in-hell" rhetoric he had heard at other churches in the past, and when he met and got to know Joan, as well as her faith, he decided that Catholicism was more "logical" rather than over-the-top emotional, which suited his personality fine. He had always had a relatively strong personal faith, but had never really found a religious organization with which he had felt comfortable.

Stu and Joan had been "opposites" as children—he had had a rural and somewhat-rugged upbringing, whereas she had been raised in traditional

Deep South society, but they recognized that the primary quality that had attracted them to each other for a lifetime commitment was a mutual spirit of adventure.

On one occasion after they had been seeing each other exclusively, he was visiting the house where Joan and her friends lived, and abruptly announced to the residents that Joan had agreed to marry him. She hadn't, but Joan didn't deny it at that point because she didn't want to shoot him down in front of all of her acquaintances. However, Stu's proclamation represented a turning point for their relationship—Joan reckoned that if Stuart Roosa had enough moxie to announce his intentions in such a bold manner, he was willing to commit to a lifetime with her, and for all intents and purposes, her relationship with her Mississippi beau ended right then.

The time came when Joan and Stu decided to marry, and Joan went through the unenviable but necessary obligation of informing her (former) Mississippi boyfriend face-to-face that she was going to marry someone else.

Another traditional part of the bride-to-be's Southern upbringing was for the prospective groom to ask her father for his daughter's hand in marriage.

Roosa made plans to fly his F-100 into Columbus Air Force Base, about 70 miles south of Tupelo. Before he left Langley, however, he found out the location of the Barretts' home.

And the first "contact" for Joan's parents and others by Lt. Stuart A. Roosa of the United States Air Force occurred when his Super Sabre buzzed their house. To his credit, Roosa's brashness didn't include lighting off the afterburner again, but when the plane roared over the Barrett home, some of the Barretts' servants were so terrified that they jumped under the house's raised front porch, cowering beneath the structure.

When the Air Force pilot came to the Barrett house for the requisite social obligations, the servants dubbed him "Mr. Lieutenant," and that would be Roosa's sobriquet among them from then on whenever he visited, regardless of what rank he had attained.

Stu discussed his intentions with Doc Barrett regarding the veterinarian's youngest daughter, but Stu reported that Barrett was such a talker that the young pilot wasn't sure whether his would-be future father-in-law had said yes or no.

Roosa's confusion aside, Dr. John Barrett was so impressed by Stu's flying abilities that before his future son-in-law returned to Virginia, the veterinarian presented Roosa with a list he had hastily compiled of houses in the area owned by social and business acquaintances. Barrett wanted those houses "buzzed" as well.

—⁓—

Joan Barrett and Stuart Roosa became husband and wife on September 21, 1957 in a traditional Catholic ceremony in Tupelo. Attending the bride were her two older sisters, Gloria and Patti, both of whom were already married. Stuart's brother Danny served as best man. In the group photo, the groom, attired in a formal Air Force outfit, looks to be all of fifteen years old.

The couple took a brief honeymoon to Chattanooga, Tennessee, a town replete with Southern history, and soon after they returned to Virginia, Stu went on a TDY to Italy. Joan was able to join him later, sailing across the Atlantic on an ocean liner.

Two weeks after their wedding, however, an earth-shaking event had occurred that would forever change the course of human history, and it would also alter the career path of Stuart Roosa.

On October 4th, a basketball-sized, polished aluminum sphere that weighed approximately 184 pounds became the first object to be lofted into orbit around the planet. Sporting four long antennae that made it look somewhat like a chrome-plated octopus, the contraption did little more than transmit a plaintive beeping noise to validate its existence high over the Earth, which it circled every 98 minutes.

The gizmo was harmless, as far as its pure function went. However, the successful launch of the world's first artificial satellite had a cataclysmic effect across the globe, and it was especially traumatic in the halls of power in Washington, D.C.

For the satellite, named Sputnik, had been launched by the Soviet Union. *The Communists had beaten the United States into outer space!*

As it turned out, America could have orbited a satellite first, but redundancy and infighting between branches of the military, as well as other machinations, kept delaying attempted launches of more than one configuration of missile.

The Soviets, on the other hand, knew that their still-under-development R-7 intercontinental ballistic missile had enough power to place a satellite into orbit, and the "Reds" proceeded to do exactly that.

The Space Race, with the Moon as the ultimate prize, was underway.

Boulder, Tachikawa Air Base, Olmstead Air Force Base

When Roosa's assignment with the 510th was completed in 1958, the Air Force Institute of Technology program sent him back to college to attain a degree. Such a move was something that Joan had also encouraged Stu to do, and the couple would spend two years in Boulder, Colorado, where he would earn a Bachelor of Science degree in Aeronautical Engineering at the University of Colorado.

The young Air Force officer and his wife settled into an apartment, and Joan became pregnant. The couple's first son, Christopher Allen, was born on June 29, 1959. The baby was delivered in a public hospital, and Stu snuck in after visiting hours were over to gaze at his new son and visit with Joan, only to be shooed away by a nurse. "Christopher" was a name that Joan happened to like.

Joan didn't like Boulder, however, proclaiming it to be too windy. It was also said that she also couldn't relate to any area where snow was still on the ground when spring arrived. Nevertheless, she dutifully settled into the responsibilities of motherhood.

Vance Brand, another student at Colorado, already had a business degree from that institution, but was now also working on the same degree that Roosa was seeking. Brand was also a Marine Corps aviator, and had served in Japan, flying FJ Fury aircraft before he went into the Reserves.

"I went back to college for three years, and got an aeronautical engineering degree, at the same time Stu did," Brand remembered. "We knew each other, but we didn't socialize much because of studies, and I was working on the side. I met Joan when I visited their apartment once; I think my visit was connected with studies."

Roosa was his usual focused and studious self while at Boulder, and would ultimately graduate with honors. However, one incident during his school days at Colorado resulted in what was the only "C" grade Stuart Roosa ever received in his life—he took exception to a pronouncement from a particular professor, and abruptly stood up in the middle of the classroom and called the teacher a Communist.

After Brand acquired his Aeronautical Engineering degree, he went to work for the Lockheed Aircraft company as a test pilot. He and Roosa would meet again in early 1966.

During Roosa's time at Boulder, the National Aeronautics and Space Administration (NASA) announced seven military pilots as astronauts for the Mercury program, America's initial effort to launch a human being into space. Scott Carpenter, Gordon Cooper, John Glenn, Virgil "Gus" Grissom, Wally Schirra, Alan Shepard, and Donald "Deke" Slayton were introduced to the public in Washington on April 9, 1959.

—◦◦◦—

Roosa may have gotten lucky regarding the overseas assignment that was up next after he earned his degree. Unlike some pilots, he didn't end up at some God-forsaken remote outpost in the Arctic or in a steaming Equatorial nation, but was instead assigned to Tachikawa Air Base in Japan, from 1960-1962.

Located near Tokyo, the base bustled with activity, as it was one of the nerve centers of the Air Force's Far East outposts for monitoring the military activities of North Korea, the People's Republic of China, and the Soviet Union.

However, Roosa had pretty much of a "desk job" during the Japanese assignment, and it must have frustrated him. His title was Chief of Service Engineering for the Air Force Logistics Command (AFLC). He was overseeing the distribution and containment of parts and other items, and he had nothing to do with day-to-day flying, but would be able to take a plane up for a brief time on rare occasions.

Joan went to Japan with Stu, and, having been a History major in college, readily adapted to the foreign assignment, absorbing the Japanese culture with enthusiasm. She enrolled in a cooking class soon after their arrival, as she would do at other locations throughout Roosa's Air Force career. Stu considered his wife's Japanese cooking to be among her best culinary accomplishments.

The couple would go to various events in Tokyo, and enjoyed traditional Japanese dining, even donning kimonos for such experiences.

While in Japan, the Roosas' second and third children, both boys, were born. John Dewey Roosa, named after both grandfathers, came into the world on January 2, 1961, and would be nicknamed "Jack." Stuart Allen Roosa, Jr. (who would be addressed by his middle name) was born on March 12, 1962.

And while the Roosas were at Tachikawa, the Soviet Union's space program stamped another unforgettable date into the chronology of human history. On April 12, 1961, Soviet military pilot Yuri Gagarin became the first human being to journey into outer space, making a single orbit around the globe in an automated spacecraft known as Vostok. It was another propaganda coup for the U.S.S.R. that was devastating for the United States, and once again, Washington reverberated with angst and blame, since it appeared that the U.S. could have put a man into space earlier.

Navy aviator Alan Shepard became the first American in space three weeks after Gagarin's flight, riding a Mercury spacecraft on top of a Redstone rocket to an altitude of approximately 115 miles on May 5th. Unlike Gagarin's flight, however, Shepard's flight was sub-orbital, and lasted just 15 minutes.

—◦◦◦—

Roosa's first Stateside assignment after returning from Japan was at Olmstead Air Force Base in Pennsylvania. The base was located on the Susquehanna River in Middletown, about eight miles from the state capital of Harrisburg, and Roosa's assignment in the Keystone State began in July of 1962.

Stu was flying again, but the circumstances were somewhat unique, as he was a maintenance flight test pilot. The squadron to which he was assigned did flight checks for supersonic jets such as F-100s, F-101s, and F-102s that had been in regular service after a specific number of flight hours, and had then been delivered to a facility at Olmstead for refurbishing. It would be easy to have pronounced such servicing to be "scheduled maintenance," but assuring that something as complicated as a jet aircraft was once again flight-worthy was meticulous work.

Other aircraft that were brought to the facility needed outright repairs. Accordingly, the flight checks could be dangerous if some critical part hadn't been serviced and/or replaced properly. More than once, Roosa would limp back to base in an airplane that had lost its power, or that had experienced some kind of malfunction.

—⁓—

Not long after Roosa began his assignment at Olmstead, he was assigned to do a TDY in southern Florida during the Cuban Missile Crisis.

In October of 1962, the United States and the Soviet Union stood "eyeball-to-eyeball" upon the revelation that the latter country was placing nuclear missiles in its client nation of Cuba that were easily capable of hitting targets in the United States. U.S. spy plane photographs showed missiles and launch facilities some 90 miles from Key West, Florida, and President Kennedy ordered a blockade of the island nation until the missiles were removed. The dangerous scenario moved the two superpowers close to the brink of nuclear war, and the entire world watched and waited for a resolution.

Reconnaissance aircraft would land in Key West following their overflights of Cuba, and the film from such flights would be quickly transferred to another jet, to be ferried to Washington for immediate processing and analysis.

Roosa was one of two pilots assigned to transport the spy film to D.C. He was issued a pistol, in case his courier jet had to divert because of bad weather and the pilot had to protect the film—an unlikely occurrence, but the priority of such images was obvious. Moreover, Roosa recalled that he and the other pilot were never going to divert, because the mission was too important.

The crisis abated when, in what could be presented as a tit-for-tat agreement, the U.S.S.R. agreed to remove its offensive missiles from Cuba, and the U.S. stated that it would not invade Cuba, and removed Thor and Jupiter offensive missiles from selected European nations (America's missiles in Europe were seen as becoming obsolete anyway).

—⁓—

Back on regular duty at Olmstead, Roosa demonstrated that he was proficient enough regarding flying skills to have been selected to fly an F-102 in area air shows. Yet his basic duties consisted of checkout flights for repaired or refurbished aircraft, and in one scary incident, he ended up calling on his faith.

He was about to take an airplane up when the crew chief informed him that the fuel pump for the left wing external tank was inoperable, but it wouldn't be needed for the short flight that was scheduled. Roosa signed off on a checklist that noted "EXTERNAL FUEL PUMP INOP."

However, while Roosa was aloft, the weather turned bad, and the "short flight" took much longer than anticipated. He was going to need the fuel in the left wing external tank after all, or else he would have to eject in stormy weather.

So he prayed, then hit the fuel selection switch, and the pump started working, even though the light on the control panel indicated that it wasn't.

Roosa was able to land safely, and considered the safe resolution of the incident to have been divine intervention. He would tell his wife, children, and others that he thought the Lord had His hand in that crisis.

—⁓—

While the Roosas were at Olmstead, Joan became pregnant with their fourth child, and once again, her traditional Southern upbringing would manifest itself, regarding the birth of their final offspring—Mrs. Roosa insisted that no child of theirs would be born on "Yankee" soil. Christopher had been born in Colorado, and Jack and Allen had been born in Japan, so those locales didn't figure into Southern heritage and history the way Pennsylvania, a Union state during the Civil War, did.

Accordingly, Joan and the three boys went to Mississippi to live with her parents while she awaited the birth of her child. By then, Doc Barrett had retired from his practice, and he and Mary Ethel had started a dairy farm in an unincorporated community called Sessums, located several miles south of Starkville.

Late in Joan's pregnancy, Stu would drive all the way from Pennsylvania to the Magnolia State to briefly visit on weekends, practically turning around once he arrived. At one point, he asked her "Do you think maybe you could have the baby this weekend?"

Rosemary Roosa was born in Starkville on July 23, 1963. The date was on a Tuesday, which meant Stu had to wait all week before he could drive to Mississippi to see his new daughter. Originally, the couple had agreed to name the infant Mary Ann if their newborn was a girl, and Roosa even sent flowers to Joan, and flowers "To Mary Ann from Daddy," only to discover when he arrived in Starkville that Joan had decided to name their daughter Rosemary.

—*∿*—

Joan knew of Stu's ambitions to become a test pilot, and the aforementioned spirit of adventure that they shared meant that she was supportive of such aspirations.

One of the Roosa children recalled a family story that on one trip out West (exact year unknown), their route had happened to take them near Edwards Air Force Base, the isolated mecca for test pilots in the high desert of California, northeast of Los Angeles. Stu was driving, and Joan, sitting in the front passenger seat, spotted a sign in the distance indicating that the next intersection was the exit for the state highway to the base.

She reached over towards the steering column, and without speaking, flicked on the turn signal, in a simple-but-meaningful gesture that indicated she knew that if Stu's career was going to advance like they both hoped, he would ultimately need to end up being assigned to test pilot school at Edwards.

Edwards Air Force Base—ARPS Class 64C

Roosa's career began to get on even more of a fast track when he was selected for Class 64C of the U.S. Air Force Aerospace Research Pilot School (ARPS). The class would be known as "64 Charlie" in military lingo, and the designation meant that the class would be the third to begin in 1964 (differing from an Undergraduate Pilot Training class number, which indicated a scheduled conclusion instead of a beginning order). The curriculum and flight testing would last for a year at Edwards Air Force Base.

Edwards was a legendary air base that drew its history from its isolation and almost-always perfect flying weather year-round. Originally a primitive collection of Quonset huts (and not much else) known as Muroc Army Air Field, the base was located at Rogers Dry Lake, and had been used for secret air projects during World War II (the first military jet flew there in late 1942). It was at that location that the United States military began to develop plans to break the sound barrier, using a secret, rocket-powered airplane known as the X-1. Major Chuck Yeager had accomplished that goal on October 14, 1947.

Danny, age five, left, and Stuart, age three, right, at Yellowstone Park. Courtesy of Dana Roosa.

The Roosa family in Claremore, 1941, soon after they returned there. Courtesy of Dana Roosa.

Twelve-year-old Stuart's love of airplanes had already germinated when this photo of him, left, cousin Olenda Reeves, center, and Danny, right, was taken on a summer trip. Roosa family archive.

Stuart, second from left, and other Class of 1951 members "commandeer" an excursion boat during a senior outing at a lake near Claremore. Courtesy of Jimmie Dollard.

Forest Service workers at Blister Rust Control (B.R.C.) Camp 52, summer 1951. Left to right: Dave Finney (a Chicago native not in college), Roosa (Oklahoma A&M), Okie Reiley (Oklahoma A&M), Jimmie Dollard (Oklahoma A& M), Bob Gonia (University of Minnesota). All of the individuals except Reiley lived in the tent in the background. The bag on Dollard's belt contains lunch, which workers packed each morning from selections on a table. Courtesy of Jimmie Dollard.

1953: Cave Junction, Oregon smoke jumper crew and staff pose in front of their single-engine Norduyn Norseman airplane. Among the persons who can be identified in the back row are Jim Oleson, third from left; Roosa, fourth from left; Bob Wood, sixth from left; Jimmie Dollard, ninth from left. Courtesy of Jimmie Dollard.

Roosa is shown during his summer as a smokejumper with his car, a light green 1952 Ford, on the road to Crater Lake. Dollard said that Roosa wanted his picture taken in this "canyon" of tall trees in the background. Courtesy of Jimmie Dollard.

Roosa climbs aboard a yellow-and-blue North American T-6 trainer at Spence Air Base in southwest Georgia as his instructor waits in the rear seat of tandem cockpit. Roosa family archive.

With a T-33 jet trainer at Williams Air Force Base, near Mesa, Arizona. Roosa family archive.

Lorine and Stu pose during a vacation in 1956, shortly after he was assigned to the 510th Fighter Squadron at Langley Air Force Base, Virginia. Courtesy of Dana Roosa.

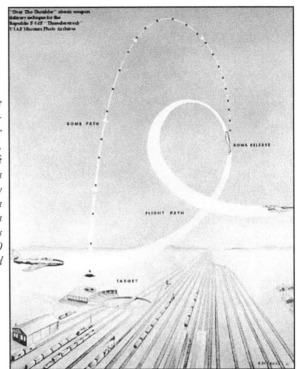

This official Air Force diagram shows the "Over-The-Shoulder" maneuver for The F-84F Thunderstreak, by which the aircraft was supposed to deliver a nuclear bomb to a target by lobbing it backwards. Roosa practiced this dubious idea in the F-84F as well as its replacement, the F-100 Super Sabre, while assigned to Langley. USAF

Wedding day, 1957. Courtesy of Dana Roosa.

Stu, Chris, Jack and Joan enjoy a traditional Japanese meal (replete with appropriate dress) during Stu's assignment to Tachikawa Air Base near Tokyo. Roosa family archive.

Roosa poses in front of a sleek F-104 Starfighter at Edwards Air Force Base, California. Courtesy of Stephanie Smith, USAF AFMC AFFTC/H, Edwards Air Force Base, California.

Aerospace Research Pilot School (ARPS) 64C, Edwards Air Force Base: front, left to right: Stroup, Hull, Larson, Roosa, Hartsfield, Moore; back, Fredericks, Wuertz, Duke, Armstrong, Hoag, Worden. Courtesy of Stephanie Smith, USAF AFMC AFFTC/H, Edwards Air Force Base, California.

Clad in a flight suit, Stu poses with his parents in 1966, around the time he was named as a Group 5 astronaut. Courtesy of Dana Roosa.

Group Five astronauts visited the Morehead Planetarium and Science Center at the University of North Carolina in Chapel Hill soon after their selection in 1966. Roosa is the fifth individual from the top. Wolf Witz, Wilson Library collection, University of North Carolina.

Astronauts from Group Five admire the handiwork of an indigenous Indian during jungle training in Panama, conducted from June 12-16, 1967. From left, Don Lind, school commander Major Jerry Hawkins, Al Worden, Roosa, Bruce McCandless, Vance Brand, John Bull. NASA

Although he never walked on the Moon, Roosa examined basalt during a geological training field trip to Iceland in July of 1967. NASA

This group shot from the Iceland geological trip includes astronauts from groups 2, 3, 4, and 5. Roosa is second from the left. NASA

74

Astronauts go through desert training in southeast Washington State, August 1967. NASA

Charlie Duke, Jim Lovell, and Roosa pose outside Command Module #007A prior to occupying it for 48 hours in a flotation test in the Gulf of Mexico, April 5-7, 1968. NASA film—scan by Ed Hengeveld.

The "boilerplate" Command Module rotates to a different position during its flotation test, as NASA technicians aboard the Retriever monitor the procedure. NASA

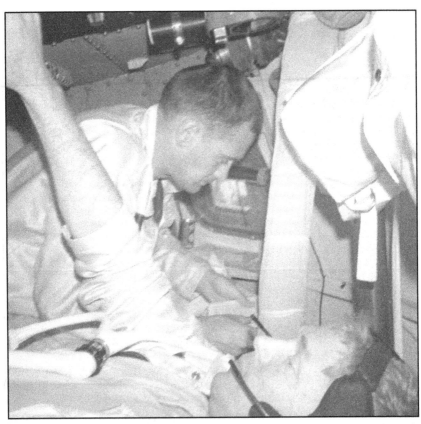

Duke and Roosa (shown), and Lovell, who took this photograph, endured miserable conditions for two days inside the floating Command Module. NASA

This photo taken from the window of the Command Module 007A during its flotation test shows the choppy seas that the three astronauts had to endure. NASA

Accompanied several dummies, Chuck Billings (left), Roosa (center) and Art Porcher (right) prepare to test the slide-wire basket egress system at Cape Kennedy on January 25, 1969. NASA

At the end of the slide-wire basket test, Roosa prepares to exit the test model via a knotted rope, as NASA officials and technicians observe. Billings is already on the ground. NASA

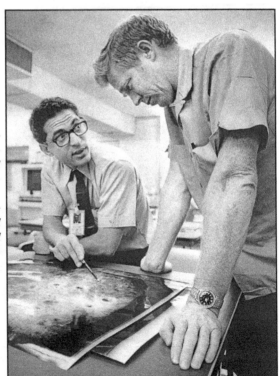

Geologist Farouk El-Baz emphasizes a landmark to Roosa during specialized training that Command Module Pilot received regarding planned observations and photography of the Lunar surface while in orbit. El-Baz is pointing out an area that was photographed from Apollo 12 that was slated to be overflown by Apollo 14. NASA

Mitchell, Shepard and Roosa pose in front of Apollo 14 as it slowly rolls from the Vehicle Assembly Building to Launch Pad 39A on November 9, 1970. NASA

Reproductions of the Apollo 14 mission patch, top, and the infamous "Beep-Beep" patch designed by the backup crew. Willie G. Moseley.

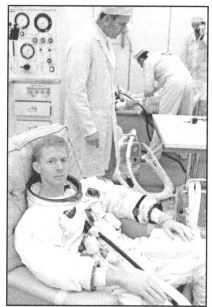

Roosa appears to be relaxed after donning his space suit on launch day. Deke Slayton is seen in the background. NASA

79

Completely enclosed in space travel gear, Mitchell, Roosa and Shepard head down the hallway of the Manned Spacecraft Operations Building to the van that would transport them to the launch pad. Slayton is also seen in the background of this photo, having changed into standard clothing. NASA

Roosa grasps his mother Lorine's hand upon exiting the Manned Spacecraft Operations building. Other Roosa family members seen in the photo are father Dewey Roosa (w/ flattop haircut), sister-in-law Wilma Roosa (brunette with sunglasses). The top of niece Dana Roosa's head (dark bangs and eyes) can be seen just above Lorine's right shoulder, and the child's arm reaching out just behind Lorine belongs to niece Janette. The identity of the blond child with the dark coat in the forefront is not known. UPI wirephoto.

The base had received its new moniker in December of 1949, being named after test pilot Glen Edwards, who was killed while testing an aircraft known as the YB-49 Flying Wing a year and a half earlier.

By the time Roosa and his fellow class members arrived there in the summer of 1964, Edwards was a sprawling, modern facility, but was still the ultimate assignment for pilots. Speed and altitude records were still being broken, as men of valor still sought to fly faster and higher in all types of exotic aircraft that were being tested.

Accordingly, the route to such excitement and glory necessitated a high ranking as a graduate of an ARPS class conducted at the same base.

Now a colonel, Yeager himself had returned to Edwards as commandant of the school in 1962.

Yet for all of its growth and legendary status, Edwards was still somewhat isolated in the desert.

—ᴡᴡ—

Two of the other members of 64 Charlie had had different paths to the cockpit compared to Roosa's experience, but Charlie Duke, Hank Hartsfield, and Roosa became lifelong friends.

Born in Charlotte, North Carolina, Charlie Duke had had a regimented but laudable education, graduating from the prestigious Admiral Farragut Academy in St. Petersburg, Florida, and the U.S. Naval Academy in Annapolis, Maryland.

He had decided to be a pilot in his junior year at Annapolis, and had become an Air Force pilot instead of a Navy aviator.

"It was *really* decided when I took a physical in my *senior* year," Duke recalled. "The Naval Academy doctor found astigmatism in my right eye, and said I wasn't qualified for Navy aviation, but I was okay for the Air Force. So I volunteered to be an Air Force pilot. Incidentally, nobody's ever seen the astigmatism again, and I always passed all of the flight physicals that I ever had."

Already commissioned as an Air Force second lieutenant, Duke would also train at Spence Air Base several years after Roosa had gone through the Georgia facility.

Henry "Hank" Hartsfield had garnered a commission and a career as an Air Force pilot via another route. A native of Birmingham, Alabama, he had participated in Army ROTC at Alabama Polytechnic Institute in Auburn while majoring in Physics. His college alma mater would be re-named Auburn University in 1960.

As it turned out, the Air Force needed pilots, so when Hartsfield was a senior, he took numerous tests at more than one Air Force base, and upon graduating, was commissioned into the USAF. He reported for pilot training after spending a year in graduate school, participating in more intensive physics studies at Duke University.

Perhaps their friendships developed because Duke and Hartsfield had Southern roots, and Roosa, as a country boy from Oklahoma, considered himself to be semi-Southern. The three friends had a shared appreciation of traditional Southern values, as well as a propensity for intense study in both the academic and flying facets of the ARPS.

As for his initial impressions of Roosa and why they became close friends, Duke recounted, "We both had a similar outlook, and we hit it off right away. We were compatible, and had similar personalities—competitors, 'hard-chargers.' Our friendship developed very quickly, and our wives were good friends. The competition was tough between us and several other guys in our class. Stu was very smart, and a very good pilot. He was very focused; working very hard to be number one in the class, as were a lot of other guys. That was a very important year for us, and we all studied very hard. But Stu never had a 'dour' or 'serious' side to his personality; I never saw him in a 'down' mood, or depressed. He was easy to talk to, and he felt comfortable about where he was and what he was doing. His confidence seemed to 'radiate' from him. He was always friendly; and he was 'almost-Southern', so to speak, so that was another reason we gravitated towards each other. By the time we got to NASA, we were referring to ourselves as 'the Dynamic Duo'."

Duke and Roosa enjoyed mutual recreational efforts during off-hours—hunting, fishing, golf, and especially flying. Their families also enjoyed visiting national parks and skiing, as there were a lot of activities within an easy distance. "Three hours to the coast, three hours to the mountains," Duke said.

—⁓—

As might be expected, the entire 64C class was made up of highly-skilled pilots, and while competition was formidable between the members of this "best of the best" assemblage, the entire class had a sense of commitment and camaraderie.

"Because we were all already accomplished pilots when we got there, there really weren't any washouts," Duke said of the ARPS class. "It was not like going through flight school."

Another 64C class member, Al Worden, had already graduated from a test pilot school in Farnborough, England.

"That's when I met Stu," Worden said of his experience at the ARPS. "When I got back from England, there was already a class in progress.

I was already certified as a test pilot, so I'd been through (what was considered) the 'upper part' of the Aerospace Research Pilots School. I actually became part of the class while I was also instructing at the same time. Unfortunately, I did not start with that group; they did their basic stuff before I got there, so I was always a little bit on the outside of the group, even though we all did things together. However, I don't recall that ever being a problem with anybody, but it was kind of strange that I was an instructor, yet was in the class."

Worden and Roosa were classmates, but were not close friends, yet Worden had an appraisal of the red-headed Oklahoman's personality and how Roosa focused on his studies and flight training:

"I would put Stu in the category of 'keeping-his-eye-on-what-had-to-be-done-in-the-class'," Worden opined. "I did not see Stu as a researcher, I did not see Stu as a guy who was trying to 'uncover' or 'discover' new things. I saw Stu as a guy who learned what he was supposed to learn in class, and he was very good at that."

Students in 64C also included members from other branches of the U.S. military. A Marine aviator named Joe Wuertz had a daily ritual of removing a framed photo of the Commandant of the Marine Corps from his desk drawer each morning, placing it on his desktop during the academic sessions. He would dutifully place the photo back in his desk when the class concluded.

"Those of use who were near the top of the class really had to study," said Duke. "It wasn't a cutthroat or backstabbing type of competition; it was open and robust, even if you were trying to eke out an advantage that was only a tenth of a point."

Hartsfield: "Anytime we had a big test coming up, the whole class would go into a night session, where the stronger students, including Stu and me, helped the weaker students prepare."

—〜〜—

Flight training was, of course, exciting and intense, as students flew models such as the T-33, T-38, F-101, F-104, F-106, among others. As for larger multi-engine aircraft, Duke recalls the B-57, and Hartsfield recalls familiarization flights on C-130s and B-47s.

Examples of test applications included the use of the T-38, a supersonic trainer, for roll characteristics, due to its rapid roll rate.

"He was a hell of a pilot," Worden said of Roosa's abilities. "In T-38s, he was very 'business-like,' and was very good at what he did."

When the class began flying F-104s in "zoom" maneuvers, each class member would strain to garner a few hundred feet more of altitude.

And it was also an exciting time to be an ARPS student at Edwards, considering the flight programs that were underway down the runway at the Flight Test center.

"Edwards had evolved into a business-like, state-of-the-art facility," Duke recounted. "Every program had plenty of simulations, as well as engineering goals on each flight. It was never 'Just-take-a-new-airplane-up-and-see-what-it'd-do.' Every flight was planned to expand the envelope of each aircraft a little bit farther."

The X-15 program was in full swing, and the cutting-edge rocket plane flew numerous times during 64C's year at Edwards.

"It was always a thrill to watch it land on the lake bed," said Duke. "A couple of those flights were above 50 miles altitude, which qualified the pilot as an astronaut."

64C members watched the XB-70 Valkyrie bomber, which had been built at nearby Palmdale, California, land at Edwards for the first time (the landing produced a brake and tire fire that was quickly extinguished, according to Hartsfield).

The super-fast and super-secret SR-71 Blackbird was also being tested. Its capabilities fascinated Edwards pilots and ARPS students, as Hartsfield remembered: "Some of the pilots we knew from earlier ARPS classes had gone over to Flight Test, and would fly chase for the SR-71 in an F-104, inspecting doors, etc. before it went on its test run. The chase planes couldn't keep up once the SR-71's run began, of course, and one chase pilot recalled landing, then asking how the SR-71's test run went, to be informed it had landed at McCoy Air Force Base in Orlando about 45 minutes after it had taken off at Edwards!"

The F-111, a medium-range multi-function fighter-bomber with variable-sweep wings that could be adjusted in mid-flight, made its first flights at Edwards in December of 1964.

—⟋⟍⟋—

Roosa and Duke often flew in the same two-seat aircraft to take in sights such as Mount Whitney, tallest peak in the continental United States (14,505 feet), which was located around 150 miles north of the base.

They even got into competitions just between the two of them—sometimes in a tandem cockpit T-38, sometimes in separate aircraft. In one contest, they had a timed climb to see who could get to 25,000 feet the fastest, and then stabilize the aircraft within plus or minus two knots, and plus or minus 20 feet. Stu went first, then Charlie, and Duke beat Roosa by less than ten seconds.

Roosa and Duke also competed in one-on-one precision landing duels, usually when they were flying in a T-38. The object of such a contest was to select a particular stripe on a runway in advance, and each pilot would see how close he could come to touching down, at the requisite landing speed, on that particular marker.

"You didn't want to slam (the airplane) onto the ground just to hit the stripe," Duke said. "You'd want to be on-speed and land the right way."

And Roosa's 64C friend detailed the reasons for such extracurricular competitions between classmates:

"For test pilots, flying has to be very precise—plus or minus two knots airspeed, plus or minus ten feet of altitude. Our planes had very sensitive altimeters, and very sensitive air speed indicators that were more precise than equipment on standard aircraft. We even combined altitudes and air speeds in such competitions, using a stopwatch. Sometimes he won, sometimes I won. Stu was very competitive, but not in a 'ferocious' way, and we always congratulated each other, whether it was an official test or something that just he and I were doing. It was an 'attaboy'-type of relationship."

Still, flying experimental aircraft could be dangerous, as was the training for such assignments. Yeager still flew unique airplanes himself on occasion, and less than a year before 64C arrived, had survived an ejection from an out-of-control NF-104, which had an added rocket engine. The incident was vividly depicted in Tom Wolfe's legendary tome *The Right Stuff*, and was also incorporated into the movie version of the book.

While 64C was active, two Edwards instructors were killed in a crash in Colorado, and another plane came apart at 40,000 feet while trying for an altitude record. An F-106 also crashed.

—⌇—

The Hartsfields and Roosas lived next door to each other on base, and the Dukes lived right down the street. The relationships of Joan, Fran Hartsfield and Dotty Duke would become as close as the relationships of their husbands. The Dukes were younger than the Roosas, and their first son was born during Charlie's ARPS assignment. Joan, who had given birth to four "stairstep" children within four years and one month, was somewhat of a mentor to Dotty regarding motherhood.

"Edwards was fighter pilot heaven," Charlie observed, "but it was a little difficult for the wives, because it was such an isolated place—not much shopping except for the commissary and a little base exchange. Most of the 'decent' shopping was in Lancaster, about 30 miles away."

Dotty was originally from Atlanta, so she bonded with Joan, another Southern lady.

"We just had a lot in common," Dotty said, "including things that we enjoyed doing together."

Dotty also recalled that while many Air Force wives ultimately wouldn't have fond memories of Edwards A.F.B. because of its isolation, her perception was that outwardly, Joan didn't seem to mind the assignment. Joan would later admit that like most of the other wives, she didn't care for the location, in spite of how such an assignment was enhancing Stu's career.

"Of course, she had been married into the military for awhile," said Dotty, "and I was new, because I hadn't been married for too long, and she already had a bunch of children. So she was used to living in different places as part of the military way of life."

And it was at Edwards that the three Roosa boys began to realize what their father did for a living. Chris, Jack, and Allen all have vague childhood memories of playing in the back yard and hearing sonic booms on a regular basis, and of being taken to the flight line, where they heard the loud whine of jet engines, and smelled the exotic aromas of jet exhaust and fuel.

"At that time, there were a lot of unique airplanes there," Chris recalled, "and Dad would take us out onto the flight line at times. One time, we got to watch the X-15 land; we got to see the B-70 at an air show; the SR-71 was around."

Even Allen, who was three years old, recalled "...seeing my dad in a flight suit. I remember riding with him in the Econoline van that shuttled pilots out to their aircraft; I remember it didn't have any doors on it. When we pulled up to his jet, that's when I knew he was a pilot."

ARPS class members participated in various outdoor activities, such as climbing Mount Whitney (only a couple of students didn't make the trip).

64C also had its share of parties, which were usually held at a member's house.

One memorable soirée started at the home of Joe Wuertz, who had invited the class to his home in November to have a drink in honor of the Marine Corps anniversary.

Wuertz most likely meant for the occasion to be informal, but several Air Force class members decided to pull a bit of a "gotcha" on the proud Marine, and showed up wearing their formal dress uniforms.

When Wuertz answered the door, he was dressed casually, and was "absolutely shocked," according to Hartsfield. The Marine officer made his guests wait for a few minutes while he scrambled to put on his own dress uniform.

The group then went to dinner at a restaurant near Lancaster, and when they arrived, they were almost the only customers in the establishment. The dining room, which happened to have a large fireplace, was cold, but a complaint to the owner went unheeded. The room had a large number of folding wooden chairs, and after a second complaint, the owner threw a number of them into the fireplace and lit them, and the blaze soon warmed up the room.

Worden also recalled a particularly wild party at the Roosas' home on base, but the Air Police weren't called.

Another 64C member had an elite-sounding name, Barron Fredericks III. His nickname within the class was "Duke," but his real name would serve the Roosas, the Hartsfields, and Fredericks and his wife Theresa well on one occasion when they made a jaunt to Las Vegas.

The three couples had wanted to see Frank Sinatra's show, but found out it was sold out.

Fredericks got on the phone, and using his full name, apparently made the theatre management think he was some kind of royalty, and the Roosas, Hartsfields, and Fredericks quickly acquired six seats close to the stage.

—✺—

After a year of intense academic work and cutting-edge flight tests, the top four finishers in final rankings were separated by less than a point. Pete Hoag was the "top stick" of 64 Charlie, followed closely by Hartsfield, Duke, and Roosa. Hank and Charlie are not sure about the exact rankings of the individuals in second, third, and fourth place, and it doesn't matter to them.

"Members of our class have always said we had the best class ever to go through the school," said Hartsfield. "We all worked hard, and it paid off. We generated four astronauts, but in the main, we always felt that we all got along well, and we were never cutthroat in our actions. We cooperated and helped each other academically."

Duke: "We didn't see the fact that four of us from 64C ended up as astronauts to be ironic, but we were very proud of our class. I think it's the only class that had four astronauts selected, and three of us got to fly on Apollo. There were also three members of that class who became generals, and that was something else to be proud of; everybody else—at least, the Air Force class members—made colonel."

ASTRONAUT

Application and Selection

It came as no surprise that Roosa, Hartsfield, Duke, and several other ARPS Class 64C graduates remained at Edwards for their next assignments, beginning in September of 1965.

Roosa was assigned to Flight Test, as was Duke. Hartsfield remained at the ARPS as an instructor. Among the aircraft that Roosa flew during his short tenure at Flight Test was the pre-production version of the F-111.

According to Duke, most 64C students didn't really discuss applying to NASA to be astronauts, but they had talked about how it would be exciting just to be *chosen* for a program that was even more exotic—and potentially more dangerous—than flight test operations at Edwards.

The original seven Mercury astronauts were now demi-gods among pilots as well as the general public, and such had been the case since they were selected (i.e., even before any of them flew into space). All of the original seven astronauts had been hurled into the void in a primitive, single-man, bell-shaped Mercury spacecraft, except for Deke Slayton, who had been grounded due to a heart condition. The launch sites for NASA's space program were at Cape Canaveral, on the Atlantic coast of the Florida peninsula.

Soon after the initial 15-minute sub-orbital flight of Alan Shepard on May 5, 1961, U.S. President John F. Kennedy had challenged the nation to complete a lunar landing mission by the end of the decade.

"I believe that this nation should commit itself to achieving the goal, before this decade is out, of landing a man on the Moon and returning him safely to the Earth," Kennedy told Congress on May 25th. "No single space project in this period will be more impressive to mankind, or more important for the long-range exploration of space; and none will be so difficult or expensive to accomplish."

Astronaut Group 2 was announced in September of 1962, and was known as the New Nine. One of them would die in a plane crash before he ever flew on a mission.

Group 3 was presented to the public in October of 1963, and had fourteen members. Four would perish before they had an opportunity to go into space.

Cape Canaveral's moniker was changed to Cape Kennedy in late 1963, following Kennedy's assassination on November 22nd of that year.

In 1964, Alan Shepard was grounded due to an ear condition that caused dizziness and nausea.

In early 1965, six astronauts with scientific and research backgrounds (instead of test pilot experience) were chosen as Group 4. Doctorates were required.

The ambitious-if-interim Gemini two-man project was already underway in 1965 when NASA put out its notice concerning recruitment of a fifth group of spacemen shortly after 64C had graduated.

Considering the time frame NASA was dealing with in its effort to meet Kennedy's goal of landing on the Moon by the end of the decade, it was possible that some members of the newest group of astronauts, which would become known as Group 5, would have a chance to be chosen to journey to that desolate but fascinating world. The dream of such a voyage had fascinated the human species since it first developed the ability to reason, and plans for a series of epic flights were rapidly taking shape.

Stu and Joan were actually on a vacation by themselves in northern California when they heard about the announcement of applications being accepted for the next group for astronauts. They turned around immediately, and headed back to Edwards so Stu could begin the paperwork as soon as possible.

—⁓—

Around the same time, another astronaut "option" also beckoned many of the Edwards test pilots, but it was to be a siren call to an ultimately-cancelled military program that most likely meant bitter disappointment to the astronauts who had been chosen for it.

The "militarization of space" had its advocates and detractors in the early days of the fabled Space Race. One Air Force space program, the X-20 Dyna-Soar project, had been proposed just after the Soviet Union lofted Sputnik into orbit in 1957.

Conceived as a re-usable "space plane" that would fly military missions in orbit and re-enter the atmosphere with a heat-ablating shield on its underside, the X-20 looked remarkably like NASA's Space Shuttle that would first fly in the early Eighties.

The Dyna-Soar program was cancelled on December 10, 1963, but the Air Force announced its successor, the Manned Orbital Laboratory, the same day.

Known by its acronym, MOL (and pronounced "Mole"), the Manned Orbital Laboratory's concept proposed to use a bell-shaped, modified Gemini two-man spacecraft instead of a "space plane." The spacecraft would be sent aloft attached to an orbiting space station, which, although touted as a test facility for human endurance in space, was an obvious "spy-in-the sky."

Accordingly, many Edwards test pilots were in a quandary about whether to apply to the NASA space program or the Air Force space program, or both.

Duke recalls that he and Roosa were informed that if they applied for the MOL program, they would probably be selected. However, the uncertainty of military space flight took them down the other path:

"Stu and I—and maybe Al Worden as well—decided we would take our chances with only NASA. The future of manned space flight with the Air Force was sort of tenuous; they had already cancelled the Dyna-Soar program, and we didn't know if the MOL program would actually get to fly."

"If you applied for both (programs), the Air Force would decide which one to nominate you to," said Hartsfield. "I applied for both. However, Charlie and Stu had told me not to apply for both programs. I got selected for the MOL."

Roosa and Duke went through the NASA astronaut selection process together. They went to Houston for interviews, then to Brooks Air Force Base in San Antonio for a physical and psychological testing (to include Rorschach ink-blot tests).

"We spent the better part of a week there," Duke recalled, "and I guess maybe a half a day was spent with a psychiatrist or psychologist. The big thing about the Rorschach tests was that you weren't supposed to see anything sexual or weird; you should just breeze through without giving complicated answers...one would look like a butterfly, or a cloud formation, or a giraffe. Simple as that, but if you looked closely, you could have gotten something more complicated out of some of them."

Other processes included centrifuge testing, encephalogram (brain wave) tests, and cardio-vascular and vestibular testing for endurance and balance.

"We had a whole day of electro-cardiogram tests, where we were strapped to a table that would roll and rotate into an inverted position," said Duke.

Candidates were also subjected to odd tests that Duke described as "right-hand-in-hot-water, cold-water-in-your-ear stuff" that the would-be astronauts didn't understand.

The mid-Sixties astronaut candidates did not, however, have to endure a plethora of over-the-top type of initial testing that had been done on earlier groups of would-be spacemen, as depicted in *The Right Stuff* (the book *and* the movie).

Cuts in the list of prospective astronauts were made, but Stu and Charlie remained in the chase, as did several other Edwards pilots.

Because of their unique experiences, smoke jumpers tend to keep in touch with each other, communicating on a regular basis for years after their on-duty firefighting days have ended. Jim Allen says that Roosa was no exception.

"I heard from Stuart quite often," Allen recalled, "and he was very good about letting us know about his flight training."

In the winter of 1965-66, the former Cave Junction Air Project Officer received a call from the Federal Bureau of Investigation district office in Eugene, Oregon, asking if he knew Stuart Roosa. When he confirmed his acquaintance with the Air Force pilot, the FBI representative asked for an interview with Allen concerning details about the CJ-53 smoke jumper.

"I told them I had a trip planned to Portland the following week, and being that Eugene is between Cave Junction and Portland, I said that I would be glad to stop by their office on the way," Allen said. "When I got to the FBI office, they asked me about my recollections of Stuart. I told them what I knew, including that I remembered his intelligence and leadership qualities very well."

"During the course of the conversation, they asked me if I knew why I was being interviewed. I told them that I had recently read where pilots were being considered for astronaut positions, and I assumed that might be the reason; they concurred. They asked me how I could remember him so well, when I hadn't seen him for several years, and I replied that it was because he was an outstanding young man. Several of their questions concerned how I thought he would be at meeting the public; they said it was important, as he would be in the 'limelight' if he was selected for the astronaut program. I assured them that I thought he would do very well."

Roosa and others went through numerous interviews and tests, and continued to "make the cut." At one point, another candidate stationed at Edwards, Joe Engle, received a letter at his duty station from NASA, requesting that he continue to the next phase of the selection process.

Roosa received no such letter at his own duty location, and figured he was out of the running.

However, when he arrived at home that evening in a glum mood, Joan gave Stu his own copy of the same letter Engle had received. NASA had sent the missive to Roosa's home address, and his relief at being informed he still had a chance to become an astronaut made him—as well as Joan—realize just how much he wanted to be selected.

The finalists were invited to Houston for interviews with NASA officials, including Deke Slayton, who had assumed a primary role in NASA's Astronaut Office as the Director of Flight Crew Operations.

When Roosa's final interview took place, Slayton left in the middle of the encounter to take a phone call, so Stu assumed once more that he was not going to be selected, and was dejected, yet again.

But Slayton knew one of Roosa's commanders at test pilot school, and that officer had highly recommended the redheaded Oklahoman. Slayton had apparently already decided to accept Roosa prior to the final interview.

The fateful phone calls from Slayton came in March of 1966, giving each newly-designated astronaut 30 days to report to Houston.

"We had a big party that evening," Duke recounted. "Others who were at Edwards at that time but weren't 64C graduates were also selected—Ken Mattingly, Ed Mitchell, Joe Engle. There was a lot of celebrating going on, because we knew we'd been selected for the greatest job you could have as a test pilot. We were practically shouting from the rooftops."

Worden recalled that Roosa didn't particularly raise hell when the Group 5 list was announced. Stu seemed to take the selection in stride, underlining Worden's opinion of Roosa as "a very matter-of-fact guy."

One might also wonder what the thoughts were of the wives of the newly-selected members of Group 5. While some of them were undoubtedly grateful to be able to depart from the dusty, wind-swept isolation of Edwards Air Force Base, their husbands' new assignments, while exciting, were obviously dangerous.

Officially announced on April 4, 1966, the members of Group 5 were, in alphabetical order, Vance Brand, John Bull, Gerald Carr, Charles Duke, Joseph Engle, Ronald Evans, Edward Givens, Fred Haise, James Irwin, Don Lind, Jack Lousma, Ken Mattingly, Bruce McCandless II, Edgar Mitchell, William Pogue, Stuart Roosa, John "Jack" Swigert, Paul Weitz, and Alfred Worden.

Someone noted that some previous astronaut groups had acquired nicknames, and an unknown cynic came up with the tongue-in-cheek moniker "The Original Nineteen" for Group 5. The sardonic sobriquet stuck.

Two months later, Hank Hartsfield was in the second group of astronauts to be assigned to the Air Force's MOL project.

Houston, Early Training

Most of the wives of those Original Nineteen members who had been stationed at Edwards Air Force Base were delighted with the move to Houston.

"My wife had grown up in Atlanta," Duke recalled, "and was pleased when we moved to the piney woods of the Houston area!"

The Roosa children were too young to realize at the time what an important career step this was for their father, but Chris and Jack recall their dad bringing home a photo of the home where they would be living in the suburbs of the south Texas metropolis of Houston.

Likewise, Allen remembered one facet of the move—the family traveled from California to Houston in a long station wagon, and the boy would have trouble figuring out that Texas was such a large state. He was flummoxed about why it took so long to get to Houston after they had entered the Lone Star State in its Panhandle.

Rosemary's earliest memories about her father's occupation began in Houston.

In the early Sixties, Vice-President Lyndon Johnson had been a fervent supporter of space exploration, and had gotten NASA's Manned Space Center, the massive new nerve center of the country's space program, built in his home state. Johnson was now President, and was still committed to the United States' effort to beat the Soviets to the Moon. Accordingly, the Houston area to which the Roosas moved in 1966 was a sprawling metropolis that reveled in the excitement of the Space Race, and the astronauts and their families were the darlings of local society.

The Roosa family moved to a community known as El Lago, located close to the Manned Space Center. Numerous astronauts and NASA employees and their families ultimately resided there, as well as in nearby locales such as Clear Lake. The Roosa children would attend an elementary school that would later be named for astronaut Ed White, and other students included the children of astronauts Neil Armstrong, Fred Haise, and Joe Engle, among others. They would also become good friends with Judy and Keely Hartsfield, daughters of Fran and Hank Hartsfield, who eventually moved a few blocks away. Dotty and Charlie Duke and their children lived less than a mile away.

"We grew up in Houston, after he joined NASA," Chris said. "There were other astronauts living in the same neighborhood, and there were other astronauts' kids going to the same school. Some of their fathers had more seniority, and had already gone into space, but it wasn't like your father was the President of the United States. Most of the families in the neighborhood worked at NASA—engineers, astronauts, and support persons. NASA was the 'up-and-coming' industry just outside of Houston at the time."

Jack: "When I was in the second grade, I began to notice what my dad was doing; why he was gone from home so much. When we were in school, classes would stop for a launch. Teachers would roll a black-and-white TV set into the classroom, and the whole school would get quiet during a countdown. It was particularly important for *that* elementary school, since it was near the NASA facility, and a lot of the children of NASA employees, including astronauts, went there. You started to realize 'Hey, my dad's part of this.' While my recollections are from a child's perspective, the older I get, the more impressed I am with what the Mercury, Gemini, and Apollo programs accomplished."

—⁓—

The Original Nineteen started out with four months of classroom indoctrination—understanding the Apollo spacecraft systems, NASA organization (and its plethora of acronyms), public relations.

"We were like sponges," said Duke, "sopping it all up."

"Stu wasn't real talkative," said Roosa's former Colorado classmate Vance Brand, "but I wouldn't say he was 'super-quiet,' either. He had a good sense of humor, and he was very even-tempered, in the sense that you'd apply that term to a pilot—he was 'cool and collected.' He was actually a very adventurous sort of guy, and very sure of himself. I always had a lot of respect for him; he was obviously a real asset to the Apollo program; he performed well, and was a very confident individual."

One of the earliest trips the Original Nineteen made as a group was to the Morehead Planetarium on the campus of the University of North Carolina at Chapel Hill, visiting the facility on June 10, 1966. The planetarium hosted a training program for astronauts, focusing on celestial navigation and constellation recognition, throughout the entire Mercury-Gemini-Apollo era.

The journey to the Moon had been through numerous proposed scenarios before NASA had opted for a concept called "Lunar Orbit Rendezvous," which would send two conjoined spacecraft to Luna. The Group 5 astronauts began to study the systems, rockets and spacecraft that would ultimately propel some of them to another world.

The delivery system for the mission would be the powerful Saturn V (Roman number "five") three-stage rocket system, which would become the most potent and complex missile of its time. The Space Race was getting more arduous, as the size of the rockets and scope of planned missions increased. The Soviets were known to be scrambling with their own Moon-designated super-rocket, the N-1, but it never flew successfully.

The Saturn system would loft the two spacecraft into orbit, after which the last stage would fire again, boosting the astronauts and their spacecraft towards the Moon in a maneuver called Trans-Lunar Injection (TLI).

One of the two spacecraft was actually comprised of two units itself, consisting of the Command Module (CM), the conical-shaped cockpit and primary living quarters for the voyage, and a cylinder-shaped section known as the Service Module. The complex interior of the Service Module contained oxygen, batteries, and other essential components, as well as the Service Propulsion System engine (SPS), the rocket that would be used during transit to correct trajectory, as well as to place the two spacecraft into lunar orbit and to break the CSM free of lunar orbit once that phase of the mission had been completed. Collectively, the Command Module and Service Module were known as the CSM.

The Lunar Module (LM) was a four-legged, ungainly-looking contraption that would detach itself from the CSM to take two astronauts, the mission's Commander (CDR) and the Lunar Module Pilot (LMP) to the surface of the Moon, while the third astronaut, the Command Module Pilot (CMP) remained in orbit around the Moon by himself.

However, CMP duties on Apollo lunar missions also included navigating the spacecraft to its rendezvous points with the Moon and Earth during the outward and return voyages, respectively. Moreover, CMPs would have plenty of planned geological surveying and photographic assignments to keep them busy while they were orbiting solo around the Moon.

The Lunar lander had originally been known as the Lunar Excursion Module—a.k.a. LEM—but the "E" was phased out.

The LM was to be stored in the third stage of the Saturn. Once the Saturn's third stage had boosted the spacecraft out of orbit and into a trajectory that would result in a rendezvous with the Moon, the CSM would detach itself from the third stage, turn around, and dock with the LM, which would then be extracted from its storage compartment. The critical procedure was known as TD&E, the initials of which represented its chronological order (Transposition, Docking and Extraction). TD&E was also the responsibility of the CMP.

The LM also had two distinct units as well. When the two astronauts had completed their work on the Moon, they would blast off in the upper half of the LM, known as the ascent stage; the lower half of the LM would serve as a launch pad and would remain on the surface. The LM would rendezvous with the CSM, and link back up. Astronauts would transfer the samples they had collected on the lunar surface to the Command Module, after which the now-unmanned upper half of the LM would be disconnected, and would be redirected for a crash landing back on the Moon.

The fuel tanks for the SPS engine on the CSM were designed to furnish enough propellant to get the conjoined Apollo spacecraft into orbit around the Moon, and to blast the CSM back to Earth in a reciprocal maneuver called, not surprisingly, Trans-Earth Injection (TEI). There would just enough leftover fuel to make mid-course corrections on the return flight, if needed, just as such adjustments would have been made on the outward flight, if needed.

As the spacecraft approached the planet, it would be traveling several times faster than a bullet. The Service Module would be jettisoned, and would burn up upon re-entering the Earth's atmosphere.

The angle for re-entry had to be extremely precise, as it was a one-shot effort for the CM—the cone-shaped spacecraft, all that remained of the mighty, multiple-staged Moon mission, would come barreling straight in, instead of orbiting prior to re-entry. It would have had to slow from over 25,000 mph to 17,000 m.p.h. to go into orbit, but such a maneuver was impossible, due to the lack of fuel. The Command Module had to plunge into the atmosphere in an exact profile, angle-wise, through a narrow "corridor." If it entered at too deep of an angle, it would be incinerated. If it came in too shallow, it could skip off the upper atmosphere like a flat rock on the surface of a lake, and would bounce back into outer space... permanently. There would be no second chances.

—⁓⁓—

On October 3, 1966, technical assignments for Group 5 members were announced. The so-called "Dynamic Duo" was placed in the Booster and Flight Safety Branch, which was under the auspices of Group 3 astronaut C.C. Williams.

The assignment to the Booster and Flight Safety Branch meant Roosa and Duke would be spending a lot of time in Huntsville, Alabama, where the powerful Saturn rocket had been under development since 1958. Originally, the Army's Redstone Arsenal in the northern Alabama town was responsible for such rocket science, under the direction of former German scientist Wernher von Braun, who had helped to develop the V-2 missile during World War II. The Huntsville facility had been turned over to NASA in 1960. Moreover, von Braun and other German scientists were now American citizens.

Roosa was disappointed. He commented at the time that boosters were not the most cutting-edge part of the program, and he and Duke fretted that such an assignation might stymie their careers, or take them down a dead-end road. The twosome didn't think "Huntspatch"—a play on the L'il Abner comic strip's backwoods locale "Dogpatch"—was where they needed to be in order to compete for a spaceflight, since very few astronauts had any experience with rockets and missiles. Most were fighter pilots; they knew aircraft front-to-back, and some had even been involved with aircraft design, but rockets that were supposed to facilitate human travel into outer space were still new, so the reasons Roosa and Duke were dubious about what they could contribute were valid.

"I felt like we had sort of missed out," Duke reflected. "It wasn't as exciting or as dynamic as being involved with the development of the Lunar Module or the Command Module. We thought we were 'sucking hind tit', if you will, but it turned out to be a very interesting time, and I was the 'booster guy' in Mission Control for the last two Gemini flights."

And while Huntsville natives and longtime residents also jokingly referred to their town as "Huntspatch," the area was indeed not as glamorous and exciting as Cape Kennedy or Houston.

What's more, the Command Module for the Apollo program were being built in Downey, California by the North American Aviation company, which became North American-Rockwell in 1967, and the Lunar Module was under development at Grumman Aircraft Engineering in Bethpage, New York, on Long Island just east of New York City. Obviously, those locales would also have offered more entertainment opportunities than the north Alabama community.

Soon after Roosa and Duke were assigned to boosters, C.C. Williams was tapped to be the LMP backup crew member for the Apollo 9 flight. Other backup crew members for that flight were Pete Conrad, commander, and Dick Gordon, CMP. Original Mercury astronaut Gordon Cooper took over as branch chief for the Booster and Flight Safety Branch. Williams's LMP backup selection for Apollo 9 made it likely that he would have been on the Apollo 12 prime crew, but he would be killed when his T-38 crashed near Tallahassee, Florida on October 5, 1967.

Over an approximately two-year period, Duke and Roosa would fly into Huntsville on a regular basis for design reviews with Marshall Space Flight Center personnel, including von Braun and his staff, and the two astronauts would also meet with contractors that were building the Saturn booster. They would also occasionally visit the CM and LM contractors, as well as sub-contractors. Likewise, other astronauts would visit Huntsville.

The plans for the rocket engines designed to send Americans to the Moon meant that an unprecedented amount of power would be necessary to heave the CSM and LM into orbit, then break the spacecraft free of the Earth's gravitational pull and send them to the Moon. The Saturn V's three stages and their systems were designed as follows:

FIRST STAGE (S-IC): Built by the Boeing company, five Rocketdyne F-1 engines. Thrust: 7,648,000 lbs. Most of its weight was propellant

(RP-1 rocket fuel and liquid oxygen/"LOX")—empty, the S-IC weighed approximately 288,000 lbs.; fully fueled, it weighed over five *million* lbs.

SECOND STAGE (S-II): Built by North American Aviation, five Rocketdyne J-2 engines. Thrust: 1,000,000 lbs.

THIRD STAGE (S-IVB): Built by the Douglas Aircraft Company, one Rocketdyne J-2 engine. Thrust: 225,000 lbs. This stage had two different ignition sequences. The first burn would achieve Earth orbit for the third stage and its two spacecraft, and the second burn, Trans-Lunar Injection (TLI), would boost this stage and the two spacecraft out of Earth orbit towards the Moon.

The first stage would use RP-1 rocket fuel, while the second and third stage used liquid hydrogen as a propellant. All three stages used hyper-cold liquid oxygen as an oxidizer.

Astronauts were almost always present for test firings of rocket boosters at Huntsville. They had to make progress reports for NASA engineers, and were required to keep the Astronaut Office apprised of any changes, as well. Stu and Charlie would meet with von Braun in a "general meeting" environment, but did not work closely with the legendary rocket scientist.

Ed Buckbee, a NASA public affairs officer, had joined that organization in 1959, and had been in Huntsville since 1960. His duties included working with astronauts assigned to monitor work on boosters, and scheduling astronauts for speeches and other appearances.

"I would pick up the astronauts at the airport when they flew in by commercial airliner," Buckbee recalled, "or would meet them when they got out of their T-38s. Stu and Charlie were stereotypical young astronauts, still 'learning the ropes.' We took them out to the test bed to watch their first Saturn V (S-IC) test firing, and when it went off, they actually jumped back, with a look on their faces that read 'Wow, this thing's got some *serious* power!' It went on for the full two and a half minutes; we were about 2000 feet away, and you could feel the shock wave and the heat. This was what they were going to ride, and I'm sure it made an impression on them."

"It *was* powerful," Duke said of the incident. "You could feel that vibration, just like it would later feel when it lifted off at the Cape."

Buckbee set up speeches for astronauts in a five-to-six-state area around Huntsville. Not all of them were gifted orators, and many of them were giving speeches before they had even flown into space. The longtime NASA public affairs official praised Roosa's speech-making abilities:

"Stu had a real 'down-to-earth' speaking style; he'd talk about his childhood and how he'd been fortunate to get a chance to fly and to get into the astronaut corps; he was very patriotic—country, flag, etc. He had that special spirit that a lot of the astronauts had, and he had a good way of expressing it. If he spoke to a school, he encouraged kids to be good students. He always gave a good presentation, and always came off very well."

At the time, Roosa was an astronaut who hadn't flown, and was trying to become comfortable with such a status, as was the case with other astronauts in the same situation—how do you act if you haven't been in space?

"I remember he wasn't really at ease with the press," said Buckbee, "which was also typical of a young astronaut who hadn't flown yet. They didn't want to make a mistake in something they said, which might be misquoted. Some of them got 'burned'; they'd been misquoted or said something that was taken out of context, or had said something in what they thought was a private situation they didn't want the press to hear, but there had been a reporter listening in behind them. That's one reason people like me would tag along—to help the astronauts feel more comfortable around the press, and to help them learn how to handle such situations."

Roosa and the other astronauts would, of course, end up giving speeches around Houston as well, and would ultimately end up giving speeches for the rest of their NASA careers, and usually, beyond their active astronaut days.

—///—

Roosa did indeed settle into his role as one of NASA's frontline representatives to the general public, affirming the general stereotype of astronauts as patriotic, family-oriented heroes, even if they hadn't flown into space yet, and even though the nation was undergoing profound socio-political changes in the turbulent Sixties.

"Stu would probably have been considered pretty 'square' in those times," said astronaut Walt Cunningham, who flew on Apollo 7. "He and I were on the same side, politically; I'd say he was very, very conservative, as am I. (We had) traditional values; he had the same kind of priorities I did, which were usually very right-wing."

Joan adapted better to Houston than some of the other astronaut wives did, and settled into raising the four Roosa children while her husband spent even more hours and days away from home. She became the disciplinarian, eschewing the "wait until your father gets home" stereotype.

She also went about joining the right organizations to help further Stu's career, and cooperated in cultivating displaying the image of astronaut wives that NASA sought to impart. She and Stu both recognized that she could, and would, be a big contributor to his success.

And the astronauts and their families were hugely popular among the residents of Houston area—everybody wanted to meet and associate with a spaceman, even if he hadn't been into space.

"When we first moved there, it was kind of exciting," Dotty Duke averred. "We were invited to sports events and activities at the Astrodome, and got 'wined and dined' a good bit."

—⁓—

Stu's parents had taken to traveling extensively, living out of a small travel trailer that they pulled behind their automobile. At one point, Lorine and Dewey parked their trailer behind the home of their younger son's family in El Lago, and resided there for several months.

Older brother Danny had served in Korea in the Air Force, and had then attended the University of Arizona, garnering a Bachelor's degree in Business as well as a Master of Business Administration (M.B.A.). He had worked for many years with the Montgomery Ward retail store chain, becoming a store manager, and eventually his family, which consisted of his wife, Wilma, and daughters Dana and Janette, moved to California. Beset with a serious illness, Danny began studying to be an accountant. Eventually his family returned to Oklahoma, where he set up a successful certified public accounting firm.

In spite of Stu's hectic schedule and Joan's obligations to four children, they managed to keep in touch with family members, and would visit with Danny and his family, two or three times a year, whether the older brother's family was in California or Oklahoma. They also visited Lorine and Dewey in Tucson whenever possible, if the elder Roosas weren't out on the road.

—⁓—

Any trepidation that Roosa might have had concerning how the boosters assignment might affect his chances at garnering a flight into space may have been assuaged somewhat when he was Capsule Communicator (CapCom) in the blockhouse at Cape Kennedy on November 11, 1966 for the launch of Gemini 12, the final flight of that interim program. The call sign for the CapCom at the Cape was "Stoney," and was a standard moniker; i.e., it was not unique to Roosa, who called out "Lift-off" when he saw the booster leave the pad. Now, he was getting closer to the action.

The same month, the Astronaut Office began assigning Group 5 astronauts to support crews for the Apollo program, with a public announcement being made in late December. Original Nineteen members began to be able to determine if they would end up specializing as LMPs or CMPs, but the ultimate decisions were, and always would be, Slayton's. The astronauts were never sure of the "how" and "why" of such diversion into the Lunar Module or the Command Module, but one guideline had to do with weight on the LM—the limit for a CDR or LMP was 175 lbs., but most of the Original Nineteen didn't think there was a "better" or "worse" path concerning LMP or CMP assignments. They simply wanted to get on a flight if at all possible.

The year 1967 was shaping up as an exciting annum for members of the Original Nineteen, and for NASA overall.

But before the first month of that year was over, the entire American manned space program would be devastated by a disaster that threatened its very existence and continuation.

Apollo 1

Almost any former NASA astronaut, technician, and official can recall where he or she was on Friday, January 27, 1967 at 6:31 p.m., and many average Americans would recall the occasion in a similar manner, just as they remembered where they were or what they were doing when President John Kennedy had been assassinated in November of 1963. The calamitous events that happened on Launch Pad 34 would potentially doom the Apollo program, and would shake the confidence of NASA and the entire nation to its core.

The Apollo 1 crew was made up of Mercury and Gemini veterans Gus Grissom, Ed White, who had become America's first space walker on the Gemini 4 flight in June of 1965, and Group 3 rookie Roger Chaffee. The trio was preparing for the liftoff of America's first three-man space shot in less than a month.

And Stu Roosa happened to be in one of the most important locations for the Apollo program when the tragedy occurred, as he was once again "Stoney," the CapCom in the blockhouse a little over 500 yards from Launch Pad 34, where a "plugs-out" full simulation of a countdown to a launch of an Apollo spacecraft (#012) atop a Saturn 1B was in progress. The third communication center was the Automatic Check-Out Equipment (ACE) Control Room, located five miles away on the Cape Kennedy complex, and technician Skip Chauvin was on duty there.

Development of the Apollo Command Module had been fraught with quality control problems, and Grissom's entreaties over the last several weeks and months to make corrections had apparently fallen on deaf ears. On January 27th, there had even been talk of Deke Slayton, who was also at the Cape, climbing into the Apollo Command Module during this particular test to observe, but that scenario didn't come to pass.

The rocket system and spacecraft measured 224 feet tall, and there were several NASA and North American company technicians in the "White Room," the enclosed portion of the launch tower that surrounded the spacecraft.

The simulation had even included Slayton having breakfast with the Apollo 1 crew, just like a launch day, which was scheduled for February 21st. Moreover, pure oxygen was being used in the interior of the Command Module, as would also be the case on launch day.

In addition to Slayton and Roosa, other key personnel in the blockhouse included Joe Shea, the Manager of the Apollo Spacecraft Program Office (ASPO), and Rocco Petrone, Director of Launch Operations.

And the test was proceeding badly, dragging on through numerous holds, which were primarily due to poor communications. A plethora of annoying, crackling static began to fray the nerves of launch personnel and the crew.

It was suggested that the test be cancelled and re-scheduled, but Chauvin declined.

By 6:30, the astronauts had been sealed in the spacecraft for over five hours, and Grissom had gotten so frustrated that he testily inquired how the astronauts would be able to communicate from the Moon if they couldn't even talk between three locations near each other on Earth.

It was to be one of the last understandable comments ever heard from the veteran of the Mercury and Gemini programs.

6:31 p.m.: Looking at camera monitors in the blockhouse, Roosa, Slayton, and others thought they saw a brief, bright flash through a window on the spacecraft. It was difficult to understand the crew's exclamations because of the communication problems, but what sounded like an alarmed exclamation from Roger Chaffee slashed out of the loudspeaker, quickly followed by White exclaiming "We've got a fire in the cockpit!"

The crew quickly tried to follow standard escape procedures, but they were rapidly overwhelmed by the blaze that was being fed by the pure oxygen atmosphere. Chaffee's plea of "We have a bad fire! We're burning up!" was abruptly punctuated by what sounded like a scream.

Then, nothing...except static.

A recording of the transmissions indicates that the time of Chaffee's initial cry of alarm to the sudden and permanent silence from Apollo spacecraft #012 measured 18 seconds.

Stunned, Roosa and Chauvin continued to struggle to get through to the crew on the radio, as personnel in the White Room tried in vain to get to the hatch on the spacecraft, only to be driven back by the raging heat.

Roosa ran outside the blockhouse, and strained to see the top of the launch pad several hundred yards away, praying that the astronauts had gotten out.

Rising internal pressure finally caused the hull of the spacecraft to rupture (the hatch remained sealed), and smoke billowed from its interior.

Once the fire had been extinguished, and the dangerous and literally-potentially-explosive situation in the White Room had been stabilized, Roosa accompanied Slayton to the launch pad. They had been advised that the hatch had finally been removed, and what Roosa and Slayton viewed inside the spacecraft was not pleasant, but the bodies of the three dead astronauts were in positions that indicated they had been attempting to open the hatch following the procedure they had been trained to do. Stu also noted that their spacesuits were still white. Grissom, White, and Chaffee had been asphyxiated, and would probably have survived what actual burns they had received.

—⁓—

Even though he had been assigned to Lunar Modules, Ed Mitchell, another Original Nineteen member, happened to be on an indoctrination trip along with several other astronauts at the North American company's Command Module construction facility in Downey when the Apollo 1 fire occurred. He recalled being paged over the public address system at the Los Angeles airport as he and the other astronauts were preparing to return to Houston. The phone call for Mitchell was from Deke Slayton, informing him of the tragedy at the Cape.

Charlie Duke was in South Carolina to give a speech when he got word.

Other astronauts in other locations were informed of the calamity, and left their assignments to converge on Houston.

—⁓—

Roosa dutifully participated in the methodical post-fire investigation, the conclusion of which indicated that an exposed electrical wire under Grissom's seat had sparked, initiating the inferno.

Stu would later recall that when Chaffee was yelling about the fire, the immediate "unreality" of the emergency didn't register with the "Stoney." Roosa remembered a quick thought of "Chaffee is gonna hate to hear this tape in the morning," because somehow, in those brief seconds, Stu's own psyche wouldn't let him accept the fact that the crew was actually perishing. He would experience some pangs of guilt for that personal reaction, which was perhaps understandable, but at the time, he kept it to himself.

He also resented some of the news reports that indicated the bodies had been charred, pronouncing such journalistic irresponsibility to have been a disservice to the late astronauts' families.

Other astronauts had been lost in airplane crashes, and while the veterans and rookies of the Astronaut Office all knew that a fatality in a spaceflight program would eventually occur, the idea that America's first astronaut deaths in an actual spacecraft happened during a simulation seemed to add to the surreal numbness that enveloped NASA.

The CapCom who had been on duty when the Apollo 1 fire occurred would have nightmares about the tragedy for years, and Stu also made it obvious that he did not want to discuss his experience, even with family members, but there would be a few exceptions.

Duke recalled that he and Stu talked briefly about the fire, but not in detail.

"We never did talk about what the inside of the spacecraft looked like," Charlie recalled. Duke himself has never listened to the recording of the transmissions that took place during the tragedy.

On one occasion, Roosa abruptly informed his son Chris that there were only two people who knew the real story about what had happened— Deke Slayton and himself. And Roosa said nothing more about that pronouncement.

Another time, he told Jack that "...the investigation team got it wrong." Again, Roosa's comment was out of the blue, and when Jack asked for an explanation, his father said that the investigation team "...didn't nail down the final analysis correctly." Jack didn't press for further details at the time.

But whatever additional clandestine and/or classified information Roosa knew about one of the darkest days in American space history, he took to his grave.

And history could forever ponder whether the voice of Stuart Roosa may have been the last sound astronauts Grissom, White and Chaffee ever heard.

Post-Apollo 1 Training

After the Apollo 1 fire and the subsequent investigation, training for astronauts eventually got back on track.

Roosa attended a two-week training session in late May and early June of 1967 at Ellyson Field, part of the Pensacola (Florida) Naval Air Station. The short autorotation course involved landing techniques with helicopters that were supposed to simulate, in a primeval manner, the landing of an LM on the Moon's surface. According to a news publication of that facility, Roosa was the last Apollo astronaut to participate in the curriculum.

After completing the autorotation course, Roosa began jungle training several days later.

Outdoor training in survival techniques for all types of hostile environments, as well as geology field trips to examine what were thought to be somewhat-Moon-like areas of the Earth, followed the initial classroom work for each adventure.

Jungle training was conducted in Panama. Small groups of astronauts from both the Apollo and MOL programs would be dropped off in the middle of the jungle, and had to fend for themselves, constructing primitive shelters and finding their own food.

"We were dropped off by helicopter on a mountain there and had to live off the land," one astronaut said of his Panama experience. "One guy shot a toucan, and we cut down a palm and dug out the heart-of-palm, which is kind of stringy, so that night we had toucan noodle soup."

Redbugs/chiggers were persistent pests for the astronauts during jungle training.

Bruce McCandless, another Original Nineteen member captured a fer-de-lance (*Bothrops Atrox*), a very aggressive and very venomous snake. He managed to bring it back into the United States, and donated it to the Houston Zoo.

Not surprisingly, Roosa relished all facets of outdoor training, not just the jungle work.

"Stu kind of knew his way around; he was an 'outdoors' guy," Al Worden confirmed.

One astronaut was reportedly a bird watcher, so it was obvious that he loved the jungle training for a unique reason, to the point that he would wander off when he spotted an interesting member of the avian kingdom.

The jungle training session for the group that included Roosa also had the dubious bonus of enduring a flash flood. When that facet of training was completed, the astronauts floated down a river on rafts that were similar to the ones that would be utilized on Apollo spacecraft.

"He was exceptionally talented when it came to training for desert and jungle survival," Duke recalled. "He was knowledgeable, and felt right at home. He knew how to skin animals, and how to prepare them as food. I was also an outdoorsman, so we both felt comfortable in those environments."

Domestic geological trips for astronauts included outings to Big Bend National Park in Texas, Grand Canyon, the Meteor Crater and the San Francisco Peaks near Flagstaff, Arizona, and other locations.

In July of 1967, astronauts from Groups 2, 3, 4, and 5 journeyed to Iceland to do more geological field work near volcanic sources, as there was speculation about how much volcanism the Moon had experienced during its existence, and the astronauts hoped to find rock samples that would provide answers. Duke described Iceland as "...a very fascinating country; the interior is absolutely barren except for a few oases."

In August, desert training was done for several days in the southeast corner of Washington State. Initial classroom orientation was held at Fairchild A.F.B. in Spokane, after which the group was transported to an area near the tri-state juncture of Washington, Oregon, and Idaho.

Duke described the area as dry, rolling desert with a lot of scrub brush.

"I remember it as being sort of boring," he said. "We were just sitting in the shade for most of the day, trying to build solar evaporator water collectors. You'd dig a big hole, take part of the parachute to make a funnel that was supposed to feed collected moisture into something like a Sterno can. Ours never worked very well."

"It was a great training program to get our group ready for Apollo." Vance Brand said of the rugged but important outdoor training. "After that, we all split off into specialization—Command Module, or Lunar Module, but up to that point we had all gotten the same training, under the assumption that any one of us might walk on the Moon someday."

—⁓—

One result of the Apollo 1 disaster was the assignment of Duke and Roosa to the Emergency Egress Working Group. Stu would also find himself working, individually or with other astronauts, with NASA workers in tests of a myriad of spacecraft systems and other innovations beside egress innovations. For example, many astronauts, including Roosa, tested space suits and other gear in vacuum chambers at contractors' facilities.

From April 5-7, 1968, astronauts Jim Lovell, Charlie Duke and Roosa were ensconced for 48 hours in the #007A Apollo Command Module as it floated in the Gulf of Mexico near Galveston, in what was termed a post-landing systems qualifications test. The test had nothing to do with egress, but was designed to measure the seaworthiness—such as it was—of an Apollo Command Module, and the three astronauts volunteered for the assignment.

Lovell, a Group 2/"Next Nine" member, was already a veteran of two Gemini flights, including the longest, which lasted fourteen days, so the two-day stint in a "roomy" Apollo Command Module (compared to a Gemini spacecraft) shaped up as an easy assignment for him. Moreover, he didn't mind the flotation facet, as he was a Navy aviator.

CM #007A was a "boilerplate" test example, instead of a fully-completed Command Module, meaning that many of its interior appointments and instruments were mockups instead of "the real thing." The control panels inside were cosmetic phonies, and the only real electronics consisted of the radio with which the crew communicated with NASA technicians floating nearby.

"I don't know why we ever volunteered for that," Duke recalled with a self-deprecating chuckle. "And we were asking ourselves the same thing soon after we got in there! Maybe Lovell talked us into it, and we thought it would be good training. But once the humidity went up, we were miserable...and it was a miserable 48 hours. It was boring; about all we could do was talk with each other or sleep. We couldn't check out any systems because the instrument panels were mockups. I took some (motion sickness) pills. It was hot and sticky; just awful. We survived it, but it was probably the worst thing I ever did when I was in the space program."

The spacecraft's long-term flotation capabilities/seaworthiness were examined in more than one position (right-side-up was known as "Stable I"/"apex up" in NASA terminology; upside-down was known as "Stable II"/"apex down"). A NASA motor vessel, the *Retriever*, was on station nearby for the duration of the test. While sealed in the spacecraft, Roosa became seasick, and reportedly described the experience as "pretty miserable" himself.

When the test was reported in the April 26, 1968 edition of the Manned Space Center's in-house periodical the *Roundup*, the story was headlined "Yo, Ho, Ho and a Bottle of Marezine."

Marezine is a motion sickness medication.

As for escape systems, one example of Roosa's involvement was his participation in a new multiple-person "slide-wire basket" egress system from the top of the Apollo launch tower. "Passengers" in the slide-wire basket could potentially include technicians in the White Room.

NASA's previous method for a quick egress from the tower, which had been in use for several years, had been a simpler slide-wire device. Evacuees would hook themselves onto the wire in a type of harness/vest, and would zip down the wire individually, looking to some observers like some kind of bizarre troupe of circus performers. That procedure was ultimately deemed to be too dangerous.

The "basket" was simply a larger, trapezoid-shaped apparatus that was designed to carry nine persons. If an emergency occurred before the spacecraft was sealed, astronauts and White Room personnel would jump into such baskets and zoom down a wire to an armored personnel carrier that would then haul the "escapees" to a nearby bunker.

An alternative plan envisioned only technicians escaping in slide-wire baskets if the astronauts were already sealed in their spacecraft. After the launch tower had been quickly evacuated, the rockets on the Launch Escape Tower (LET) above the spacecraft would fire, separating the CM from the rest of the rocket, and sending it to a high enough altitude so its parachutes could be deployed. Interestingly, the rockets on the Apollo LET escape system were more powerful than the Redstone missiles that had hurled Alan Shepard and Gus Grissom into their sub-orbital space flights in 1961.

Roosa and two NASA employees, Chuck Billings (Safety Representative) and Art Porcher (Design Engineering Representative), were among numerous individuals who tested the slide-basket system. NASA photographed a Roosa-Billings-Porcher test conducted on January 25, 1969, from the top of a mobile launcher from which Apollo 9 would be launched the next month. Several dummies accompanied the threesome during the test.

Roosa and Duke also tested a type of insulated "slide tube" egress system, which may have reminded some observers of something seen at a water park.

Duke: "If you didn't use the slide-wire basket, the other way off the pad was to run across the swing arm to the elevator. You'd jump in and hit a free-fall button that would take you down into the 'catacombs' below the pad. Then, you'd open the door of the elevator, and off to the right was a slide tube. The idea was to slide down the tube ramp into the blast room."

The blast escape room, which had been nicknamed "the rubber room," had a six-inch thick steel door, sat atop two dozen giant springs, and was constructed with steel, concrete and sand. The underground facility had its own air supply, and padded seats with belts, to keep occupants secure in case of an on-pad explosion of a Saturn V. It was stocked with provisions, in case the launch pad collapsed on top of the shelter, and its occupants had to be dug out. Accounts vary as to how long the provisions were supposed to last.

The "rubber room" was never an active/frontline concept at the Apollo launch pad, but the success of the slide-basket system meant that it would still be in use decades later, during the Space Transportation System (STS) program, the re-usable, airplane-like spacecraft of which was known as the "Space Shuttle."

Astronauts are usually portrayed as having strong personalities, due primarily to the stereotypical "fighter jock" mentality, so it wasn't any surprise that the competition to get on a flight was often fast and furious, which at times seemed to detract from a sense of camaraderie among the potential space travelers. Once a particular crew was named for a particular mission, however, the rest of the astronauts would close ranks behind the prime crew. Walt Cunningham's perspective is noteworthy:

"It was not only dog-eat-dog, but some of us—like me—never figured that out. I was not a political player, and later, I realized that politics was a very big factor. I'd just always figured that if you did the best you could, it was bound to be noticed. But when you were on a crew, the backup crew was very supportive, as was the support crew. Everybody wanted the program to be a success, and everybody wanted every mission to be a success."

Roosa also eschewed any scurrilous in-office "political" machinations, and opted for the do-your-best-and-maybe-you'll-get-noticed approach, letting his assignments and results speak for themselves.

"I never saw Stu playing any kind of politics," Cunningham concurred. "He and I got along so well because we both thought of ourselves as fighter pilots first, and fighter pilots always go all out to do the best they can. I never saw him doing any kind of finagling."

—⁓—

On some Saturdays, the three Roosa boys would accompany their father to his NASA office if Stu had some weekend work to do. On more than one occasion, the boys would grab three secretary chairs (which had wheels), and would have "chariot races" through the halls of the deserted office building. They would be stopped by security personnel, but would be very respectful to such authorities. Once it was established that they were the children of an astronaut, they're be "released" with no disciplinary action (and no complaints to their father).

And being such an offspring occasionally did have other advantages: Some of the NASA employee parents would help their own children as well as other neighborhood kids with science fair projects, which turned out to be very elaborate and impressive for that day and age.

—⁓—

Naturally, Roosa became interested in hunting in various parts of Texas, as did other astronauts. At one event at a renowned hunting ranch located about 75 miles west of Austin, Stuart met an individual with whom he would develop not only a close friendship for the rest of his life, but a business relationship as well.

"I first met Stu Roosa on the Dos Arroyos Ranch, owned by my friend Bob Phillips, who was a safari client of mine," recalled legendary hunter

Bert Klineburger. "We hit it off at once. It was just one of those 'instant rapport' things. We had a lot in common about our interests in hunting."

To say that Klineburger epitomizes the term "big game hunter" is an understatement. Owner of a world famous safari company and other business ventures that reached around the globe, Klineburger had been at the forefront of international hunting since the mid-1940s, and also had a highly-successful taxidermy business in Seattle with his brother. He has also written more than one book about his experiences.

Klineburger counted many affluent business leaders, as well as numerous astronauts, among his clients and friends. He attended several launches at the Cape during the halcyon days of the space program.

"I had been invited to some of the Apollo launches by my friends and safari clients Dick Dobbins and Wayne Ewing of the Arrowsmith company of Los Angeles," said Klineburger. "They were making some special components—really special, high-tech stuff—for the rockets that would take our astronaut friends into space. There were cocktail parties sponsored by companies that were doing work on the space program, and I was able to meet a lot of the astronauts, and a lot of other people in NASA. But I actually met Stu at that hunt at the Dos Arroyos Ranch."

Klineburger proudly noted that he developed friendships with many other astronauts, including Jim Lovell, Charlie Duke, Deke Slayton, Wally Schirra, Gordon Cooper, Frank Borman, Tom Stafford, Rusty Schweickart, Jim McDivitt, Walt Cunningham, Bill Anders, Gene Cernan, Ron Evans, Jack Lousma, Jack Swigert, Joe Engle, Joe Allen, Dave Scott, Vance Brand, Paul Weitz, Ed White, and Hank Hartsfield.

In later years, Roosa and Klineburger would later attend many unique hunts together, and their interest in a mutual business venture would take them to more than one country in Africa. Other astronauts went on African safaris with Klineburger as well.

"Stu and Charlie Duke were probably the most committed (astronauts) about hunting," said Cunningham, who also hunted with Roosa, "and Stu kept it up over the years. And hunting skills are definitely an asset to flying—since he was a good hunter, he was a good pilot."

—∿∿—

Stu's ARPS Class 64C comrade Hank Hartsfield wouldn't move to Houston until after he had been through a disappointing experience with the Air Force's MOL program, which would end up being cancelled a little over a month before Apollo 11 landed on the Moon.

The two primary contractors for MOL were Douglas Aircraft, which merged with McDonnell in 1967, and General Electric.

"I spent a lot of time at Douglas, along with a couple of other MOL guys," Hartsfield recalled. "The way I found out the program was cancelled was unbelievable—I happened to be in my little MGB, which didn't have a radio. June 10, 1969, I was on my way to (McDonnell-) Douglas, and was listening to a portable radio I kept in the car, and a news report said that the Secretary of Defense had cancelled the Manned Orbital Laboratory program. I changed to the other news station that I liked to listen to, and heard the same thing. The general that headed the program had asked the Defense Department to hold off on the announcement until he told his people, but they said they couldn't do that."

There were fourteen MOL astronauts in the program when it was cancelled, and those under 36 years of age were offered the opportunity to transfer to the NASA astronaut program. Seven of the fourteen MOL astronauts were younger than 35, and took the offer. In addition to Hartsfield, they were Richard Truly, Karol Bobko, Robert Crippen, Gordon Fullerton, Robert Overmyer, and Donald Peterson. All would eventually fly in space on the Space Shuttle, but at the time of the MOL cancellation and the transfer of Hartsfield and others to NASA, the Shuttle was still in the proposal/very early planning stages.

Hartsfield: "We went to Houston, and met with some astronauts. Tom Stafford showed us around; they were willing to evaluate us about joining the NASA program. As it turned out, we met back up with the Roosas, and we bought our house in Houston in 1971 in the same neighborhood where they lived. While they were in Houston, we often went out to eat or went 'tonking,' where we would dine and dance."

Apollo 9

Following extensive redesigns and modifications to the Command Module, the Apollo program returned to business in mid-October of 1968, when Apollo 7, sitting atop a Saturn 1B, took Wally Schirra, an original Mercury astronaut, and rookies Walt Cunningham and Donn Eisele on the first manned Apollo flight, which lasted 11 days, and indicated all of the systems for the CSM were now functioning appropriately.

Construction of a space-worthy LM, however, was behind schedule, and in an audacious move, NASA proposed sending three astronauts into orbit around the Moon in a CSM only, on what would be only the third launch of a Saturn V (unmanned test flights had been conducted in November of 1967 and April of 1968).

The memorable flight took place during the Christmas season of 1968, when Frank Borman, Jim Lovell, and Bill Anders became the first humans to leave Earth orbit and travel to the closest other world in space, fulfilling at least part of a dream that had been part of the human experience for eons.

Roosa's initial opportunity to make a decent impression on the NASA higher-ups during a manned flight came when he was named as a CapCom for Apollo 9. That mission is arguably the most unsung or underrated in the history of the Apollo program, as it was a complete test of the LM and CSM, including docking, extraction of the LM from the third stage, flying both vehicles independently, and re-docking, albeit in Earth orbit. The crew for the mission consisted of Jim McDivitt, CDR, Rusty Schweickart, LMP, and Dave Scott, CMP. The trio had been the original backup crew for Apollo 1.

And perhaps it was because they were both redheads, but on more than one occasion, Schweickart and Roosa got into intense and borderline-heated discussions about their respective socio-political views. Roosa was a stereotypical God-and-country conservative, while Schweickart was described by Walt Cunningham as "...probably the most liberal person I knew, except for his wife."

The backup crew for Apollo 9 was made up of Pete Conrad, commander, Dick Gordon, CMP, and Alan Bean, LMP. That trio would become the prime crew for Apollo 12. Backup crew members would be in Mission Control during simulations of crucial maneuvers, regardless of which flight shift was on duty.

Ron Evans, also an Original Nineteen member, was also named as a CapCom. Other Original Nineteen members had also begun making inroads into being considered for spaceflight—the three support crew members for Apollo 9 were Jack Lousma, Edgar Mitchell, and Al Worden.

The third-echelon support crew might have seemed to some to be glorified "gofers," as their duties often consisted of running errands for prime crew members, doing background work, getting checklists ready, and visiting contractors. Nevertheless, it was an initial step in getting involved with the internal workings and training for a particular mission; i.e., the cliché about "it'll look good on your résumé" was usually applicable, and most astronauts who had not flown yet looked at an assignment to a support crew as a good sign.

Roosa was never on a support crew (although CapComs were sometimes referred to as support crew members in the media, and support crew members could and did serve as CapComs), and he would ultimately never serve on a backup crew, either.

What is sometimes not acknowledged is that CapComs assigned to certain spaceflights would go through many of the practice sessions of those missions while the assigned astronauts were in simulators. Specific CapComs were assigned to specifics shifts of personnel (teams) in Mission Control, and Roosa worked long and hard along with others in the nerve center during the simulations of the Apollo 9 mission, preparing for the important test of the two Apollo spacecraft.

"Most of the CapCom training was done at Mission Control in Houston," Charlie Duke would recall about his own (later) CapCom experiences, which were similar to what Roosa had gone through with Apollo 9. "We would do 'full-up' simulations, which were known as 'integrated sims,' where the crew was in the simulator in the Kennedy training building in Florida, and we were in Mission Control—Building 30 in Houston—and we would 'fly' various stages of the mission. There were some guys who were called 'sim sups' (pronounced 'soups'), who would interject failures into the system—we could be practicing (lunar) descent, rendezvous or liftoff. We went through all phases of the missions. But we were also involved with the crew in procedures development, and understanding emergency procedures."

Stu also would have garnered some notice when, in a first-of-its-kind assignment, McDivitt designated him as a liaison for the Apollo 9 crew to NASA officials. He was authorized to speak for the crew regarding policies or issues, and relayed decisions and specifics from NASA authorities to McDivitt, Schweickart, and Scott, who were intensely training for a mission that had the most complicated flight profile of any NASA manned space effort up until that point in time.

Roosa was the CapCom for the launch of Apollo 9 on March 3, 1969. The two spacecraft were named for their respective silhouettes: *Gumdrop* was the moniker for the CSM, while *Spider* was the LM's designation—not particularly flattering names, but practical.

Both of the spacecraft performed well, and the LM flew as far as 111 miles from the CSM before re-docking. However, like all Apollo flights (past and future) the mission did have several problems that had to be worked through, and Roosa would stay in Mission Control long after his own shifts at the CapCom console had been completed to monitor the proceedings.

However, Duke doesn't necessarily believe the extra time spent in Mission Control influenced upper echelon NASA officials in Houston, because the practice of CapComs remaining there after a shift change was common:

"Stu was, like me, one of the CapComs who would stay around once we got off shift if there was something exciting coming up. The more experience you got in Mission Control—even if you weren't on duty—the better off you'd be, but I don't think the 'voluntary overtime' had any influence (on NASA higher-ups); it was just something that everybody did, and it was part of your job. I think the recognition of your abilities—by Shepard, Slayton, and others, when it came to selecting crews—was more of an 'overall view' of what you'd *done* in other jobs that you were doing; *how well you'd performed* as a CapCom or in a support crew or ancillary duties. We were all qualified for spaceflight, so a lot of the 'extra' duties were almost *expected*; we all did it because we *wanted* to do it."

Nevertheless, Roosa's efforts apparently caught the eye of Deke Slayton and others, as he was named "Most Valuable Player" for the Apollo 9 mission following its successful conclusion. In addition to participating in the ritual of cigars being lit by Mission Control personnel, Roosa was chosen by the flight directors to hang a replica of the Apollo 9 patch, measuring 18 inches in diameter, on the control room wall.

Slayton told Roosa that he had known more about the flight plan than the flight directors had. By doing his job efficiently, thoroughly, and staying in the loop even after he was technically off-duty, the redheaded CapCom had managed to get himself noticed by important NASA officials who would be making future decisions about Apollo crews that would go to the Moon.

———∿∿∿———

Apollo 10 was a full-out dress rehearsal for a Moon landing, with astronauts Tom Stafford and Gene Cernan, both Gemini veterans, separating from the CSM while in lunar orbit and piloting the LM to within 47,400 feet of the surface of the Moon. CMP John Young, also a Gemini veteran, remained in orbit.

Stu was delighted that Charlie was selected to be a CapCom for Apollo 10, and in a precedent-breaking move, Duke was assigned as a CapCom for Apollo 11 as well.

Roosa was out of any early rotation opportunities for Apollo 11, the historic voyage that was designated to culminate in a landing on the Moon for the first time. He brought his family to Cape Kennedy to witness the launch, and the Roosas were able to meet Charles Lindbergh, another pioneer in the history of flight.

And when the *Eagle*, Apollo 11's LM, landed on the Moon, it would be Charlie Duke's voice that responded to Neil Armstrong's "Houston, Tranquility Base here—the *Eagle* has landed" with an emotional but eloquent (and briefly tongue-tied) "Roger, Twan...Tranquility, we copy you on the ground. You've got a bunch of guys about to turn blue; we're breathing again. Thanks a lot."

APOLLO 14

Apollo 13 Selection...Er, Make That Apollo 14

It's almost as if the application of the term "mercurial" to describe the personality of Alan Shepard is an odd-but-accurate pun.

America's first man in space, Shepard had been one of the original seven Mercury astronauts that had been announced with great fanfare to the public in April of 1959. A native of New Hampshire and a crack Navy aviator, he had made his fifteen-minute sub-orbital flight aboard *Freedom 7* in May of 1961.

Even while the Mercury astronauts were in training, Shepard acquired the reputation of being able to ooze charm, expectorate cockiness, or abruptly summon up frosty hostility at will. Such personality traits might, at times, be expected in a career field as dangerous as test piloting, but Shepard's countenance could unexpectedly and instantly shift 180 degrees, and contradictory terms such as "Smilin' Al" or "The Icy Commander" are part of the Shepard legend.

Shepard had been grounded in 1964 due to an inner ear problem, and had been appointed Chief of the Astronaut Office in Houston, as Slayton moved up to Director of Flight Crew Operations. While it was gratifying for Shepard to be able to remain with NASA, the probability that he would never journey into space again seemed to sharpen the edges of his unpredictability, so much so that another legend says that every business day, Shepard's secretary in the Astronaut Office would place one of two portraits of her boss on display—one in which Shepard was smiling, the other in which he was scowling—to alert visitors to the office as to what kind of mood Shepard was in.

"He had sort of built this 'fence' around himself, and he didn't want many people to break through," said Eugene Cernan, a Group 3 astronaut who had been a spacewalker on Gemini 9 and who had orbited the Moon as LMP on Apollo 10.

One Apollo astronaut, when asked to recall Shepard's temperament, paused before uttering a somewhat-diplomatic, one-word description: "He could be very...'direct'."

Ed Buckbee remembered trying to deal with Shepard on public relations issues while America's first spaceman was grounded.

"He *could* be the 'Icy Commander,'" said Buckbee. "He was grounded for ten years between his Mercury flight and Apollo 14, and he was not a happy camper, because he couldn't fly. So during that time, he was not an easy guy to work with. When I was in NASA Public Affairs, I had to deal with him a lot when he was in the Astronaut Office; I'd have to get permission from him to get one of his astronauts to go give a talk or an interview, or to visit a school or organization. He could turn you down flat, and didn't have to give you a reason, unless it was something like 'We don't have time for that'."

Interestingly, Roosa figures into the legend of Shepard's unpredictable moods. Reportedly, on more than one occasion prior to the Apollo 14 assignment, Stu spotted Shepard walking down the hall in his direction, and the Chief of the Astronaut Office had a dark expression on his face, so Roosa quickly ducked into a nearby office.

The point needs to be made that Roosa probably wouldn't have taken evasive action due to any intimidation or outright fear of Shepard, but considering the competition at the time to get a flight, he was most likely seeking to avoid any type of encounter that might have been construed by Shepard in a negative manner, or perhaps Roosa just didn't need the aggravation.

A variant of this anecdote was seen in the 1998 television mini-series *From The Earth To The Moon,* in which Roosa, portrayed by George Newbern, approaches Shepard's office, but spots the "scowling" portrait of his boss in a frame on the wall just outside, and quickly turns away, muttering "Y'know what? I can come back."

Shepard's secretary then abruptly inquires: "Stu, are you flying to the Cape Friday?"

"Yeah, why?" Roosa responds.

A quick shift to the next scene shows Roosa in a blue NASA flight suit, waiting on the tarmac at Houston's Ellington Air Force Base beside one of NASA's T-38 jet trainers. Shepard (portrayed by Ted Levine) arrives, scowling in real life, and without uttering a word, climbs aboard the airplane as Roosa's passenger.

One could surmise that such a scene was exemplary of how Shepard was able to take note of Roosa's stick-and-rudder capabilities for future reference.

—w—

Inner ear surgery on Shepard would ultimately return America's first space traveler to flight status. He had missed out on all of the two-man

Gemini flights, which meant that controversy would ensue when, in April of 1969, he reportedly told Slayton he wanted to command the next assigned lunar prime crew, which would be Apollo 13. Shepard had not done any backup work with previous Apollo crews...and neither had Stuart Roosa, who was to be named as the mission's Command Module Pilot.

Ed Mitchell had been on the support crew for Apollo 9, and was the backup Lunar Module Pilot for Apollo 10, and had now rotated, as was the tradition, into eligibility for a prime crew three flights later.

Slayton and Shepard had a lot in common, of course, and made a lot of decisions together, particularly about who got a seat on a spaceflight. Shepard may have been a hero from the early days of the Mercury program, but Slayton's decision to comply with Shepard's unprecedented request/demand obviously had its detractors among the astronaut corps and elsewhere within NASA.

Walt Cunningham: "It was R.H.I.P.—'rank has its privilege,' and it bred a lot of resentment at the time."

"I didn't have a problem with that; some people did," Gene Cernan said of Shepard's abrupt leap into a prime crew assignment. "A lot of people thought that flight was going to be Gordon Cooper's. There's no question that Shepard pulled a lot of weight."

Slayton's official choice of Shepard as Apollo 13 commander may have been made a bit easier because of the behavior of Cooper, backup commander for Apollo 10, who was the only other Mercury Seven member remaining in the Apollo program. Cooper had reportedly agitated NASA higher-ups by taking a laid-back attitude regarding training during the Gemini program, and he had also gone against guidelines for astronauts to stay away from dangerous extra-curricular activities, signing up to drive in a race at the nearby Daytona Speedway. When Slayton forced Cooper to withdraw from the race, Cooper grumbled out loud about the incident.

Accordingly, Cooper didn't rotate from his assignment as the Apollo 10 backup commander into the prime crew commander's slot on Apollo 13.

What's also intriguing about the selection of the original Apollo 13 crew is the fact that because of his lofty position within the Astronaut Office, Shepard, as the prime crew commander, had unprecedented input concerning who he wanted on his team.

"Deke assigned everybody," Al Worden said of crew selections, "but a lot of times, those assignments—even if you had started out as a support crew member—meant that you got assigned to a crew with the consensus of the commander of that flight."

Mitchell's memory about being informed that he and Roosa were in line for the LMP and CMP positions on the Apollo 13 prime crew is a bit nebulous, as he recalls it being announced to astronauts and other

NASA staff members in a standard manner, perhaps at a general astronaut meeting, within the halls of the Manned Space Center.

The popular anecdote, however, is that Shepard had called the two Original Nineteen members to his office and informed them that if they didn't mind "...flying with an old retread," the three of them were going to be the prime crew for Apollo 13.

Roosa, having never been on a backup crew, reportedly asked for clarification, wanting to know if the Chief of the Astronaut Office had indeed said "prime," which Shepard curtly confirmed.

Another variant to this episode had Roosa asking Shepard something like "What about backup?," or some similar inquiry that indicated Roosa couldn't fathom not having to go through backup rotation first, to which Shepard snapped "I don't fly backup to anybody!"

("That sounds exactly like something he'd say," Ed Buckbee said of Shepard's retort in the latter version.)

There are two primary schools of thought about the "who and why" regarding Shepard's selection of Mitchell and Roosa. The first is that he wanted the best people he could get for the mission—Mitchell had indeed rotated into prime crew eligibility, but he was also brilliant regarding navigation and rendezvous techniques. The Apollo 14 LMP would later recall that Shepard reportedly told more than one confidant that he chose Mitchell "...because I want to come home." Roosa was good at analyzing flight anomalies and taking appropriate action. Shepard also liked Stu's attitude about what the Apollo program was doing, as well as his other flying skills and patriotism. Mitchell and Roosa were most likely considered by Shepard and others to be the top unassigned Lunar Module and Command Module experts.

"There's no question that Stu was pretty good when it came to stick-and-rudder," Mitchell recalled. "He was certainly one of the best of our group."

The flip-side explanation for Shepard's choices is that by choosing two rookies, America's first spaceman would have more of the spotlight on himself, and Al Shepard could still come on like the self-assured/cocky fighter pilot and hero if and when he needed to. Mitchell recounted that members of the press would often refer to the crew as "Al Shepard and those other two guys."

And like Shepard, Mitchell was Navy. Shepard's choice of Roosa, an Air Force captain, may have also surprised some people, who might have expected another all-Navy crew (like Apollo 12's crew of Pete Conrad, Alan Bean, and Dick Gordon).

"Shepard would have wanted crewmen of the same (types of) personalities even if he had not chosen (Mitchell and Roosa)," Cunningham opined, "but it was considered 'Shepard's flight' all the way through."

Nevertheless, Shepard's own experience in space had only consisted of a 15-minute sub-orbital hiccup, so it wasn't surprising that some wags referred to the crew as "the three rookies."

"Shepard's choices probably shocked a lot of people," said Buckbee, "but I think he took a little pride in the fact that he wasn't second-guessed on his choice of a crew. He never regretted his selections, and therefore didn't have to apologize for who he selected."

—⁓⁓—

Original Nineteen member Dr. Edgar Mitchell had joined the Navy in 1952, following graduation from college. He had become an aviator and had flown missions from aircraft carriers, but had also demonstrated an intense technical ability regarding navigation and other piloting issues, so it wasn't any surprise that he became a flight instructor.

He earned a master's degree from the Navy's Postgraduate School, and in the early '60s, enrolled at Massachusetts Institute of Technology, as the Navy acknowledged and encouraged his prowess—particularly, his research on space exploration. Mitchell garnered a doctorate of Science in Aeronautics and Astronautics at M.I.T., becoming one of the first to earn such a degree. His 1964 doctoral thesis, published through M.I.T.'s Experimental Astronomy Laboratory, was titled "Guidance of Low-Thrust Interplanetary Vehicles."

"After Sputnik, NASA had asked the leading technical institutes, like M.I.T., Princeton, and Caltech, to set up graduate programs in 'Aero 'N Astro'," Mitchell recalled, "and frankly, nobody knew what the hell was out there. I was one of the first ones to go through that program; it was only a couple of years old at the time."

While he was at M.I.T., Mitchell did some teaching as a graduate assistant, and one of his students was Charlie Duke, who was getting a Master's degree in the same field.

After attaining his doctorate, Mitchell originally thought he would be going to Houston to work with NASA's Guidance and Control division, having requested such an assignment, but the Navy had other ideas.

"They essentially shanghaied me," he said. "I got a call from the Pentagon while I was on the way down (to Houston). I was visiting my mother-in-law in Pittsburgh; my orders had been changed, and I was sent to Los Angeles to work with the Manned Orbital Laboratory program under Jack Van Ness. I was technical director for the Navy's participation. After a year of working with that, I knew that it wasn't going to go anywhere, so I petitioned my boss to help me go to Edwards, because that's where most of the astronauts were being selected from."

Mitchell got his assignment to the ARPS at Edwards, but his technical brilliance meant that he had to wear two hats there, and he would cross paths with MOL astronauts, most of whom, like Hank Hartsfield, had been through an earlier ARPS class themselves.

"I finagled my way out there," Mitchell said of Edwards. "I'd already been at China Lake (a huge Navy weapons testing facility in California, north of Edwards), essentially as a test pilot, but when I got to Edwards, I was teaching Advanced Propulsion Techniques, so I was both an instructor and a student who went through the 'space' portion, which was what I was interested in. As it turned out, all of the MOL guys came through Edwards; I was teaching them fuel optimization techniques."

Mitchell acknowledged that he and Roosa "...may have passed each other in the halls" while they were both at Edwards in the mid-'60s. Roosa would have been wrapping up his own test pilot class and beginning his test flying assignment around the time Mitchell, who was a member of Class 65B, arrived.

Charlie Duke recalled a role reversal from M.I.T., as he was Mitchell's instructor on one of the space courses at Edwards. Mitchell's student status in the "space" facet of test pilot training didn't end until early 1966, but he had already applied for the next astronaut group, as had numerous other pilots at Edwards.

—⁓—

Mitchell was the oldest member of the Original Nineteen, and refers to himself as having been "the senior guy" in that group; he had attained the rank of Commander while at Edwards.

Once the NASA assignments got underway, he demonstrated his technical expertise almost immediately, and was quickly dubbed "The Brain" by other astronauts. Although the appellation was used behind his back, Mitchell knew about the nickname. He also had an interest in paranormal activity and extra-sensory perception (E.S.P.), and when he was chosen for the original Apollo 13 crew, he privately resolved to attempt personal E.S.P. experiments during his flight.

Mitchell recalled that when the Original Nineteen had begun their familiarization courses regarding Apollo systems and applications, he was already knowledgeable with much of the curriculum because of his own education.

"In fact, there were times when I was kind of helping the teacher," he said.

His initial impression of Roosa was similar to Worden's perspective— Roosa wasn't particularly a standout with an overly-extroverted personality, but would concentrate on doing what needed to be done to get a job done accurately and thoroughly.

When Roosa and Duke were assigned to boosters at Huntsville, Mitchell had been among the Original Nineteen members who had gotten involved with the development of the Lunar Module. Mitchell would ultimately furnish important contributions and input, working long hours at the Grumman facility on Long Island.

—⁓—

The would-be Apollo 13 crew began training in secret, before the official announcement of its lineup. NASA didn't want any announcement that Alan Shepard was returning to space to dilute any publicity for the upcoming Apollo 11 flight. Such secrecy was actually standard, as it would usually be around two months between the time a crew selection was made—during which time training would commence—and the date that a public announcement was made.

As it turned out, however, the crew of Apollo 13 would ultimately become the crew of Apollo 14. Slayton submitted his office's selection of Shepard, Mitchell and Roosa for Apollo 13 to NASA headquarters, and was turned down. George Mueller, NASA's head of manned spaceflight, let it be known that since Shepard had been out of action for so long, America's first spaceman needed a more-extensive training period, but it was also said that Mueller took exception to the perceived buddy system between Slayton and Shepard, which had placed Shepard on Apollo 13 without a turn in backup rotation. Some longtime members of the astronaut corps, including individuals directly involved with Apollo 13 and Apollo 14, supported Mueller's move.

Accordingly, the crews of Apollo 13 and Apollo 14 were reversed, and the new Apollo 13 crew consisted of commander Jim Lovell, who had already been into space on two Gemini flights as well as Apollo 8, and two Original Nineteen rookies, Fred Haise (LMP), and Ken Mattingly (CMP).

Haise had been on the backup crews for Apollo 8 and Apollo 11 as well as the support crew of Apollo 9, and he recalled being informed at the Apollo 11 debriefing of the switch in crews for the Apollo 13 and 14 missions.

Mattingly had been on the support crew for Apollo 11, but stepped into simultaneous training with backup CMP Bill Anders when, in early 1969, Anders announced he would be retiring as an astronaut in August of the same year to take a job with the National Aeronautics and Space Council, an advisory organization to the Executive branch of the federal government. Mattingly trained alongside Anders in case the Apollo 11 flight was delayed past July, after which Anders would be gone.

"Deke Slayton gave Al (Apollo) 13 before consulting with management," Jim Lovell said of the decision to swap the crews. "We thought he would not have enough training time for the mission. NASA management thought so too, and that is why they slipped him to Apollo 14."

As for a prime crew made up of three astronauts with a grand total of 15 minutes in space between them, Lovell was more conciliatory about Shepard's return:

"With enough training time, no one was worried. After all, (Neil) Armstrong had only minimal space time—Gemini 8—when he landed on the Moon."

The crew now designated for Apollo 14 instead of Apollo 13 had a differing point of view about being bumped backwards by one mission.

"Of course, we didn't like it, initially," Mitchell said of the NASA decision. "We had Deke and (flight director) Chris (Kraft) on our side, but 'the boss said so,' so that's the way it was."

―⁓―

Fred Haise, a native of Biloxi, Mississippi, had a somewhat-similar path to an Apollo spacecraft as Roosa, in that he only had two years of college before heading to aviation training, albeit it with the Navy. Unlike Roosa, however, Haise's two collegiate years were spent at Perkinston Junior College just north of his hometown, where he garnered an Associate degree. Around the same time Roosa was getting a Bachelor degree at Colorado, Haise was accomplishing the same thing, as he earned an aeronautical engineering degree from the University of Oklahoma, graduating with honors in 1959.

Haise was a civilian who had already been doing research work at the NASA facility at Edwards Air Force Base when he attended the ARPS there (Class 64A, in which he was selected as the outstanding graduate), and was back with NASA at the same facility when he was chosen to be an astronaut.

Like Mitchell, his early and intense work with the development of the Lunar Module had resulted in very early assignments on Apollo support and backup crews.

Haise was a firm believer in the rotation from backup crew to prime crew three missions later, noting "Once I did backup on 11, I knew I was going to fly on Apollo 14."

―⁓―

Stu told Joan about his selection, and Joan informed their children, but admonished them to keep it secret until the public announcement.

The youngsters did exactly as they were told, but several weeks later, one of Chris's classmates walked up to him at school and said, "Hey, Walter Cronkite says your dad's goin' to the Moon."

"I had to tell my mother the secret was out," Chris recalled. "Walter Cronkite broke the story. I was afraid she would think I leaked it, but she told me not to worry, because she already knew the word was out."

The crews for Apollo 13 and Apollo 14 were both officially announced to the public on August 6, 1969. Backup crew for Apollo 13 consisted of John Young, commander, Jack Swigert, CMP, and Charlie Duke, LMP. Support crew members were Jack Lousma, Vance Brand, and Bill Pogue, all Original Nineteen members.

The backup crew for the Apollo 14 mission was made up of Gene Cernan, commander, Ron Evans, CMP, and Joe Engle, LMP. The latter two were also from the Original Nineteen, indicating that Group 5 astronauts were making inroads into the Apollo program.

Moreover, Engle was already an astronaut, but had not earned the distinct gold insignia by riding a rocket into space from Cape Kennedy. Instead, he had been designated as an astronaut for having flown the X-15 rocket plane beyond an altitude of 50 miles (264,000 feet), which was recognized as the boundary separating the Earth's atmosphere and outer space. On June 29, 1965, he had flown the X-15 to an altitude of 280,600 feet, and had become the youngest pilot ever to qualify as an astronaut. Three of his sixteen flights in the X-15 exceeded an altitude of 50 miles.

Cernan's assignment to the Apollo 14 backup CDR slot might have been considered somewhat surprising, as it had included some audacious moves on his part. He had actually turned down the LMP backup position on the new Apollo 13 team, which, if the standard three-mission rotation was applied, would have meant that he would be scheduled to walk on the Moon on the Apollo 16 mission. Cernan had informed Slayton that he thought he deserved his own command of an Apollo mission, and the head of Flight Crew Operations was understandably nonplussed that someone would decline an almost-certain opportunity at being a moonwalker. While Cernan was adamant, he also knew he was taking a huge gamble regarding whether or not he would ever be a prime crew CDR himself.

"Turning that down was the biggest risk I ever took in the space program," Cernan recalled. "Deke never guaranteed anybody anything."

Accordingly, of the six astronauts on the Apollo 14 prime and backup crews, only Cernan had any orbital (and beyond) space experience.

The public relations profile for Roosa cited his 4,300 flying hours (3,900 in jet aircraft), and his experiences at Edwards Air Force Base and as a CapCom for Apollo 9.

The support crew for Apollo 14 was not announced in the August 6th press release, but would consist of Phillip Chapman (a Group 4 scientist), Bruce McCandless (Original Nineteen), Bill Pogue (again), and Gordon Fullerton (a transfer from the MOL program).

As for Roosa's perspective on having to remain in lunar orbit as a CMP instead of walking on the Moon as a LMP, Duke says the subject never came up between the Dynamic Duo before Apollo 14 flew.

"He never intimated to me, in any way, that he didn't want the (CMP) job," said Duke, "or that he had wanted to be an LMP. He was really focused, and was pleased that he was flying. He took his role as CMP very, very seriously."

As for the dearth of space flight time for Shepard, Mitchell, and Roosa, Duke opined, "I didn't think anything about Shepard having one fifteen-minute flight and two rookies being on the original (Apollo) 13. When you think about it, *all* of the flights after the *actual* (Apollo) 13 (flight) had two rookies. Shepard was extremely sharp, and he picked two guys he thought he could work with, and that he thought were the best in their respective jobs, CMP and LMP…and they worked very well together; Alan was not an autocrat; the crew was able to express themselves."

—∿∿—

As the 1970s began, NASA was already feeling the heat regarding funding for lunar missions. The space agency also had plans for several missions to a still-in-the-works space station called Skylab, and money could be saved by flying fewer missions to the Moon.

On January 4, 1970, NASA cancelled the Apollo 20 Moon shot. Apollo 18 and Apollo 19 would later be axed on September 2nd of the same year.

As events would transpire, NASA traditions and protocol would probably have resulted in Roosa being involved in a dramatic way in one of the cancelled Apollo flights, had those last three Moon missions been retained.

—∿∿—

After Roosa had been selected as the Command Module Pilot for a specific mission, he met, trained under, and developed a lifetime friendship with a geology specialist whose affiliation with NASA would probably have been considered unusual, if not outright controversial, given the international times of the mid-Sixties.

Farouk El-Baz was an Egyptian citizen, with a doctorate in Geology, who worked for the Bellcomm company, a subsidiary of American Telephone &

Telegraph (AT&T). At the behest of NASA Administrator James Webb, AT&T had created Bellcomm specifically to assist NASA in communications facets of the space program. El-Baz was assigned to train CMPs to do landmark tracking, photography, and other geological surveying tasks while they were in orbit around the Moon.

The timing of El-Baz's employment was somewhat of a paradox, as he joined Bellcomm in March of 1967, and the Six Day War in the Middle East, between Israel and several Arab nations, including Egypt, occurred in June of that year. While the geologist did not let such events affect his work or his relationship with NASA, he would be required to sign a statement of commitment to become a U.S. citizen as soon as possible. El-Baz would be naturalized in 1970.

Originally, Bellcomm employees were supposed to assist NASA Headquarters only, and were not to associate with astronauts or speak to the press. El-Baz's abilities soon meant a dispensation for him regarding such policies, in an era when the United States had no diplomatic relations with Egypt, while the Soviet Union had advisors—military and otherwise—firmly positioned in that Middle East nation.

Some NASA officials grumbled about whether El-Baz could be trusted, but they were rebuffed by Rocco Petrone, who appreciated the Egyptian's abilities and loyalty.

CMPs had originally been instructed by Harrison "Jack" Schmitt, one of the Group 4 scientist-astronauts. Schmitt and Jim Lovell developed procedures for landmark tracking that would first be demonstrated on Apollo 8, the first flight to the Moon, in December of 1968.

Schmitt relinquished his role at the advent of the new decade, due to new priorities:

"Early in 1970, after being told I would soon have a backup crew assignment, I began to spend more time in simulators, and less time with the upcoming crews. So the transition was gradual during that period."

Accordingly, El-Baz's primary duty was to concentrate on training CMPs on specific missions, regarding how to recognize landmarks, photograph important areas for consideration as future landing spots, etc. His knowledge and enthusiasm for the Moon program quickly won over the astronauts with whom he worked.

The geologist recalled that the first CMP with whom he worked extensively was Ken Mattingly, scheduled for the Apollo 13 flight, and word of the geologist's positive attitude and abilities began to spread through the astronaut ranks.

El-Baz's first encounter with Roosa occurred when they met just outside the Astronaut Office building at the Manned Space Center. Stu asked the bespectacled Egyptian if he was Farouk El-Baz, and after getting confirmation, said, "Well, I want you to make me as smart as Ken...Hell, no, I want you to make me *smarter* than Ken!"

Training techniques utilized by El-Baz included coordinating what he called "flyover exercises" by CMPs, during field trips by other astronauts who had been designated as future Apollo CDRs and LMPs. Airborne CMPs would make geological observations and would take photographs, just as they would do while orbiting the Moon. In some locales, the CMPs would be required to fly T-38s up to an altitude of 25,000 feet, to simulate the speed at which they would be zooming over the lunar surface.

Perhaps not surprisingly, El-Baz quickly acquired the nickname of "King" among the CMPs, being so named after the deposed Egyptian monarch King Farouk, who was overthrown in a 1952 military coup.

As for his particular association with Roosa, El-Baz would recall, "Apollo 14 was the first mission to the relatively-rugged lunar highlands. Stu and I spent vast numbers of sessions on what we theorized the highlands featured along his track. Furthermore, he was to take pictures with the advanced Hycon camera, particularly high-resolution images of potential sites in the southern highlands for a later mission, Apollo 16."

And the conservative fighter pilot and the Egyptian geologist forged a mutual respect for each other that transcended the business in which they were associated.

"Although Stu was born in Colorado, he was more of a typical Southern gentleman," El-Baz remembered fondly, "warm and uncomplicated. Because of the enormous time we spent together, we began to know each other as individuals, not just as team members of the vast Apollo program. We spoke about his childhood, and his training as an Air Force pilot. We had occasions to meet each other's families, and to get to know the kids."

El-Baz and Roosa ultimately discussed geo-politics as well. Although El-Baz's home country was practically a Soviet client state, the geologist was not interested in such machinations, and Roosa opined that Egyptians would never become Communists anyway, because they were too smart and too civilized.

—ww—

Apollo 13 blasted off on April 11, 1970 at 1:13 p.m.—13.13 in military time. The Commander and Lunar Module Pilot of the new Apollo 13 crew had been assigned a landing site in an area known as Fra Mauro, named for a 15th century Italian mapmaker and monk. It is located close to the equator and close to the center of the near side of the Moon, some 225 miles south of the spectacular Copernicus crater. The area was the first mission to the a more-rugged "highlands" area of the Moon, and was chosen due to the proximity of what was believed to be a relatively "new" crater called Cone Crater—it was thought to be only around 25 million years old—and geologists believed that the impact that had formed the "new" crater would have exposed material from below the surface.

The CSM for the Apollo 13 mission had been named *Odyssey*, and the LM was named *Aquarius*.

And the disastrous explosion of an oxygen tank aboard Apollo 13 when the spacecraft was some 200,000 miles from Earth would jeopardize not only the lives of the three crewmen en route to the Moon, but the entire Apollo program. It would also cause some "what if" speculation about what would have happened if the original crews of 13 and 14 hadn't been swapped.

There had also been a last-minute change in the crew of Apollo 13, as CMP Ken Mattingly was pulled from the flight due to possible exposure to measles. Backup CMP Jack Swigert was now occupying the center seat in the Command Module.

Vance Brand was a CapCom during the Apollo 13 mission, and recalled "I had been at the Cape to help strap the crew in on launch day. I got into the CapCom rotation after I got back to Houston."

Ed Mitchell recalls the luck of having been in Mission Control, standing behind the on-duty CapCom (Jack Lousma) when the ominous "Houston, we've had a problem" transmission was received:

"As soon as we were sure—and this was within minutes—that it was a real problem, and not a telemetry problem, I got into a quick conference with the flight director, and it was decided that I should immediately go into the Lunar Module simulator and start working on what the crew would have to do, using the Lunar Module as a 'lifeboat'."

Other astronauts quickly converged at the Manned Space Center, taking turns in Command Module and Lunar Module simulators, meticulously searching for ways to conserve battery power and oxygen on the crippled spacecraft, which was now trying to limp home. Such participants included Roosa, and even Neil Armstrong.

"I spent a good bit of time in the simulator," Armstrong confirmed, "as did many other astronauts."

Harrison Schmitt spent time in simulators at Cape Kennedy.

"I happened to be working full time in the simulators at the Cape, since I knew they would not be in use after 13 launched," Schmitt recounted. "When the accident occurred, the simulator operators and I immediately went to work on procedures that might be needed, such as platform alignments using the crescent Earth. Once the actual procedures were finalized in Houston, we ran them on the Cape simulators as a final check, as those simulators were slightly more up to date than the ones in Houston. As a result, I spent the entire emergency working at the Cape."

Charlie Duke: "We all spent hours and hours working during the Apollo 13 crisis; we didn't have to be there, but we were."

The wives of the astronauts pitched in to assist the three women whose spouses were in the stricken spacecraft. Joan had become good friends with Marilyn Lovell, wife of the Apollo 13 CDR, but would end up at the Haise residence, where the Apollo 13 LMP's wife, Mary, was eight months pregnant. The astronaut wives' informal organization meant that they were supportive of the families in the same astronaut group as their own husbands.

Reporters were congregating outside the Haise residence, of course, and at one point, Joan smuggled the Haise children away from the house in the Roosas' large station wagon, taking them out for ice cream in an effort to give the youngsters a break from a very tense and very public crisis that was being followed around the globe.

The 1995 movie *Apollo 13*, directed by Ron Howard and starring Tom Hanks as Jim Lovell, Bill Paxton as Fred Haise, and Kevin Bacon as Jack Swigert, is a thrilling presentation of the most dramatic and complicated rescue in human history. However, the film takes a bit of poetic license with some of the characters, and Stu Roosa figured into the incongruous mix in a peripheral manner (and in more than one facet).

Two CapComs are portrayed in the movie—the one who receives the "Houston, we've had a problem" message is portrayed by Brett Cullen, who resembled the real-life Jack Lousma. However, the credits only refer to Cullen's character as "CapCom 1."

Actor Ned Vaughn has the role of "CapCom 2" (and again, that's the only character name in the credits), and curiously, the second CapCom is a thin-faced redhead that resembles Stuart Roosa. However, Roosa was not a CapCom for the Apollo 13 flight, but his children noted that "CapCom 2" even had his hair styled like their father.

Actor Gary Sinise portrayed Ken Mattingly (but looked nothing like the bumped-from-the-flight CMP), and was shown spending long hours in the Command Module simulator. However, Roosa and others also worked in the CM simulator (and Roosa had already been training in the CM simulator before the Apollo 13 and 14 crews were switched).

Armstrong offered an opinion about generalities being proffered in movies, and cited a scene in *Apollo 13* where he and Buzz Aldrin are shown sitting with Lovell's mother as the Apollo 13 Command Module prepares to re-enter the Earth's atmosphere.

"A movie watcher can only keep about a dozen characters in his/her mind without mixing them up," Armstrong said, "so the screenplay writer must simplify many situations. I believe I did visit with Mrs. Lovell, but the movie presented her as not recognizing me. I had met with her a number of times and I think she knew me pretty well."

Roosa would later admit that while the crisis was ongoing, he had ominous reservations that the Apollo 13 crew would be able to return to Earth alive. When the return was successful, he observed that every pilot wants to fly a successful mission, and that while the mission of Apollo 13 *ended* successfully, the full mission had, of course, not been completed.

Moreover, the crew of Apollo 14 would later discuss, among themselves, what the scenario might have been had the order of crew flights remained the same, instead of the lineup of Apollo 13 and Apollo 14 being reversed. They came to the conclusion that their reactions and performance, as well as the actions of the earthbound NASA scientists, astronauts, and Mission Control personnel would have been the same under similar circumstances, and that the outcome of the mission would also have been successful.

The heroic and Herculean efforts of the technicians at Mission Control and elsewhere, astronauts in simulators, and of course, the crew of Apollo 13, all working under extreme duress, is an American legend, and *Apollo 13* is an uplifting, "feel-good" movie that appropriately chronicles what is considered by many observers to have been NASA's finest hour.

In real life, however, the future of the Apollo program itself was in serious doubt.

Post-Apollo 13 Training

To say that Apollo 14 had something to prove was an understatement.

"We realized that if our mission failed—if we had to turn back—that was probably the end of the Apollo program," said Mitchell. "There was no way NASA could stand two failures in a row. We figured there was a heavy mantle on our shoulders to make sure we got it right."

The Apollo service module had to undergo extensive redesigns due to the Apollo 13 disaster. Modifications included the addition of another oxygen tank in a previously-empty section of the Service Module, as well as a back-up battery.

And the delay had a perhaps-ironic benefit of allowing Shepard, Mitchell, and Roosa to practice even more extensively. Including their training period prior to the Apollo 13 emergency—and it also needs to be remembered that the crew was held back when Mueller insisted that Shepard needed more training time—the crew of Apollo 14 would spend a total of nineteen months preparing for their lunar journey.

They would also consult closely with the Apollo 13 crew following their return.

Lovell: "The Command Service Module was completely modified after the 13 accident. Apollo 14 was a major test flight to verify these changes, and was to land at Fra Mauro, the destination of Apollo 13."

—w—

Recalling his own Moon experience in a self-penned book titled *Carrying the Fire*, Apollo 11 CMP Michael Collins referred to the crew that consisted of Neil Armstrong, Buzz Aldrin, and himself as "amiable strangers," and the same term could have been applied to the crew of Apollo 14. Shepard, Mitchell and Roosa didn't discuss socio-political issues or other contemporary topics among themselves, keeping their training sessions focused and business-like. Like the Apollo 11 crew, 14's threesome tended to go their separate ways once their working day was over.

Mitchell noted the differences in the personalities of Shepard, Roosa, and himself while the crew was training. He would ultimately use a geometric analogy to describe the Apollo 14 crewmembers:

"If you consider personality types in a 360-degree circle, we were 120 degrees apart from each other. We represented three totally different styles, which wasn't a surprise; we always thought that, but never really discussed it because we *knew* we had different personality profiles. But we had a great respect for each other. We realized that we made up a good crew together; we were very professional, and we treated each other as professionals. But we were not 'buddy-buddy,' like (Apollo 12's) Pete Conrad, Al Bean, and Dick Gordon. We just did our job."

And Shepard actually appeared to have mellowed out, personality-wise, for the mission. While he was still the commander for the upcoming flight, and would assert his authority if and when it was needed, he dutifully did his share of the grunt work along with his two crewmates, although it was said that he wasn't enthusiastic about geological assignments and training. Gone was the semi-imperious, moody façade from his days of being grounded. Alan Shepard was keenly aware of what he and his associates would need to accomplish, and that the eyes of the world would be focused not only on the success of the Apollo 14 mission, but how the return to the cosmos by America's first space traveler would be perceived.

When the prime and backup crews of Apollo 14 had been announced, Gene Cernan, in another personally daring move, had taken it on himself to converse one-on-one with Shepard about the capabilities of Apollo 14's second echelon. His assertion took place in Shepard's office, with the Apollo 14 CDR exhibiting his "Icy Commander" countenance, but Cernan's strategy worked.

"I don't know where I got the courage to say it," Cernan recalled, "but one day I told Al my crew was going to do everything it could his crew ready to fly, '...and by the way, we're going to be able to do it better than you can, and I'll be able to do it better than you individually.' That kind of broke the ice, because I don't think anyone ever told Al Shepard they were better than he was."

The positive change in the personality of the mission commander wasn't lost on Roosa, either, and for all of the internal controversy about Shepard leapfrogging into an assignment as commander of a prime crew, Roosa ultimately respected the way his superior dedicated himself to training.

Chris: "It was certainly felt that this had to be a mission that would get the program back on track, and my father always said that you could not have picked a better person to command a mission with that much importance than Alan Shepard."

Shepard had been a tough boss as head of the Astronaut Office, and was firm yet fair, according to Charlie Duke, who also recalled that as the training for Apollo 14 developed, the general feeling among astronauts was that they were glad to see him get back on flying status.

The Apollo 14 commander was also polite and friendly to Lorine and Dewey when Stu's parents were introduced to Shepard, and Roosa was touched.

As the flight drew closer, Roosa began to take his family to the Manned Space Center more often on weekends, to familiarize the children with the "how" and "why" of his training. The Roosa kids were impressed with the giant water tank in which astronauts could simulate working in the weightlessness of space, although Roosa himself didn't train for a spacewalk on Apollo 14.

―――

Obviously, Shepard, the commander, and Mitchell, the LM pilot, worked a lot more with each other, practicing Lunar Module flight patterns, or working outdoors in some location that had some similar characteristics to the surface of the Moon. Roosa would often work solo on Command Module flight profiles. The threesome would all be together for simulations of launch, earth orbit, and lunar rendezvous.

One of the primary assignments for an Apollo Command Module Pilot is to navigate the spacecraft from the Earth to the Moon and back. Roosa would train to use a sextant and eyepatch in sighting the stars for such duties.

The delay in the U.S. moon program due to the Apollo 13 disaster would mean that Roosa would ultimately spend approximately 1000 hours in the Command Module simulator. By comparison, another Apollo CMP reportedly had spent less than 500 hours in the same "sim" before his own Moon voyage.

The confident Apollo 14 CMP made it known to his fellow crew members and other NASA personnel that his goal was to break the record for the transposition, docking and extraction (TD&E) procedure to remove the LM, but Roosa was enough of a pragmatist to realize that his actions would need to be methodical and accurate, regardless of how long the extraction took.

Seating arrangements in the Apollo Command Module had the CDR (Shepard) in the left seat (facing forward), the CMP (Roosa) in the center seat, and the LMP (Mitchell) in the right seat. For TD&E of the Lunar Module, the CMP and CDR would change seats, and the Command/Service Module would disengage from the third S-IV-B stage. Four Spacecraft LM Adapter (SLA) panels would fold open then fall away, exposing the LM, which was stored inside the S-IVB.

TD&E was, of course, more complex than it may have appeared, and required a lot more practice than average space buffs might have thought... and like similar procedures on Earth, it had an implicit sexual inference as well.

After disengaging from the S-IVB, the CSM would rotate 180 degrees along its horizontal axis, using the small Reaction Control System rockets (RCS) thruster rockets that were placed on the exterior of the Service Module in four groups of four. The CSM's probe extended outward from the docking ring on the "nose" of the Command Module, and the CMP would maneuver the probe into the docking port of the LM. Three small capture latches on the probe would snap outward to establish a preliminary docking ("soft dock") with the receptacle. The initial capture would be confirmed onboard the CSM by an indicator on the control panel that flipped to change from a solid color to a striped configuration. Such a display was called a "barber pole."

The probe would then be retracted back into the nose of the CSM to pull the two spacecraft together, at which point twelve major, permanent latches on the CSM's docking ring would be fired to secure the dock ("hard dock"). The LM would then be pulled out of the S-IVB stage.

The conjoined CSM and LM would be known collectively as Apollo 14. Once they disengaged while in orbit around the Moon, separate call signs for the CSM (*Kitty Hawk*) and the LM (*Antares*) would be used. Roosa had selected *Kitty Hawk* for the CSM in honor of the North Carolina community where the Wright brothers had first flown less than 70 years earlier. Antares is a red giant star in the constellation Scorpio.

All Apollo crews practiced numerous emergency procedures during their many months of training. One morbid-but-plausible possibility was that the two moonwalkers would be unable to ascend from the lunar surface, and that the CMP would have to return the spacecraft to Earth and re-enter the atmosphere by himself. Such a training procedure had been in effect since the beginning of the moon landing missions facet of the Apollo program; Cernan described it as "...a scenario from Day One."

A variant of that phase of the mission considered an LM ascent stage launch that had gone wrong, leaving it stuck in a lower and/or aberrant orbit around the Moon. Roosa decided privately that if such an event happened on the real mission, he would do everything he could to rendezvous with the crippled LM. He would expend the extra fuel necessary for such a maneuver, and he might even die in an effort to rescue his fellow crew members, but he would have been determined to try.

And as a matter of historical trivia, Stu Roosa was on deck to become the first space rookie to orbit the Moon solo. Slayton had originally wanted only veteran astronauts in the center seat, primarily due to the ominous responsibilities a CMP would have if something happened to the two crew members slated to walk on the surface. That precedent would actually have been broken by either Ken Mattingly or Jack Swigert on Apollo 13, but it turned out that Roosa would be the first space neophyte to soar around Luna by himself.

Likewise, Mitchell would become the first Original Nineteen member to walk on the Moon. Had the Apollo 13 mission been successful, that distinction would have been attained by Fred Haise.

As training for the Apollo 14 flight progressed, the crew made motivational tapes and videos for the NASA technicians. Shepard, Mitchell, and Roosa addressed the camera in a positive and conversational manner, urging the employees to keep up the spirit of the space program.

"Of course, we're depending on you, the members of the checkout and launch team at KSC (Kennedy Space Center), to guarantee us a safe, flawless launch and flight aboard Apollo 14," Roosa said in one such video. "That means every functional component on of the Saturn and Apollo checked, tested, and operating as designed."

—◦◦◦—

Shepard had laid out a sketch of an idea for the mission patch, which depicted an official astronaut pin soaring to the Moon (reportedly, Shepard wanted the concept to represent a tribute to the entire astronaut corps). It was an appropriate idea that was well-received.

However, another patch connected with the same mission may actually have been more memorable for space buffs than the official one.

In a cocky but good-natured move, the backup crew for Apollo 14 had taken to calling itself the "First Team," asserting they were ready to step in immediately if something happened to one or more of the prime crew members...and that attitude was an attempt to validate Cernan's memorable assertion to Shepard that the backup crew was going to be better than the prime crew.

"I look at Apollo 14 as 'my fourth flight that I never flew'," said Cernan. "The prime crew and the backup crew had a great rapport. We worked our butts off, but we probably had more fun, and probably had the best relationship there ever was between backup and prime crews. Stu and Ron (Evans) really worked well with each other on procedures and lunar geology."

Moreover, the backup crew also had the distinction of being the only threesome of its type to design and create its own mission patch, which lampooned and actually plagiarized the design of the *official* Apollo 14 patch.

Cernan asserted that the use of the cartoon characters of the Road Runner and Wile E. Coyote in the backup crew patch was a "gotcha" that was directed primarily at Shepard. The coyote was shown in the layout as zooming to the Moon (instead of an astronaut pin), but the creature differed from its Warner Brothers Looney Tunes/Merry Melodies counterpart in that it was an older animal with a grey beard and glasses (Al Shepard was now 47 years old). It also had red fur (a jab at Roosa) and a slight paunch (poking fun at Mitchell's physique).

The backup crew patch also displayed the Road Runner (with a "First Team" streamer on its tail), already standing on Luna, having beaten the coyote to the surface of the Moon. The backup crew patch was embroidered with "Beep Beep" and the names of Cernan, Evans, and Engle. Apparently, this off-the-wall effort had also been well-planned, just like any legitimate mission patch.

Shepard's response to the backup crew patch was to reference a single-panel cartoon that was seen during that era. The drawing was obviously unauthorized by Warner Brothers, as it depicted Wile E. Coyote having finally captured the Road Runner; the coyote was throttling the fleet-footed bird by the neck, snarling "'Beep Beep,' your ass!" The succinct phrase would also become Shepard's standard retort whenever he discovered one of the backup patches that had mysteriously appeared in a locker or storage area during training.

And the "First Team," aided and abetted by co-conspirators, would ensure that plenty of 'Beep Beep' patches accompanied the Apollo 14 crew all the way to the surface of the Moon.

Final Preparations

On one trip to the Cape Kennedy complex, Roosa took his entire family into Launch Complex 39's gargantuan Vehicle Assembly Building (VAB), where they were allowed to examine the Command Module close up. He emphasized that he would be inside the spacecraft for over a week, and told his wife and children that if he happened to perish during the mission, he wanted them to know that he had died doing something that he loved to do.

Chris: "Early in our lives, he'd made it very clear to us that this was what he wanted to do, and that if he was to die, we were to go forward with life, knowing that it was how my father wanted to live his own life."

Jack doesn't recall his father making a statement *before* the mission about the possibility of his death, but remembered a *post-flight* conversation where Roosa stated that if he had died, it would have happened while he was serving his country in a unique way.

"I wasn't worried," Allen recalled. "I was eight years old, and I thought my dad was the greatest pilot in the world."

Rosemary was in the second grade, and doesn't recall any fear for her father's safety at the time, either. However, she had drawn a picture of her father in outer space, which caused her teacher to call Joan to the school for a parent-teacher conference. The teacher thought Rosemary had drawn her father in a coffin, and told Joan that Rosemary was apparently afraid that her father was going to die in space.

Joan asked to see the picture, and upon examining it, informed the teacher that her daughter wasn't that good of an artist, because Rosemary had simply been trying to illustrate her father inside a spacecraft.

However, like members of other astronaut families, Joan and the children had already had to deal with the possibilities of catastrophe concerning Stu's career, but the oldest Roosa son also had a practical perspective on that facet as well, as the launch of Apollo 14 loomed.

"People want to talk to you about 'Were you scared?'" said Chris, "but you'd grown up with the idea that your dad was going to ride on a rocket. It's not like my father was a shoe salesman who was picked out of the blue, placed on a rocket, and would then have to figure out what to do. We just knew that as an astronaut, my dad would probably be getting onto a rocket at some point."

On November 9, 1970, the Apollo 14/Saturn V assembly, as tall as a 36-story building, rolled out of the VAB on the proportionally huge crawler-transporter that crept along the crawlerway towards launch pad 39A, some three and a half miles away.

The crew of Apollo 14 was photographed in front of the giant rocket. Roosa and Mitchell wore suits and ties; Shepard, standing in the middle, was dressed casually in a Ban-Lon shirt, and sported a stereotypical Smilin' Al grin. The threesome also answered questions from the press.

The business-like attitude of the crew carried over to their perspective regarding the rollout. While the sight of a Saturn V was impressive to most observers, Shepard, Roosa, and Mitchell didn't gawk, and didn't find the scenario of the slow-moving giant to be intimidating. They had all seen Saturn V launches in person before, and had been training hard for over a year. It would still be almost three more months before the Apollo 14 launch, so for them, the rollout was an event that they took in stride as part of the process.

—◦◦◦—

Apollo astronauts were allowed to take along personal items, including small souvenirs such as patches and pins, to present to family and friends when they returned from their flights. The items were stored inside each astronaut's Personal Preference Kit (PPK, somewhat like a zippered kit containing personal shaving items, etc.), and the idea of owning something that had been flown to the Moon was enthralling to most space buffs. In addition to such items as a brooch that he intended to present to his mother, other pins, and the Air Force pilot wings he had won in 1955, Stuart Roosa's PPK would contain hundreds of tree seeds as a tribute to his days as a smoke jumper with the Forest Service.

Ed Cliff, head of the Forest Service during Roosa's training days for Apollo 14, knew that the CMP had been a smoke jumper, and asked Roosa to transport the seeds in his PPK. The concept had sort of a Johnny-Appleseed-in-outer-space connotation, and Roosa agreed, opining that it would be a unique way to honor smoke jumpers and firefighters.

A Forest Service official named Stan Krugman was assigned to the project. Krugman selected loblolly pine, sycamore, sweetgum, redwood, and Douglas fir seeds, which were placed into small canisters for the flight. "Control" seeds would remain on Earth for comparison to the seeds that were to fly to the Moon. If all went well, hundreds of "Moon trees" would be germinated from the seeds that were to go on the lunar voyage.

—◦◦◦—

Because of the measles debacle with Apollo 13, the crew of Apollo 14 was quarantined for three weeks prior to the launch, long before the usual time that spaceflight crews had been pulled away from public contact.

Apollo 14 was scheduled for launch on Sunday, January 31st, at 3:23 p.m. The countdown actually began on January 25th, and was to total 102 hours with a total of 48 scheduled holds.

On January 23, 1971, a week before the scheduled launch of Apollo 14, Gene Cernan crashed a small helicopter that had been used for Lunar landing training into the Indian River near Cape Kennedy. While he wasn't seriously injured, the Apollo 14 backup CDR immediately pondered that he had seriously jeopardized his chance to command the final Moon flight, Apollo 17, as he was being transported, in a soaking wet flight suit, back to crew quarters.

Upon arrival, Cernan encountered Shepard in the dining area, and muttered that Shepard had "won," and could command Apollo 14, but following a meeting with Slayton, no punitive action was taken regarding future flight possibilities for Cernan.

Two days prior to launch, one of NASA's Lunar Landing Research Vehicles (LLRV), a LM trainer, crashed at Ellington Air Force Base near Houston. Used to simulate lunar landings, the LLRV, which was a complex, skeletal frame with a rocket motor, was known as "the flying bedstead." Neil Armstrong had barely escaped from an out-of-control LLRV on May 6, 1968, and the one that was destroyed on January 29, 1971 was the same vehicle that Shepard had been using to train for the upcoming landing at Fra Mauro. It, too, went out of control while hovering at approximately 200 feet, and NASA pilot Stuart Present, who was not an astronaut, ejected safely, but the $1.9 million vehicle was a total loss.

The same day, President Richard Nixon issued a budget statement that requested permission to cut another $217 million from the space program. The helicopter and LLRV crashes, as well as the announced budget slash, would not affect the countdown for Apollo 14, but the timing of those incidents probably seemed ominous to some observers.

—⁓—

In the final days before the launch, members of electronic and print media descended on the Cape to provide complete coverage, but they were also cognizant of the earlier and longer pre-launch quarantine that meant the astronauts wouldn't be seen in public.

"With the astronauts in perfect health, space officials are making sure they stay that way," Walter Cronkite told CBS News viewers. "The three pilots will be restricted to quarters all week, under a new medical isolation policy. No more German measles scares, such as that which knocked astronaut Tom Mattingly out of the Apollo 13 flight last spring."

Cronkite also reported that "...a supervising space official said that no Apollo crew has ever been so well-trained for a mission," and a CBS story by Bill Stout from Downey detailed the changes made to the CSM spacecraft since the Apollo 13 disaster, noting that the improvements would give the Apollo 14 crew a greater margin of safety.

However, other television stories on the pending Apollo 14 flight cited other possible "problems" besides the ones astronauts would face in outer space, and some of the reports probably came across as morbid and/or controversial to NASA officials and employees:

"More than 10,000 engineers and technicians have been laid off here in the last eighteen months," intoned ABC Science Editor Jules Bergman, reporting from Cape Kennedy, "and after the near-disaster of Apollo 13, when human error nearly cost the lives of the astronauts, the space agency suddenly realized that men in fear of losing their jobs might not be able to do their best. There are thirteen million parts in the Saturn V rocket...and while sometimes, several can fail, it only takes one critical part failing to end the mission or cause a catastrophe."

Bergman cited the motivational films and recordings the Apollo 14 crew had made for space workers, pronouncing them to be "pep talks," and also noted that"...the morale building extends to posters and bumper stickers, emphasizing togetherness, dedication, and teamwork. Morale seems to have gone up, but no one is sure, and there are reports of possible new layoffs, which is why everyone, including the Apollo 14 crew, is still worried."

Another story noted that one out of every ten homes in Titusville, the town nearest the Cape, was vacant, and that there had been four hundred F.H.A. (Federal Housing Administration) repossessions there. Unemployed NASA engineers were shown taking a real estate course.

NBC's John Chancellor also reported on the morale-boosting announcements made by the crew, citing a tape that was played three times a day, as well as 12,000 letters that were mailed from the astronauts to employees, and the issuance of motivational booklets and pamphlets.

Some reports, while noting the extensive preparation by the crew, pointed out that this was the first prime crew that did not include a former crew member of a Gemini flight.

Profiles of the crew always cited Shepard first, recalling his Mercury flight, how he overcame his ear disorder, and how he rededicated himself to training.

"To outsiders," said one report, "it is a mystery why Shepard, safely a hero and safely a millionaire, should want to risk it all now, at the age of 47."

Overall, the reporting was thorough, as newscasters and writers focused on the ambitious plan for the two moonwalkers, which included two EVAs that could last up to five hours each.

Still, the tone of a lot of the coverage wasn't particularly upbeat, as summarized by Bergman at the conclusion of one of his reports:

"No flight has been more ambitious or tougher, and the space agency is running scared. Should Apollo 14 fail, in the aftermath of the recent

Apollo 13 near-disaster, it just might mean the end of the entire Apollo lunar landing program."

―――₩₩―――

The Roosa family stayed at the Holiday Inn in Cocoa Beach prior to the launch. Security personnel monitored the children closely, even when they went to the beach to play volleyball. Signs at motels, gas stations and other businesses in the area bore the message "Good luck Apollo 14" and similar good wishes, and the astronauts' names were listed on some of them.

The night before the launch, Shepard and Cernan drove out to observe the gigantic Saturn V, under the glare of spotlights, and Cernan was assured of not only Shepard's commitment to Apollo 14, but the prime CDR's enduring commitment to the space program, as he had endeavored to return to space for a decade.

"He was determined and committed to somehow, somewhere, fly again," said Cernan. "That commitment came out loud and clear that night. A lot of people would have given up earlier. He was a good guy to work for, and in retrospect, he deserved the flight."

Launch

On launch day, the crew was awakened inside their quarters inside the Manned Spacecraft Operations Building, and had what had become a traditional pre-launch breakfast of steak and eggs, with Deke Slayton and other NASA officials joining them. Roosa's countenance in photos that were taken while preparations were ongoing indicated that at least outwardly, he was his usual matter-of-fact self.

Out on the launch pad, NASA technicians were going about their assigned duties, preparing the state-of-the-art space vehicle for its journey. An astronaut checked out the interior of the Command Module in a final inspection prior to launch.

The Roosa family went to Mass the morning of the launch. "It was a very quiet time," recalled Allen, "but after that, things got real busy, real fast—the launch, flying back to Houston in a Lear jet, and a house full of people."

The skies were slightly overcast, adding a question mark about how the weather would evolve during the day. Kennedy Space Center Launch Director Walter Kapryan, who had been in that position of responsibility since 1966, watched the skies and the weather reports intensely.

―――₩₩―――

A Sunday, January 31, 1971 souvenir edition of *TODAY—Florida's Space Age Newspaper* (a Gannett publication) featured a full color drawing of the Apollo 14 crew on its front page, and hyped the mission as the most televised ever (as eight broadcasts from the crew were planned).

One page of the special edition featured profiles of all three astronauts, and perhaps not surprisingly, Alan Shepard's profile took up the entire top half ("Veteran Pilot Dominates Every Bird He Commands"), while the brief bios of Mitchell ("He May Describe Moon In a Philosophical Way") and Roosa ("He's Best Trained to Take Pilot's Seat") were found on the lower left quarter and the lower right quarter of the page, respectively. Shepard's profile had the expected story of his battle back from his health problems, and Mitchell's interest in extra-sensory perception was noted in the story on the Lunar Module Pilot.

Roosa's profile opined that his "...red hair, freckles, and fashionable clothes leave people with the impression that he is younger than 37, and an enthusiasm he carries into everything heightens that impression."

—◆◆◆—

Standard protocol was in place for Joan and the children to be taken to view the launch, along with Shepard and Mitchell family members, from a private V.I.P. section for immediate family members, located some three miles from the launch pad. However, special arrangements had been made for Lorine, Dewey, and Danny and Wilma and their children to be stationed in a cordoned-off area by the door at the Manned Spacecraft Operations Building, where they would be able to see the three astronauts emerge and board the van that would shuttle them to the launch complex.

"It was my understanding that Uncle Stuart asked Grandma and Grandpa if there was anything special that they would like to do," said Roosa's niece Dana, "and this was what Grandma requested. Uncle Stuart pulled the strings to make this happen."

Politicians and entertainment celebrities were also on hand, including actors Kirk Douglas and Charlton Heston. The Roosa family members stood in their special area in the front of the crowd, and were asked if they minded if National Security Advisor Henry Kissinger joined them in that area. The Roosas acceded to NASA's request.

—◆◆◆—

Shepard, Roosa and Mitchell finally went through the detailed procedure of donning their space suits and bubble-like helmets. Roosa's suit weighed about 35 pounds, noticeably less than Shepard's or Mitchell's suits, which weighed about 50 pounds, as the CDR and LMP had to have extra layers of protection when they walked on the surface of the Moon.

As his helmet was locked and sealed, Stu pondered to himself that the action of being closed off into a self-contained breathing environment from added a sense of ultimate commitment to the task at hand.

The astronauts now breathed from their own portable packs of pure oxygen, which would continue for some time as their bodies were purged of nitrogen, which could potentially cause a case of the "bends," as happened to deep sea divers who surfaced too quickly. The trio relaxed for about a half hour as the transformation to their respiratory systems took place.

However, a precaution that had been one of the changes made following the Apollo 1 fire dictated that a less-combustible mixture of nitrogen and oxygen would be pumped into the Command Module on the launch pad, after it had been sealed. The mix would later be purged after the spacecraft was in orbit, to be replaced by pure oxygen.

Ensconced in their self-contained outfits, the three astronauts, accompanied by Slayton and other NASA technicians, finally walked out of the building towards the van, to rousing applause from the onlookers gathered outside. Stu quickly spotted his family members to the right of the exit, and although he couldn't communicate with them verbally, he smiled, shook hands with his father, and grasped his mother's hand tenderly.

The ride to Launch Pad LC39A was eight miles. The Roosa family members who had been at the Manned Space Operations Building were quickly bussed to an alternate V.I.P. area which was a separate area from the "immediate family" V.I.P. section. Stu's hunting compadre Bert Klineburger was also on hand at the alternate V.I.P. location, having been invited by the Roosa family.

And like a hibernating behemoth, the Saturn V, now engorged with volatile rocket fuel and liquid oxygen, awaited.

Upon arriving at the launch site, the astronauts and their accompanying technicians boarded the launch pad's elevator, and ascended to the top. As he crossed the gangplank to the White Room, Roosa noticed the several hundred pounds of ice that had formed on the side of the rocket due to the sub-zero temperature of the liquid oxygen that would be part of its potent fuel mix. Condensation swirled from the massive cylinder, hinting at the eruption that was to come.

The crew then began the well-practiced and now-common boarding protocol and procedures in the White Room—familiar to the crew, NASA officials, and millions of television viewers, who had been enthralled by such procedures ever since they had watched preparations for Shepard's sub-orbital flight not quite ten years earlier.

One tradition of manned space flights was for the pad team leader, Guenter Wendt, to be presented with a going-away gift, just prior to boarding. Shepard presented Wendt, who had been a German Luftwaffe pilot in World War II, and was nicknamed "the pad *Führer*," with a German army helmet, emblazoned with "Col. Guenter Klink," a reference to the bumbling commandant of a German prison camp in the television comedy "Hogan's Heroes." Wendt reciprocated by giving Shepard, age 47, a walking cane labeled "lunar explorer support equipment."

The crew boarded the Command Module following standard protocol—CDR (left seat), LMP (right seat) and CMP (middle seat). Most of the Command Module was covered by the Boost Protective Cover (BPC), a conical sheath designed to prevent heat or fire damage to the CM if the Launch Escape Tower (LET) was fired in case of an emergency. If the launch proceeded normally, the BPC was jettisoned after the phase of the launch during which the LET might have been used (the LET rockets would carry the BPC away with the rest of the tower).

The launch schedule proceeded normally, but light rain began falling by mid-afternoon, and Kapryan halted the countdown with just eight minutes left. The unplanned hold, a first for the Apollo program, lasted 40 minutes, until the rain clouds had moved on.

And at 4:03 p.m., the man-made beast on which astronauts Al Shepard, Ed Mitchell and Stu Roosa were astride was commanded to awaken, and it did so with a fearsome, deafening bellow, accompanied by billowing flames and smoke.

—∿∿—

The approaching dusk and the damp mistiness left by the now-departed rainstorm only enhanced the spectacular sight and the sound of the launch. Tentacles of flame erupted on either side of the bottom of the Saturn V, which seemed to sit in its own cauldron of fire momentarily before breaking free of its shackles, as four hold-down arms at the base of the launch pad and five access arms along the outside of the booster swung away. Over seven and a half million pounds of thrust lifted the raging, mechanical monster, which weighed over 6,600,000 pounds, in a slow-but-determined rise.

Stu would later eloquently recall that the launch was like a birth, alluding to the countdown as slowly breathing life into the Saturn V, and noting that once the hold-down arms were released, the rocket was alive, with a mind of its own.

Joan had instructed the children to shout "Godspeed!" when the Saturn V lifted off, and the four youngsters complied, yelling the blessing at the top of their lungs. Chris recalled that the heat of the flames that could be felt even at that distance, and the family was literally shaken by the deafening, roaring noise that finally reached their ears.

"The Saturn V took off very slowly," said Chris. "It's like a 36-story building getting airborne. There's an intense flame that pumps out from the bottom of the rocket, and it takes a while before the 'shock wave' hits you. Then you get this wall of sound that permeates through your body, and the ground shakes."

Even though the alternate V.I.P. section was further from the launch pad, the sight and thunderous sound were also overwhelming at that location, particularly to those who had never experienced an Apollo/Saturn launch in person.

For all of his memorable hunting experiences, the launch of Apollo 14 left Bert Klineburger awestruck.

"That was a fantastic thrill to see Stu blast off to the Moon," the big game hunter recalled. "It was about as close to the launch site as you could get, and was one of the most thrilling things in my life—mind-boggling; you could even feel the ground shaking a little bit."

―――∿∿∿―――

The initial reactions of the Apollo 14 crew within the first seconds after liftoff reflected almost boyish exuberance.

"Beautiful!" cried Roosa at the nine second mark, with Shepard making the same exclamation seven seconds later.

"She's going; she's going," Mitchell remarked. "Everything's good."

The five Rocketdyne F-1 engines in the first stage were performing flawlessly. The Saturn V screamed into the upper atmosphere, as blinding flames more than twice as long as the rocket itself blasted behind.

While the flight of the Saturn V appeared to be smooth to Earthbound observers, the occupants of the Command Module felt like they were on some kind of bizarre carnival ride. They were being shaken violently by the roaring projectile, and were being yanked back and forth by forces that seemed almost supernatural.

G-forces (gravity) built up due to the acceleration, making the trio feel like several times their body weight was pressing them back into their couches. The pressure maxxed out at around four and a half times ground level gravity before easing up. Roosa was so excited-yet-focused that he barely noticed the "Gs," and he was easily able to lift his arms to perform tasks such as adjusting switches.

The most memorable incident of the launch phase happened when the S-IC shut down two minutes and 45 minutes into the flight, having used some

2,350 *tons* of propellant in that time period to take Apollo 14 to an altitude of 42 miles. The moon rocket's speed was now over 6000 miles per hour.

When the staging episode occurred, Stu hadn't necessarily expected the violent behavior of the rocket, noting that it was the opposite of what happened when a jet airplane pulled Gs. In an aircraft, any increase in G-forces could be detected as they began, and could be dealt with as the Gs increased, and decreased. In the Command Module, however, the four and a half Gs abruptly subsided, and the astronauts had a moment of relief before the second stage rockets cut in, jerking them like helpless marionettes yet again.

"The first stage cutoff was the worst," Mitchell recalled years later. "What people don't realize is that you had 363 feet of spacecraft that felt like it was compressed, like a spring. It's called 'aeroelasticity,' and when a stage cuts off, you feel like you're being thrown forward, because the acceleration has suddenly stopped. Then that 'compressed spring' 'unwinds' and sends you back a bit, then the second stage kicks in and throws you back hard. We actually called that phase 'the train wreck'."

The five engines on the S-II pulled the remaining active stages away from the now hollow S-IC stage. At the three minute and 20 second mark, the LET roared away on schedule, taking the BPC sheath over the Command Module with it. Transcripts indicate that Mitchell and Roosa were immediately drawn to looking out windows, and they were apparently admonished by Shepard:

Roosa: "Better watch this! That horizon is beautiful!"

Mitchell: "It sure is!"

Shepard: "Keep your eyes on the pin, cockpit troops."

Mitchell later detailed that the first view of the horizon after the escape rockets removed the sheath was "...pretty amazing, as it would have been for anyone's first time in space. The curvature of the horizon was fascinating."

The five engines of the S-II took the spacecraft to an altitude of 109 miles after burning for six minutes. Speed was now over 15,500 mph, almost enough to achieve orbit.

Shepard announced the cut off of the S-II cut off at the nine minute, 20 second mark, and the S-IVB third stage immediately took over. The NASA public announcer noted the separation to television viewers and radio listeners who were following the launch by referring to the Apollo 14 commander: "The Shepard crew has now used up two-thirds of their Saturn stages on their way to orbit."

Following the drop-off of the S-II, the astronauts were fascinated by the plethora of ice falling away.

"Look at the flakes go," said Mitchell.

"Look at the ice up there," said Roosa.

"A jillion stars," said the LMP.

The single J-2 engine of the S-IVB boosted the remaining sections of Apollo 14 into Earth orbit, where it would later be fired again to send the spacecraft to the Moon.

The crew began checking out equipment, and Roosa assumed the role of navigator. He worked meticulously with a sextant, a monocular, a telescope, and other instruments, aligning the guidance system of the spacecraft for the upcoming second burn of the S-IVB's J-2 engine.

Transit

A little over two hours into the flight, the Apollo 14 crew was observing lightning and what appeared to be a forest fire on the nighttime side of the Earth below. Shepard was the individual who spotted the forest fire, but Roosa's reaction—if any—isn't noted in Command Module recordings. Presumably, it struck a chord with the former smoke jumper, particularly since he was carrying hundreds of tree seeds in his PPK.

The mission commander was also singing the praises of weightlessness (he'd only experienced a few minutes of it during his sub-orbital flight). Roosa would ultimately appreciate the fact that he could maneuver himself a lot easier in zero G to perform his navigation tasks than he had been able to do in the Earthbound simulator.

However, he also announced that he had "...a little stuffiness in my head...you know, it sort of feels like you're...maybe when you're pulling one and a half or two Gs with a cold."

After an orbit and a half around the Earth, the Trans-Lunar Injection (TLI) maneuver occurred at the 2:28:35 mark, and the second ignition of the S-IVB broke Apollo 14 free of Earth's gravity. Just short of six minutes later, the S-IVB shut down, having done its job. Apollo 14 was now headed for a rendezvous with Luna.

Half an hour later, Roosa and Shepard exchanged couches, and the CMP settled into the left seat to begin the Transposition, Docking and Extraction phase, for which he had practiced long and hard.

"Let's set a record, shall we?" Roosa said, averring his intent to dock with the LM and get it out of its storage bay quickly and efficiently. The CMP pronounced the upcoming procedure to be "sweaty-palm time"... and he had no way of knowing at that time how quickly his words would become stark reality.

Pyrotechnics severed the CSM from the third stage, and using a hand controller, Roosa slowly worked the small thrusters of the RCS to ease the CSM away, and began to turn it around. The four SLA panels on the upper portion of the third stage unfolded like giant metallic petals, finally tumbling off of the S-IVB as other bits of debris unleashed by the disconnection also swirled and tumbled into the void.

"Look out that window!" Roosa exclaimed.

"Yeah, look at all that crap," Mitchell said.

Peering through the gunsight-like Crewman Optical Alignment Sight (COAS), Roosa closed on the LM drogue receptacle confidently. He had practiced this maneuver time and time again in the extended training period the Apollo 14 crew had had following the Apollo 13 disaster.

"Going to break the record, man," Shepard enthused. "Take it slowly."

The probe slipped into the drogue receptacle easily, exactly as planned.

And nothing happened. The capture indicator in the CSM retained its solid color; no barber pole abruptly appeared. The CSM drifted backwards.

Roosa tried again. No capture, no barber pole.

"Okay, Houston, we've hit it twice," Roosa radioed, "and (it) sure looks like we're closing fast enough. I'm going to back out here and try it again. Well, there goes the record."

For almost two hours, the CSM attempted to dock with the LM a total of five times, but was unable to get a capture by the probe.

"One, two, three, four," Roosa counted on one attempt. "Son of a bitch—nothing! Okay, Houston, I hit it pretty good, and held it four seconds on contact, and we did not latch."

"Roger," responded the CapCom. "We're seeing it all on TV here."

Roosa sighed, and muttered a single-syllable expletive.

Technicians on the ground scrambled to come up with a workable solution, as fuel and patience began to run low. Shepard broached the idea of the crew donning their spacesuits ("going hard suit"), depressurizing the Command Module's cabin, and removing the probe to inspect it.

NASA officials also quickly began discussing contingency plans, if the LM could not be extracted. Such speculation would have included (1) whether to return the spacecraft to Earth immediately, (2) in a repeat of Apollo 13's flight, allow it to whip around the Moon only once, or (3) send it into lunar orbit and do as much research as possible from just the CSM, in a "less-of-something-is-better-than-all-of-nothing" scenario. The Apollo 14 crew was not advised by Mission Control that such conversations by NASA higher-ups were taking place, but the astronauts were fully cognizant that such alternate plans were probably being considered.

Regardless of the options, what the Apollo 14 crew was now facing was the possible extinction of the entire Apollo program if the CSM and LM couldn't link up to journey to the Moon together.

Joan and the children had begun their return trip Houston that evening, as the docking crisis was ongoing. They left not knowing whether or not the CSM and LM would be able to dock.

Ultimately, a never-before-attempted plan was sent up by Mission Control.

Mitchell recalled: "It was decided after several attempts that we would *retract* the probe *before* there was any contact, and Stu would fly the spacecraft into the docking position in the same manner, but when we got it fully into docking position, we'd fire the *permanent* latches."

The transcripts from the CSM don't reflect the tension that Roosa must have felt as he delicately and meticulously approached the LM's receptacle for the sixth time.

"About six feet out," called Mitchell. "About...two feet."

"About a foot," said Roosa. "Okay, here we go."

Thirteen seconds later, the CMP exclaimed, "Okay, *retract*."

"Nothing happened," said Shepard.

"Nothing?" Roosa asked.

One second after Roosa's single-word inquiry, Shepard abruptly changed his observation, exclaiming, "I got...got a barber pole! We got a hard dock!"

"Roger, Al," said the CapCom. "That's great. Super job, Stu."

Roosa's response was a simple "Thank you."

The collective exhalation of relief from the CSM, Mission Control, and other locations of the NASA organization probably had the force of a small hurricane. Cheers echoed through the Houston nerve center. Decades later, Mitchell would still express his admiration for his crewmate's tenacity:

"Stu did a marvelous job getting the spacecraft into the docking port, and when we fired the main latches, they worked."

The subsequent extraction of the LM from the S-IVB went off perfectly. After the procedure had been completed, Roosa entered the tunnel between the two spacecraft, and spent over an hour examining and manipulating the probe, finding no indication of what might have caused it to malfunction.

"We've cycled it four or five times, and it just goes in so easily," he told Mission Control, which was observing his inspection on television.

"What you're trying to tell me is that you haven't found what's caused the problems," said Houston.

"That's basically it," Stu responded.

Roosa also found several scratches on the receptacle, apparently caused by his docking attempts.

Mission Control finally sent word that the inspection could be terminated, but the inquiry and research as to what went wrong would continue on Earth.

"We've exhausted our imaginations for right now on the troubleshooting," Houston radioed. "We'll work on it some more overnight and will get back to you in the morning."

"We just can't seem to get it to malfunction for us at all," Stu concluded.

Although the Apollo 14 mission was now two hours behind schedule due to the docking problems, it would continue as planned, but the non-functioning capture latches would remain an ominous problem. Mitchell also recalled the possibility that other phases of the mission would be affected:

"We never got an official 'diagnosis' about why we couldn't dock. We had pulled the probe back inside and inspected it; it looked normal, and the capture latches worked properly once we got them inside. I thought then—and I still think—that moisture got inside the docking mechanism during the rainstorm while we were on the launch pad; we had a 40-minute delay. And that would have frozen those capture latches."

But what if *Antares* landed on the Moon, and the ascent stage lifted off successfully, only to be unable to dock with *Kitty Hawk* in lunar orbit once rendezvous had been accomplished?

"We had talked about that on the way out, among ourselves," said Mitchell, "and yes, it was a concern, but the capture latches were working okay once we got them back into the Command Module. If (an inability to dock) had happened, we would have had to do an EVA (Extra-Vehicular Activity) in our pressure suits, abandoning the Lunar Module and climbing into the Command Module."

Shepard and Mitchell also briefly discussed whether or not they would be able to transfer the lunar samples they would have collected while on the surface, but their conversations didn't get into any extensive details or plans, because they didn't think the post-lunar landing docking of the LM's ascent stage with the CSM was going to be a problem.

The crew also suspected that Mission Control was working on some kind of contingency plan in case the capture latches failed to work again, but no alternate ideas or instructions were ever relayed to the spacecraft.

However, the press was also speculating about further problems with the docking system, and NASA *was* addressing the potential problem in the media. The headline on the front page of the February 1st final home edition of the *Orlando Evening Star* blared "Moonwalk Plans Still Up In Air—Docking Problem May Cancel Landing."

The first paragraph of the article erroneously noted that the crew had "…probed and jiggled the docking mechanism of their lunar lander today, seeking to determine what caused it to malfunction. Experts on the ground huddled to decide whether the problem was serious enough to abort the moonwalk."

(Technically, the problem was with the probe mechanism on the nose of the CSM, not on "the docking mechanism of their lunar lander.")

The article cited officials in Houston as stating that the decision to attempt a lunar landing would go down to the wire. Director of Flight Operations Sigurd Sjoburg was quoted as saying "We have a couple of days to work this out. I don't want to speculate now on when any decision (about the lunar landing) will be made. We will have to convince ourselves in some fashion that the thing is indeed satisfactory for additional docking."

Bob Gordon, another spokesman, said in the same article that a final decision had to be made before the maneuver that would put Apollo 14 into orbit around the Moon.

And perhaps not surprisingly, the *Orlando Evening Star* story gave the Apollo 14 Commander the predominant position in the text.

"Shepard, America's pioneer astronaut, and rookies Roosa and Mitchell blasted off at 4:03 p.m. EST Sunday," the article noted.

—*~~~*—

Following the extraction of the LM, Apollo 14's S-IVB was diverted by controllers on Earth into its own course to the Moon, where its impact would be measured by seismic monitors that were either on unmanned lunar landers, or that had been placed on the surface by previous Apollo crews. Not all S-IVBs had suffered such a violent end, however—others had been placed into permanent orbit around the Sun.

As the outward journey continued, the crew of Apollo 14 was now able to get a perspective on just how out of this world their mission was taking them.

"By the time way got docked," Roosa would later recall, "we were really 'hauling the mail.' The Earth had shrunk into a sphere; it was a beautiful sight."

In the raw void of space, unfiltered sunlight could burn an object on its side that is facing the Sun, while the same object could freeze solid on the opposite/"shadow" side. Soon after the successful extraction of the LM, a differently-configured firing of the RCS thrusters put the conjoined spacecraft in a slow roll along its center axis; the maneuver was called Passive Thermal Control (PTC), which was done in an effort to keep the spacecraft with an even temperature.

The tongue-in-cheek nickname for this simple-but-critical procedure was "barbecue mode," since it resembled the rotation of a rotisserie. Apollo 14 continued its rapid, smooth, and deliberate journey.

Several hours after the docking crisis, the subject of weightlessness came up again in a conversation initiated by Shepard. Other Apollo astronauts had been troubled by nausea, but the Apollo 14 crew was doing fine:

Shepard: "I'm not having any trouble at all with the weightlessness."

Mitchell: "I'm not either, Al."

Shepard: "How are you doing, Stu?"

Roosa: "Well, so far, so good....I guess I'm a little surprised at...at the fighting to stay down."

On the home front in Houston, Joan was dealing with media representatives that were camped out in the street in front of the house. The children would take coffee to reporters as well as the Secret Service detail that had been assigned to protect the family's privacy as much as possible. She also set up a television in the family's garage for the reporters to watch.

In addition to the help of relatives and other astronauts' wives, one house guest was an entrepreneur from Coos Bay, Oregon named Bob Perkins, who was an astronaut fan that had managed to become good friends with Stu, having met the astronaut during a NASA geological field trip to the Pacific Northwest to study volcanic lava flows. To the children, he was known as "Uncle Bob," and the youngsters were impressed by Perkins's simple magic tricks and E.S.P. routine.

Another interesting aspect for the Roosa kids was that they were being allowed to skip school, a bonus accommodation (in a child's eyes) that was afforded to families whose patriarchs were in space.

"I recall that when Daddy was named to a flight, my first reaction was 'That means we won't have to go to school!'" said Allen.

On one morning during the flight, the boys climbed a tree in the front yard and "razzed" some of their friends who were walking to school.

Joan had explained to the children that they should expect a lot of attention from newspaper and television reporters. The reporting on the activities of the family was part of the coverage of the mission, but it would vanish when the flight was over.

Early one morning during the mission, Chris, age 11, went to get the morning newspaper prior to sunrise, and a plethora of flashbulbs unexpectedly exploded, sending the frightened youngster scurrying back to the house, without the newspaper.

Jack and Allen were photographed playing in a refrigerator box, and a newspaper erroneously captioned the picture that the boys were romping in a "pretend" spacecraft.

Eventually, the children began to tire of the media exposure during the flight, but they remembered Joan's earlier admonishment regarding media attention.

The family had two "squawk boxes" installed in their home (one in the living room; one in Stu and Joan's bedroom), which allowed them to listen to real-time transmissions between Apollo 14 and Mission Control, and the children were fascinated by such devices.

And as might be expected, Joan and the children visited Mission Control more than once, as did Shepard and Mitchell family members, watching the activity of the NASA nerve center from an observation room behind a Plexiglas panel.

—⁓—

An astronaut in the White Room had, as noted earlier, been the last to inspect and set up the Command Module, and had, not unexpectedly, made sure that numerous "Beep Beep" patches had been stowed away in various locations throughout the spacecraft.

Somehow, during earlier preparations, backup crew members and/or support crew members and/or certain NASA technicians—their names were never revealed—had even managed to get "Beep Beep" patches sneaked into the Lunar Module, according to Cernan, who estimated that the total number of patches in the CSM and LM was around 25, and the backup commander claimed that "Beep Beep" patches were even in the backpacks that would be worn by Shepard and Mitchell on the surface of the Moon.

"They were all over the place," Mitchell recalled with a chuckle. "They were in various storage areas; it seemed like every time we opened a particular storage bin for the first time, one of those things would come floating out."

Whenever a backup crew patch made an unexpected appearance, Shepard would respond with a rehash of his original retort: "Tell Cernan 'Beep Beep,' his ass."

—⁓—

Overall conditions in an Apollo CM were tight, but not overly claustrophobic, and the crew had been preparing for such a lifestyle for over a year and a half. Privacy was pretty much non-existent, particularly when it came to body functions. Urination involved the use of a vacuum tube, while defecation meant placing an adhesive receptacle across the buttocks in a usually-clumsy attempt to capture all of the stool, which was then supposed to be saved for analysis upon return to Earth. Some leaks occurred from both procedures, however, meaning that sanitary housekeeping, accompanied by expected odors, kept the astronauts scrambling at times.

Moreover, the trio could only take sponge baths, which didn't particularly alleviate body odor.

But things could have been worse. Jim Lovell, who had spent 14 days with Frank Borman in an extremely cramped Gemini spacecraft, thought highly of the Apollo Command Module:

"The living conditions, though crowded, were much better than Gemini. The pure oxygen atmosphere pretty much kept the odor in check. The Apollo also had a greater variety of food."

Roosa stayed busy with navigation, monitoring the spacecraft's guidance alignment on a regular basis, setting up guidelines for possible mid-course corrections. He would have the CSM all to himself at times during the outward bound portion of the journey, as Shepard and Mitchell floated into the LM to begin initial checkouts of its systems. While he appreciated the ease in which weightlessness figured into his movements, Roosa noticed at times that the phenomenon did interfere with his attempt to hold himself steady while utilizing his sextant or other instruments. Nevertheless, his navigation stayed on the money.

Housekeeping duties for the CSM were also the responsibility of the CMP. The not-exactly-spacious interior meant that Stu had to prepare "meals," which were often granulated items that had to be mixed with hot water. He also had to discard the leftover packets, all the while monitoring oxygen and fuel, and performing other tasks such as charging batteries, dumping waste, and purging fuel cells.

Crew members took photographs and made 16 mm. movies, including documentation of the activities of other astronauts, throughout the flight. One memorable movie image of Roosa showed the CMP grinning as he sported an eyepatch (used with the sextant for navigation). To what extent he may have been thinking about his senior class outing from his Claremore High School days isn't known, but some of his old classmates would have taken notice.

Another sequence from the in-flight film shows Roosa contemplating a squeeze packet full of orange liquid as it is sent floating over to him by another crew member. An initial reaction from average followers of the space program would have been that the packet contains a concoction made from a powdered drink mix marketed as Tang, as that product had been heavily advertised as a drink used by astronauts. While Tang went into outer space on at least one Mercury flight and some Gemini flights, it wasn't a standard or requisite sustenance item.

Mitchell concurred that the packet being examined by Roosa was probably some other kind of orange-flavored drink, recalling: "We didn't know about Tang until after the flight."

—_w_—

NASA had planned several windows of opportunity for mid-course corrections, but Roosa's initial navigation was on-the-money, and the first optimum time for a correction was cancelled.

Some thirty and a half hours after launch, however, Apollo 14's SPS engine cranked up for the first time, burning for less than eleven seconds for a necessary mid-course correction. A second mid-course maneuver was done some three days and five hours after launch.

Astronauts had been allowed to bring along cassettes of music for "entertainment," and a deejay for a country and western music radio station had prepared cassettes for Stu that included selections by artists such as Johnny Cash, Sonny James, and Jerry Lee Lewis, among others. However, Cash's manager had reportedly announced the intent of his client to record an album or songs that referenced Moon shots, so NASA had pulled the music by "the Man in Black," as the organization did not want businesses profiting from that type of commercial exploitation of the Apollo program.

On the other hand, Buck Owens and the Buckaroos had re-recorded some of their songs especially for the mission, and Owens even introduced them himself. As the intro to "Act Naturally" cranked up, Owens' voice was heard informing the astronauts that when they got back from their voyage, movies would be made about them; his remark was the segue to the first lyrics of the song.

Lunar Orbit and Landing

As Apollo 14 raced towards its planned orbit around the Moon, its crew would be drawn to the windows to observe the bizarre, airless world they were rapidly approaching. Understandably, some of their comments were like those of excited schoolboys rather than pragmatic space explorers.

"Oh, man, look what's out that window, too!" Mitchell exclaimed.

"Looks like a plaster-of-Paris cast," said Roosa.

"It sure does, doesn't it?" said Mitchell.

Roosa: "It doesn't even look real. I wish there was some other word besides 'fantastic' to describe it. But it does…it looks like somebody has made a cast and poured it out there."

"It's really there," said Mitchell, affirming a dream come true.

"Really wild," said Shepard.

"Man, I'll tell you, at this sun angle, I won't have any trouble recognizing my landmarks," Roosa said of his upcoming duties.

Farouk El-Baz had been a thorough and effective pedagogue for Roosa, as there were times when the CMP sounded like an excited tour guide, pointing out specific landmarks to his crewmates:

"Okay, there are the Loveletts. See, right straight over your head, there's two craters that have got sort of...you have to look...You can probably see them out your window, Ed. The two craters with the ridges in the bottom?...Those are called the Loveletts. Yes, from the copulating craters. Off to your right, you'll see Mendeleev...Tsiolkovsky's coming up in this window...."

―――

The first extended use of the SPS was the Lunar Orbit Insertion (LOI) burn. Roosa later opined that this crucial maneuver defined whether or not a spacecraft would have a Moon mission. Like other facets of the mission profile, it was a one-shot opportunity.

Mitchell was of the same frame of mind regarding LOI, and would recall that the minutes prior to ignition were tense, because for the first time, the crew would be on its own. Apollo 14 would be out of contact with Mission Control when LOI occurred on the far side of the Moon.

Around the time Apollo 14 slid into its rendezvous with Luna, one of Roosa's cassettes was in the player, and Sonny James' rendition of the magnificent hymn "How Great Thou Art" began to play. The paradox of the first lines of the hymn ("Oh Lord my God, when I in awesome wonder, consider all the works Thy hands have made") and the proximity of a barren world's "magnificent desolation" (Buzz Aldrin's comment during the Apollo 11 moonwalk) that was beneath Apollo 14 had a profound effect on Roosa.

The astronauts also noticed that the far side of the Moon seemed to be more rugged than the side that faced Earth.

Ignition for LOI occurred some 82 hours into the mission and lasted for over six minutes, placing Apollo 14 into its initial elliptical orbit around the Moon, measuring approximately 200 miles by 69 miles. During the burn, the astronauts experienced about one-half of one G, which felt unusual after several days of weightlessness.

They had arrived.

―――

The fascination of viewing the Moon continued, as Roosa invoked the name of his Egyptian geologist instructor. At one point, Stu said with a laugh, "This is the most unreal-looking real thing I've ever seen—if that makes any sense."

Mitchell did some visual surveying himself, telling Roosa, "I have got the crater King out here, Stu, if you were looking for it."

"Yes, that's one of our targets," Roosa replied. "That's one of Farouk's favorite craters."

"Pretty damn interesting one, too," said Mitchell. That one…looks like… got a rugged one right out here, with central peaks. Sure does. Really got a very complex central structure."

"It's got one of the biggest central peaks around," said Roosa. "It's a very unusual crater. But there are some dark areas in it that Farouk has gone on record as saying they are dikes."

Shepard: "What's the name of that one?"

Roosa: "It has no name. I've called it the Bright One. This is Langemak that we're just going over right down here."

The crew would excitedly look for craters they had encountered whenever their orbit brought them over the same location again, and at one point, Roosa referenced a classic 1968 science fiction movie, comparing it to his real-life observations as Apollo 14 soared over Luna.

"This is really a *2001* epic," he said. "It's unreal…Man! What a view!"

All three crew members worked on unpacking and mounting the large, high-tech Hycon camera. A frame counter was built into the state-of-the-art unit, and the operation of the camera included careful monitoring of how many frames of film were used.

Suddenly, after around 140 frames had been shot, the film magazine in the Hycon suddenly began to make ominous noises. A mechanical grinding/ratchet-like sound emanated from its interior, but the photography continued. The frame count went to 180, then the noise stopped, only to pick up again once 240 frames had been taken. The noise would continue until the film magazine was used up (420 exposures), after which the crew did some troubleshooting, with Houston sending up advice. Roosa took twenty-three frames with a second magazine, after which the problem was put on the back burner.

—⁓—

As Shepard and Mitchell busied themselves doing final checkouts of the LM, Roosa mounted cameras at specific locations in the CSM that would film the LM's separation and initial maneuvers, which would be followed by its disappearance from view as it began its descent to the Moon.

The next burn of the SPS was a new innovation in the flight plan (and was actually supposed to have been accomplished for the first time on Apollo 13). In earlier flights, the orbit for the CSM had been changed to a near-circular orbit of around 60-69 miles, depending on the individual mission, before the LM had separated from the CSM. This procedure had been known as the LOI-2 burn, and though the orbit was slightly elliptical, the maneuver was still called the "circularization burn."

However, to save fuel for the LM, Roosa now made calculations for a radically-different orbit, and Apollo 14 instead performed what was called a Descent Orbit Insertion (DOI) burn, which was designed to bring the conjoined spacecraft down to a "perilune" (low point in an elliptical orbit) of around ten and a half miles above the Lunar surface that was about 310 miles short of the Fra Mauro landing site. This new burn lasted 21 seconds. After the LM began its descent, Roosa would boost the CSM up to the circularization orbit that had been the standard for previous Apollo Moon missions.

Shortly after the DOI burn, one of Roosa's country music cassettes was in the Command Module's music system as the crew continued their assigned tasks, and the twanging "Truck Driving Man" emanated throughout the spacecraft. Keeping the mood lighthearted in spite of the intense preparation that was underway, Shepard observed that the tune was a good song. Later, music by Buck Owens and the Buckaroos rang out.

"Those guys actually sell any records of that stuff?" Shepard asked.

"He's got a TV show," Roosa retorted, referencing "Hee Haw," a music and comedy show starring Owens and guitarist Roy Clark. "It's been on several years. It's the hillbilly 'Laugh-In'."

Owens's "Tiger By The Tail" got a chuckle out of the CDR.

"Seems to be something I'm missing with this country music," said Shepard.

The Houston CapCom advised Roosa that the perilune of the spacecraft's orbit was actually 46,000 feet, or 8.3 miles, above the Moon—a bit closer, but safe and acceptable.

February 5, 1971: Preparations for the separation were completed. Goodbyes and good luck wishes were expressed, then Shepard and Mitchell entered the LM to begin their journey. The hatch in the tunnel closed, and Roosa was alone.

Following further checkouts, the LM disengaged, and Roosa tweaked the CSM's RCS system slightly to put a bit of distance between the two spacecraft. He inspected the outward appearance of the LM, assuring that everything was in place, and that the four legs of the landing gear were fully extended. He took photographs, and made sure the movie cameras onboard the CSM were running properly as the ungainly-looking LM tried out its own RCS engines, rotating along more than one axis. Shepard and Mitchell checked out the LM's performance using hand controllers that looked like the same types of devices used on Earth.

The separated spacecraft were now known by the names that had been chosen for them in advance. As *Antares* began to finalize preparations for its descent to the lunar surface, Roosa fired the SPS once again to boost *Kitty Hawk* into its circularization orbit to await the return of his two crewmates. The occupants of *Antares* didn't see any flames coming from the SPS, but did report seeing the CSM's tracking light.

"You have a mighty invisible engine, Stu," Mitchell radioed. "It didn't have anything we could see at all from here…that's interesting…we never saw your burn at all, but at the same time, when you burst into sunlight, you were right ahead of us. We were pointed right at you, but we didn't see a thing."

The Apollo 14 mission was the first to have a separate CapCom assigned to the CSM at specific times, once the LM and the CSM had separated. The three primary CapComs, one for each shift, or team, were Gordon Fullerton (Orange Control Team), Fred Haise (Gold Control Team), and Bruce McCandless (Maroon Control Team). Ron Evans was the individual who pulled most of the time talking separately with Roosa onboard *Kitty Hawk* while he was circling the Moon solo.

An internal memo dated October 19, 1970 regarding CapCom assignments had listed Fullerton, Haise, and McCandless, but also stated: "Additionally, Cdr. R. E. Evans will serve as Command Module (CSM) CAPCOM during certain periods of simultaneous, unrelated Lunar Module and CSM activities and one shift serving to restore the assigned team sequence after TEI (Trans-Earth Injection)."

Fred Haise had volunteered to be a CapCom for the Apollo 14 mission, the LM of which was to land where Apollo 13's LM, *Aquarius*, had been slated to touch down.

"I thought maybe I could be useful," said Haise, "particularly on their second EVA on the lunar surface, and could take advantage of some of the training I'd had, including helping out with some of the field geology."

―――

The crew of *Antares* would spend about four hours checking out systems and studying the lunar landscape—particularly when they whooshed over the Fra Mauro sector, eyeballing craters with names like Cone, Weird, Doublet, and Triplet. They had studied those particular indentations in the lunar surface for many months, and from lunar orbit, the craters' features were more apparent than what they had seen in photographs.

However, problems onboard *Antares* would come close to canceling the Lunar landing, as a computer glitch during a final practice run for the landing indicated that the descent sequence had not kicked in, and that the auto abort program, designed to automatically blast the LM away from the surface of the Moon, had taken over.

Some 30 minutes before the LM would need to fire its descent engine, a new computer program designed to bypass the auto abort program was quickly uploaded to *Antares*. Mitchell inserted the new instructions into the onboard computer, and noted that the LM occupants would now have to hit the abort switch manually, if such drastic action was required.

And another dangerous problem manifested itself on the final descent, as the landing radar stopped providing updates. *Antares* was intentionally flying blind, in relation to the lunar surface—its windows were facing upwards, towards the stars, as the two crewmen trusted the descent program to get them in the appropriate location at the appropriate altitude when the spacecraft rotated upright to provide Shepard and Mitchell with a visual panorama of their designated landing area.

Haise was the LM CapCom in Houston during the descent of *Antares*, and his perspective was unique, as he was participating—albeit on Earth—in yet another Apollo mission that might not land on the Moon. His communication with the LM was matter-of-fact as he informed them that they were approaching a point where the landing would have to be aborted.

"I already knew what the solution was," Mitchell recounted. "It was either recycle the circuit breaker, or recycle the on-off switch, but I did not want to make the call; I wanted the circuit guys on the ground to do that, because they had the circuits right in front of them, and they knew the circuits as well as I did. They called out to recycle the circuit breaker, which was on Alan's side of the cockpit, so he pulled it out and put it back in, but it was not reading any update to our trajectory."

The radar lock finally kicked back in when *Antares* was some 13,000 feet above the surface, and its reacquisition happened just before the crew would have been required to abort the landing.

Mitchell indicated, however, that he and Shepard had other plans:

"If we'd had to abort, it would have been my call to do such, and with the abort switch disabled, we would have had to do all of the abort functions individually. We were right on target; there wasn't any point of aborting, and when we pitched over, there was Fra Mauro and Cone Crater, right in front of us. There was no way in hell I would have aborted...and Alan wouldn't have, either."

Antares landed safely within 60 feet of its designated touchdown spot.

Shepard and Mitchell would perform their assignments on the lunar surface as planned, to the best of their ability. On their first EVA, they deployed an Apollo Lunar Surface Experiments Package (ALSEP), which was the largest array of scientific equipment that had been taken to the Moon so far, about 250 yards from the LM.

The two moonwalkers pulled a small two-wheeled cart on their geological treks to haul samples. Once again, NASA jargon had given it the moniker of modularized equipment transporter, (MET), but it had been dubbed a "rickshaw" due to its similarity to the Earthly transportation vehicle. Shepard and Mitchell did their job so well that they were allotted an extra half-hour on their first EVA.

Another scheduled-for-Apollo-13-but-seen-for-the-first-time-on-Apollo 14 facet were the red stripes on Shepard's moon suit and helmet, to allow observers to be able to differentiate between the CDR and the LMP while they were on the surface.

———∿∿∿———

Apollo CMPs worked harder than the public ever realized, particularly when they were flying solo around the Moon, fully occupied with their own flight plans. Roosa was no exception, observing and taking photos of potential future landing sites, and conducting experiments. He also had to take requests for more details from geologists, who, upon hearing about a particular discovery, would ask him for further observation and clarification.

Unfortunately, the Hycon camera continued to malfunction, and Stu struggled to repair it by himself. He bantered back and forth with CapCom Ron Evans, and later, Gordon Fullerton and Ken Mattingly, about suggested solutions. Simulations were tried on similar equipment on Earth in an effort to emulate the problem and find a solution, to no avail.

Attempted troubleshooting by Roosa overlapped into a time period when the CMP was supposed to eat, so he ate chicken salad, which did not require any preparation time. Ultimately, ready-to-eat items would make up most of his diet for the duration of his solo time around the Moon.

"I didn't have the time nor the inclination to try to mix any hot foods with water," he later said of his decision to favor open-and-serve food. "That was a good plan for me anyway, because I like those kinds of foods better."

The huge, expensive Hycon camera would never fly on another Apollo mission. Roosa would end up taking 250 mm and 500 mm photographs using hand-held cameras, as well movies of Lunar lighting phenomena; i.e., the movies were actually scheduled experiments. CapComs would stay in constant contact during photo sessions, monitoring Roosa's progress and dispensing reminders of specific procedures that needed to be done. Houston communicators would also let *Kitty Hawk* know about the events that were transpiring on the surface of the Moon.

"Did they say anything about the terrain, Ron?" Roosa asked Evans, as Shepard and Mitchell prepared for their first EVA. "It seems like I heard them say they were on something like an eight degree roll angle or something."

"Yeah, that's right," Evans replied. "And it's a little rougher than what they thought it was going to be down there. That's just a general comment on the terrain."

One of the lunar surface areas Stu would survey was the Descartes formation, also in the lunar highlands, for consideration as a future landing site.

"Descartes is an extremely easy landing site to pick up," he would later report, "with the two bright craters leading right in. There's no way one can miss it."

Roosa would also claim that he could see *Antares* sitting on the lunar surface, recalling later that he "...had no trouble identifying the area. I was looking on my map at these coordinates, and they were wrong. They had the LM over on the other side of the Triplet (crater). Then I saw the bright spot—the reflection of the LM and the shadow. There is no mistaking the LM when you see that long shadow coming out from it. I had a real good track on the LM."

—◊◊◊—

The next day, Stu would proclaim that he had even spotted the ALSEP, sitting approximately 750 feet from *Antares*.

"This time, the shadow of the LM was down," he recounted, "but I knew exactly where to look. I saw the Sun shining off the LM, and also off the ALSEP package. I marked down the coordinates of the ALSEP and phoned those down to Ron. It looked to me like the ALSEP was right out there by this crater."

His geological efforts from *Kitty Hawk* did Farouk El-Baz proud.

"Stu performed his tasks flawlessly," El-Baz remembered. "He was determined that no one would ever say that someone else would have done better, and he certainly proved it, to me, and to all others."

160

The second EVA for Shepard and Mitchell had a disappointing facet. In an exhausting trek, the two explorers were unable to reach the rim of Cone Crater, and they were turned back by Mission Control. However, they were able to gather some of the oldest rocks ever harvested from the Moon during the Apollo program.

But history would record that the most memorable incident for most observers of the Apollo 14 mission probably occurred when Shepard and Mitchell were about to re-enter *Antares* following their second EVA. Shepard removed what he pronounced to be a six-iron golf club head from a space suit pocket, and attached it to the shaft of the collector device with which he had picked up lunar samples. Then, the Apollo 14 commander took out two golf balls, dropped them to the surface, and attempted to drive them as far as he could, using a one-handed swing; his suit was so bulky that a two-handed swing was impossible.

Ron Evans advised Roosa of the golf attempt and other on-the-Moon shenanigans: "The guys are really having a ball down there on the lunar surface, throwing away their tools. Making javelins out of them and everything."

The two EVAs for the crew of *Antares* had totaled nine hours and 25 minutes.

The "squawk boxes" in the Roosa household continued to fascinate family members and others. CapComs would call the Roosa house and ask Joan if there was anything she wanted them to pass along to Stu in real time, in a "three-way" conversation—Joan to CapCom, who immediately relayed such information to Stu, who would respond while the family listened in on the "squawk box." One time, the CapCom noted that Joan was fixing lasagna, one of Stu's favorite meals.

Considering what the CMP had been dining on for several days, his mournful "Aw, what I wouldn't give to have some lasagna!" from a quarter of a million miles away was understandable.

As for sleeping while flying solo in *Kitty Hawk*, Roosa recalled, "I didn't sleep any better, any worse—as far as the solo period was concerned—as I did when we were all in there. I didn't have any pangs of loneliness or anything like that."

Nevertheless, the hard-working, "matter-of-fact" astronaut would have occasions where he was acutely aware of his solitude, particularly on the far side of the Moon, when he was out of radio contact with both *Antares* and Mission Control.

In the shadow portion of the far side of the Moon (i.e., the part that was not illuminated by sunlight or Earthshine), the number of stars that became visible presented a mind-boggling contrast between their points of light and the raw blackness of space. While constellations could still be discerned, they seemed to be closer and brighter, and millions of other stars would abruptly become visible, almost obliterating recognizable stellar formations, and adding an almost-incomprehensible type of three-dimensional view to validate the vastness and depth of the Universe. Roosa would later recall that he could almost "feel" the darkness.

The darkness also caused the temperature of the Command Module to drop slightly. Condensation formed on the bulkheads, causing a clammy environment in the interior of *Kitty Hawk*. Such a change in temperature and humidity intensified Roosa's awareness of his isolation, but his subsequent emergence into sunlight was a positive experience for his psyche. Due to the lack of an atmosphere, the change from pitch-black darkness to blinding light was instantaneous, and his attitude perked up just as abruptly.

And when he was zooming over the Earth-facing side of Luna, Stu was fascinated by the fact that he could hold up his hand and block out the view of the world where all of humanity, except for a handful of space travelers, had spent its entire existence. The views of Earth in different phases, sizes, and constantly-changing cloud patterns had enraptured the CMP since the launch, and would continue to do so for the remainder of the voyage, as he pondered the blue and white globe in its entirety, instead of looking for the location of his state or country on the planet he was viewing.

Curiously, what had ultimately brought Roosa to the realization of just how far he and his crewmates were from Earth had been the ever-increasing delay in radio transmissions from Earth. Radio waves travel at the speed of light, but the further Apollo 14 had headed outward from Earth, the longer it had taken for his transmissions to get a response. Stu estimated that a transmission from the CSM took five or six seconds to get a reply, even if the CapCom at Mission Control had responded immediately to Apollo 14. Half of that time would have been CSM-to-Earth, the other half Earth-to-CSM.

—◦◦◦—

At more than one point during his solo orbits, Roosa shut down all optional systems. Every unnecessary light was turned off, and the interior of *Kitty Hawk* was barely illuminated. The only noise was the soft whirring of a fan.

And in that darkened interior of a state-of-the-art spacecraft, the country boy from Oklahoma who had been fascinated by P-38s in the mid-1940s silently contemplated how, around a quarter of a century later, he had ended up so far from home, in the most foreign and hostile environment to which humans had ever journeyed.

Return and Quarantine

Apollo 11 CMP Michael Collins had said that the most harrowing moment for him on that historic flight happened when he was alone in *Columbia*, awaiting the launch of the LM named *Eagle* from the surface of the Moon to return Neil Armstrong and Buzz Aldrin for rendezvous.

"I would say that my dad probably had a similar feeling—'If that engine doesn't fire, those two are stuck on the Moon,'" said Jack. "He knew how lonely that (solo) trip back to Earth would have been, knowing you'd had to leave two of your comrades on the surface."

The docking problem from the TD&E phase was also still an ominous question mark to Houston, so Evans advised Roosa that in addition to going through the planned docking procedure, the LM was also supposed to supply some thrust, using its own RCS rockets, once the control panel onboard the CSM showed contact. Roosa wasn't particularly enamored with the idea—at least, not as an initial docking maneuver.

Roosa was in communication with Shepard and Mitchell as the ascent stage of *Antares* blasted off after thirty three and a half hours on the Lunar surface.

"Man!" Mitchell enthused after the ascent engine cut off.

"Okay, we made the burn," Shepard reported.

"Okay," Roosa replied. "Sound like you got a good burn."

"Boy, that's a wild ride, Stuart," Mitchell said.

"I've been told..." said Roosa, whose own chances to experience a moonwalk seemed to have been kiboshed due to NASA's cancellation of the last three Apollo missions.

Antares zoomed towards its rendezvous with *Kitty Hawk*, making one minor course adjustment en route. During the ascent and rendezvous flight, Shepard and Roosa discussed the additional procedure regarding docking that Mission Control had imposed, and decided to try a normal docking first.

"They called us from the control center a little while...well, before we left the surface," said Shepard, "and said now, on the docking, on the normal docking, the first attempt, they want us to thrust plus-X (forward) with you anyway."

"Yes, that's what they said," Roosa confirmed.

Shepard: "Okay, Well, I'll thrust plus-X four jets then, when you give me a contact."

Roosa: "Okay."

"I'm not sure I like it, but…" Shepard's voice trailed off.

"No, I'm not sure I will, either," said the CMP. "Why don't we go ahead and dock and see if we capture? And if not, I'll give you a 'go' for thrusting."

"I like that idea better," Shepard replied. "We'll just play it nominal first."

As the two spacecraft closed, other radio banter included Roosa's recollection about spotting the LM and the ALSEP package on the surface.

"I could see the ALSEP," Roosa told Shepard.

"That's what they said," the CDR responded. "Ron was telling us that. Man!"

"I got a real good track on you on my pass yesterday," the CMP detailed. "The shadow—it really showed up, man. Big long shadow coming out from the LM."

"Great," said Shepard. "You think we were pretty close to the landing site?"

"I'd say you were," Roosa said.

The docking with the CSM went off without a hitch an hour and forty-seven minutes after the LM had been launched from the Moon, and it was accomplished without the extra thrust from the LM that had been ordered by Mission Control.

Roosa passed a vacuum cleaner into the LM for Shepard and Mitchell to use on their spacesuits. The two moonwalkers attempted to clean off the lunar dust, which had a slight odor that some astronauts had likened to gunpowder.

"We had tried very hard to clean ourselves off," Mitchell recalled, "but (Roosa) still complained about it a bit."

Transfer of 94 pounds of precious lunar rock samples ensued, and Mitchell and Shepard also disconnected their respective hand controllers from the LM to keep as souvenirs.

A little over two hours later, the ascent stage of *Antares* was jettisoned. Roosa backed the CSM away using the RCS engines, and the rocket engine that powered the upper portion of the LM ignited for the last time, sending the spacecraft hurtling towards the Moon again, to suffer the same ignominious fate—for the same scientific reasons—that befell the mission's S-IVB stage and other boosters and LM ascent stages on other Apollo missions. The ascent stage crashed onto the lunar surface some twenty eight minutes later.

Just before the crew prepared to fire up the SPS to break out of Lunar orbit and head to Earth, Roosa managed to get photographs of the LM ascent stage's impact point, as well as impact photos of the S-IVB stages from both Apollo 13 and Apollo 14.

The crew of Apollo 14 didn't waste any time preparing for a return to their home planet. Less than an hour after the ascent stage of the LM impacted on the Moon, the CSM's SPS performed its final major task, the Trans-Earth Injection (TEI) burn, which began while the spacecraft was on the far side of the Moon. The engine burned for some two and a half minutes, whipping the CSM out of lunar orbit. The CSM had orbited the Moon for 67 hours, completing 34 revolutions.

Even as the Moon began receding in view, Roosa was still taking photos. On the outward journey, the crew hadn't particularly had much time to watch the Earth recede in the distance once they were on their way to the Moon. Now, with no particularly crucial duties to perform on the return trip until they prepared for re-entry, Roosa stayed near a window more often, and was impressed by how fast they were leaving Luna behind.

The fuel tanks for the SPS engine were designed to furnish enough propellant to get the conjoined Apollo spacecraft into orbit around the Moon, and to break the CSM free of lunar orbit and back to Earth. There was enough leftover fuel to make mid-course corrections on the return flight, just as such maneuvers had been made on the outward flight. Apollo 14's trajectory alignment was so good that Roosa only had to make one mid-course adjustment, and he only had to use the RCS motors.

—⁓—

The crew performed numerous scientific experiments on the return voyage, but their primary goals had been completed, and a relaxed mood permeated the interior of the Command Module.

"I didn't have as much to do," Mitchell remembered, "so I started growing a beard. When I was asked why, I said the press had been referring to 'Alan Shepard and the two other guys,' so now they were going to have to refer to 'Alan Shepard, the guy with the beard, and the other guy'."

Roosa and Mitchell had never really discussed religion, and Mitchell was (and still is) agnostic, "...because I don't think we've proved (the existence of a deity) one way or the other. But my experiences with E.S.P. were concerned with the nature of the Universe, and what we don't understand."

And as he had planned, Mitchell had done two E.S.P. experiments on the outward bound journey, and would conduct two more on the return voyage, all during his rest periods. He had actually hoped to do three experiments on each transit (one each day, for a total of six), but was too tired to concentrate on such extra-curricular activity.

Moreover, he would have what he considered to be an "epiphany" while the Command Module was returning to Earth:

"My major job had been completed; the science and the Lunar Module had been my responsibility. We still had some experiments to do, but I could also 'look out the window and be a tourist.' We were in the plane of the ecliptic of the Earth, Moon and Sun, and we were perpendicular and rotating to keep the solar balance—Passive Thermal Control, 'barbecue' mode—and every two minutes, the Earth, the Sun, the Moon, and a 360 panorama of the heavens passed by the cockpit window. In space, the stars are ten times as bright as seen from Earth, because of the lack of an atmosphere. I'd taken some astronomy courses at Harvard, because I thought those were better courses than what was offered at M.I.T....I had an ecstatic feeling of oneness with the Universe, and oneness with nature. Every time I looked out the window, I had that experience."

—⁓—

Shepard, Mitchell and Roosa conducted a press conference from outer space on their final night before re-entry. Questions had been submitted by reporters to NASA in advance, and were relayed to the crew by the CapCom. Inevitably, many of the inquiries would be directed to the two moonwalkers about their experiences on the surface.

Shepard stated that he and Mitchell had gotten within 100 yards of the rim of Cone Crater, and had been in a field of boulders that was associated with that particular crater, so they were bringing back plenty of appropriate lunar samples.

Roosa was asked about having seen the LM from orbit. His response was detailed, but understandable for viewers with a minimal amount of knowledge about the geological surveying missions of CMPs:

"The first pass that I made on the landmark tracking, I picked up the LM with no problem. It just showed up as a white spot, obviously something foreign to the lunar surface, reflecting light, but the 'ringer' was the long shadow it put out. The first pass, the sun angle was still pretty low, and you could see the shadow coming, and the shadow and the reflection clinched it as the LM. Now, you couldn't see a shape of the LM as such, but, without a doubt, the LM was there. And on the next day, as I was doing landmark tracking, it was not on the schedule to track the LM again; however, I had a landmark just prior to the Fra Mauro region, and one after it, and I was in the right attitude for landmark tracking, so I looked for the LM again— apparently this time without any trouble. The shadow had diminished to almost nothing, or it was very small, but here again then I could see the glint coming off the ALSEP. At this time, the ALSEP had been deployed so I could see the glint coming off it, and I checked with Ron Evans later and told him what I thought it was, and he agreed that that was the ALSEP location."

Another question for Roosa concerned the failure of the Hycon camera, as the CapCom relayed an inquiry about whether or not he got enough pictures"...since your big camera was broken."

Roosa responded affirmatively, citing his use of other cameras, with the caveat that he couldn't give a complete answer since the film had not been processed.

One question addressed the problems Apollo 14 had encountered, including docking, the LM's landing radar, and other anomalies that could have abruptly terminated the mission.

Mitchell took a bit of a feisty tack, insisting that he never doubted that all facets of the mission were going to succeed. Stu added his own perspective, which had been formed while in lunar orbit, adding a bit of humanity to a question about technology:

"Well, I guess we're always concerned about the operation of the equipment. That's what we're up here for—to assure that it operates to the best of our ability...we're always concerned about that, and we still are. I still have a little bit of the 'voice' left to go, and we're still concerned about a safe return. I think that anyone that's involved in this kind of a business has to be concerned until the flight's totally over."

When a question about lunar dust was relayed, Shepard divided the answer among the crew. The commander recalled that he began to see dust during the landing at around 100-150 feet above the surface, Mitchell discussed the way the material would cling to equipment and suits ("It's a nuisance"), and Roosa described housekeeping for such a potential problem following the return of the LM, averring that there was very little dust remaining in the CSM's atmosphere, which had had a bit of positive pressure added to help suppress any dust floating around in the weightless environment.

Asked for their impressions of the flight, Roosa indicated he didn't want to get into details, once again offering the perspective that the flight wasn't over yet, including the admonition "Before we elaborate too much on a post-mission conference, I'd rather wait till after re-entry."

Mitchell and Shepard concurred, and the commander said that the mission "...has been a resounding success, and I don't really think that we've been able to assess at this stage what the contributions will be, but I can intuitively tell from what we've done, what we've seen on the surface that we're bringing back a lot of information photographically and geologically, that we've left stations and other stations on the moon sending back information for scientific purposes, and I think that generally speaking, it was a smashing success."

The CapCom relayed a question about which facet of the flight had been the most emotional for each astronaut, and their responses were brief and straightforward.

167

Shepard: "Well, I think the big emotion for me is yet to come, and that's getting both feet on the carrier."

Roosa: "Okay, there's been a lot of rather tremendous sights on the mission so far, and re-entry will be another one, but I guess the first look at the Moon after you...after you burn LOI in the darkness, and you come around, pitch to an attitude where you can see the Moon and it's there below you at about 60 miles, and it looks like about 200 *feet*. And your first impression of its body is a rather tremendous thing."

Mitchell: "I think Stu's sight is my number two, and my number one impact is when we pitched over, and there was Cone Crater, right out the window. It was very impressive."

The press conference began to wind down as Shepard was asked to compare the Apollo 14 mission to his sub-orbital flight a decade earlier.

"It's very difficult to—of course, as the question implies—discuss the technical differences between the two flights," said the CDR. "And from the standpoint of personal differences, I think that for those days, the Mercury Redstone flight was just as much of an individual challenge as has been Apollo 14. I think, of course, the machinery is different, but the men with whom we worked, the individuals that helped us along, are pretty much the same, and therefore the emotions are pretty much the same. They both were a great thrill for me, there's no question about that."

The final inquiry was, not surprisingly, about Shepard's golf effort on the Moon's surface, and Mitchell wisecracked that there weren't any greens in sight.

—⁓—

Accolades for the Apollo 14 mission were already being seen, read, and heard on Earth, even as the spacecraft entered the final day of its homeward journey. The headline of the February 9, 1971 edition of *The Atlanta Journal* ("Covers Dixie Like The Dew") was exemplary, proclaiming: "Apollo Streaks For Splashdown After Smashing Lunar Success," with a sub-heading that stated "Trio's Course Perfect With Weather Ideal." The article text noted that Apollo 14's splashdown was set for 4:04 p.m. Eastern Standard Time in the Pacific Ocean, 874 miles south of American Samoa, and that the prime recovery ship was the U.S. Navy aircraft carrier *New Orleans*. Weather reports from the prime recovery site indicated that there were some clouds, winds were approximately twelve to eighteen miles per hour, seas were approximately three to six feet, and the temperature would be eighty degrees.

—⁓—

As the spacecraft approached Earth, one of the first procedures to prepare for re-entry was the discontinuance of the Passive Thermal Control/"barbecue" mode, which allowed Roosa a brief opportunity to practice navigation techniques. There would be only one opportunity to re-enter the Earth's atmosphere, and if anything went wrong with the programmed trajectory, Roosa would have to take over manually.

The Service Module, the cause of the most perilous hours in the history of the Apollo program ten months earlier, had performed flawlessly on the Apollo 14 mission, and was jettisoned some fifteen minutes before re-entry. The Command Module, now on its own, would be re-entering the Earth's atmosphere at some 25,000 mph—almost seven miles per second.

Roosa's alignment of the Command Module was precise, but he would still need to monitor the re-entry closely. Despite the lack of wings, the CM would begin to acquire aerodynamic lift as it collided with the Earth's atmosphere. Too much lift or too little lift would abruptly change the alignment, and could be potentially disastrous. The Apollo CMP had to be prepared to make quick adjustments to the spacecraft's final trajectory.

The conical projectile that was the last component of Apollo 14 zoomed towards its final rendezvous, completely committing itself to enter the Earth's atmosphere.

The friction caused by re-entry created a raging torrent of heat and fire that were deflected by the heat shield, and the CM was surrounded in a plasma sheath, known as the "airglow," which left a flaming trail behind the CM as it streaked through the ever-thickening air.

"Oh, man, are we coming down!" Shepard cried.

Roosa and Mitchell reverted to the same type of enthusiastic observation in this facet of the flight's conclusion that they had affected when they had first spotted the Earth's horizon following liftoff.

Roosa: "Okay, there's some airglow."

Mitchell: "Yes; it's starting to glow. We got a—Oh! Man, oh, man, you can see it! That sure is pretty. Back home again."

Re-entry for Apollo CMs returning from the Moon included about three minutes of communications blackout due to the airglow. During that time, G forces built up yet again. Shepard called off the "Gs" as the force increased. The "Gs" topped out at 6.75 times normal Earth gravity, and began to subside.

The spacecraft stayed stable, and was enveloped in bright sunlight as it dove further into the atmosphere. The crew watched eagerly as a mechanism on the nose of the CM snapped open to pull out drogue parachutes. Less than a minute later, the drogues pulled out three main parachutes, which abruptly bloomed overhead in a dazzling display of

169

orange and white stripes. The awestruck crew grinned like teenage males at a burlesque show.

"They look great," Shepard said, laughing.

"We got three beauties," Roosa averred.

"They look great," Mitchell echoed.

Suspended beneath the parachutes, the spacecraft slowly descended as the crew established radio contact with the *New Orleans* and its recovery forces.

Nine days and two minutes after launch, the Apollo 14 mission concluded as the Command Module splashed into the choppy waters of the Pacific. The ensuing conversation inside the spacecraft was succinct, and perhaps even a bit giddy, although Mitchell didn't have much to say other than to point out a procedure that needed to be done. Nevertheless, they all knew they had accomplished their task well.

Roosa: "We did it, Ed."

Shepard: "You got it."

Roosa: "Hey, I think we made it."

Shepard: "Hey, we did."

Roosa: "We made it...good show."

Shepard: "Okay. Ha ha!"

Mitchell: "Circuit breaker..."

"Apollo 14, this *New Orleans*," a voice intoned through the radio speaker. "Welcome home."

"Thank you, sir," said Shepard.

"Thank you, sir," said Roosa.

"We're Stable I," Apollo 14's CDR announced, referring to the upright position of the Command Module. "Everybody's in good shape."

———〜〜〜———

Helicopters quickly converged on the CM, and swimmers attached a flotation collar to the bobbing spacecraft. Inside, the crew put on respirator devices across their noses and mouths as a precaution against spreading any sort of alien germs that might have returned from the Moon with them.

Twenty minutes later, the hatch was opened and the three Moon voyagers plopped into a life raft before being individually hauled up to a helicopter hovering overhead. Following protocol, Roosa was the last crew member to exit the spacecraft. During the brief flight to the aircraft carrier, Shepard, Roosa, and Mitchell, keeping their respirators in place, changed into one-piece coveralls, and donned caps emblazoned with the name of the *New Orleans*.

Disembarking from the helicopter, Apollo 14's triumvirate waved to the crew of the *New Orleans* and media, and strode confidently to the Mobile

Quarantine Facility (MQF), a silver, stretched-out Airstream trailer that would be their first temporary home for the post-flight quarantine.

—∿—

The three-week quarantine period for the Apollo 14 crew prior to the launch and the three-week post-flight quarantine made their voyage unique among the Apollo missions. Prior to the flight of Shepard, Roosa and Mitchell, Apollo crews had been quarantined only briefly prior to the flight, and the crews of Apollo 11 and 12 were extensively quarantined post-mission only. After Apollo 14, crews for the remaining missions were only quarantined *before* their flights.

Mitchell: "We were the only flight that had a 'double dose,' before and after. We were the *first* ones to have an *extended* pre-launch quarantine, due to the measles scare. We were the *last* ones to have a post-flight quarantine. After that, NASA decided that the astronauts weren't going to bring back any 'moon bugs'."

Inside the silver quarantine trailer on the aircraft carrier, Roosa (who had been in zero gravity nine days) had a top bunk above Mitchell, and the first night, Stu rolled off, crashing to the floor (but he was uninjured). The CMP had gotten so used to weightlessness in space that he (or his body) forgot that a return to Earth meant a return to gravity.

Post-flight discussions among the three astronauts centered on how well the mission had gone, and "...how close it was to what we had practiced," Mitchell said.

On February 12th, Joan and the Roosa children went to Ellington Air Force Base (as did the Shepard and Mitchell families) and watched excitedly as the silver MQF trailer was pushed out of an Air Force cargo plane. The astronauts appeared in the rear window of the trailer, and the families conversed briefly. The crew and accompanying NASA technicians were then transported to the lunar quarantine facility that had been built at the Manned Space Center in 1967. They would be confined in that building for another 15 days, but it was larger than an Apollo Command Module or the quarantine trailer.

The Technical Crew Debriefing for Shepard, Mitchell and Roosa took place on February 17th, during which the entire mission, and its problems, were reviewed extensively by the astronauts, who must have felt at times like they were being interrogated like spies, as NASA officials and mission scientists asked detailed questions, expecting detailed answers.

Roosa reviewed the TD&E problem, as well as his inspection of the capture latches and the drogue receptacle on the docking system after the LM had been extracted, recalling that "...close examination showed that we had three deep scratches 120 degrees apart (on the drogue), just like on the capture latches, only they weren't extending all the way into the hole. When I saw this, I appeared to me that the only way for this to happen was if the capture latches were locked instead of in the cocked position."

He also discussed sleeping patterns onboard the Command Module, meals, and other facets of the flight.

One episode occurred during the quarantine at the Manned Space Center that left Roosa and Forest Service officials upset and frustrated— during decontamination procedures, the seed canisters from Roosa's PPK burst open, mixing the seeds from the five varieties, and potentially traumatizing most, if not all of them, to the point that they might fail to germinate.

—◦◦◦—

On February 26th, the morning the quarantine was over, the families, NASA officials, and news media gathered early at the facility. When the astronauts emerged, each gave a brief speech. Ed Mitchell's beard was progressing nicely, and a notable NASA photo taken at the event showed him at the microphone, as Shepard, Stu and Joan, and the three Roosa boys listened to his remarks. Rosemary, on the other hand, was staring unabashedly at her father, to whom she hadn't been this close in almost two months.

And in another positive conclusion to a unique facet of the Apollo 14 journey, the tree seeds that had Roosa had flown to the Moon would prove to be hardier than Forest Service officials might have expected.

Following the release of the seeds from quarantine, Forest Service official Stan Krugman split the contents, sending some to the southern Forest Service station in Gulfport, Mississippi and others to the western station in Placerville, California. Surprisingly, nearly all the seeds germinated successfully, and within a few years, the Forest Service had counted some 420 to 450 seedlings that sprang up from the seeds that Roosa had taken to the Moon. Roosa would also end up keeping some of the seeds for his own personal use.

Some of the "Moon tree" seedlings would be planted with control seedlings from seeds that had remained on terra firma, and comparisons between the plants indicated no discernable differences. Most of the "Moon trees" would be given away in 1975 and 1976 to many state forestry organizations to be planted as part of the country's Bicentennial celebrations, and fledgling "Moon trees" were also planted in foreign countries.

NASA: POST-FLIGHT

Post-Flight Publicity Tours and Appearances

Roosa had been a major when he flew to the Moon, but was promoted to lieutenant colonel soon after his return. For the record, his Moon voyage did not really affect such a promotion, as he was already on the Air Force's Lieutenant Colonel Select List before the Apollo 14 flight.

As was the scenario for any successful space voyagers, the crew of Apollo 14 would be doing a lot of travel following the mission. One of the primary occurrences was a trip to Washington, Chicago, and New York in early March.

The trip got off to an awkward start for the Roosa family, as their luggage was lost when they arrived in Washington. Joan had to scramble, and plans were made to attempt to bring dresses for her and Rosemary, and suits for the boys, over to their hotel from a department store. However, the luggage was later found at NASA Headquarters. Lorine and Dewey also came from Tucson to take part in the memorable event.

Tuesday, March 2nd began at the U.S. Capitol, with a report by the crew to the House Committee on Science and Astronautics, chaired by George P. Miller of California. As was usually the scenario in Congressional hearings, the Apollo 14 crew sat at a table in front of the committee, along with NASA Acting Administrator George Low. Roosa family members sat in the first row of reserved seats behind the astronauts and Low. Former astronaut Bill Anders, now the Executive Secretary of the National Aeronautics and Space Council, was also in attendance, as were other Washington-based space officials.

The hearing was actually the first of seven that were conducted in March, as Congress began examining what to do about NASA's financial allocations for fiscal year 1972. Later meetings would include appearances by Wernher von Braun and Neil Armstrong, among others, but NASA knew that the appearance of its most recent Moon voyagers at the first meeting would be a plus for the space organization.

Included in Miller's initial statement was the introduction of the astronauts' family members:

"I am pleased to welcome to the first hearing on the fiscal year 1972 NASA authorization Dr. Low and the crew of the Apollo 14 lunar mission, astronauts Alan Shepard, Stuart Roosa, and Edgar Mitchell. Your outstanding success in Apollo 14 has again provided the world with an example of perseverance, skill, and dedication. It is fitting that we open our hearings today with the Apollo 14 crew, because they have shown through this flight how quickly man's capability I space can be multiplied by adequate support. I know that I speak on behalf of the committee in congratulating you on this great personal and national triumph of man and technology."

"I would like also to recognize a number of people in the room with us today. First, would the parents of our Apollo 14 astronauts please stand." (Applause followed each introduction.)

"Now I would like to recognize those ladies who also flew with our astronauts, at least in spirit—the wives of our Apollo 14 astronauts, Mrs. Shepard, Mrs. Roosa, and Mrs. Mitchell. I would also like to introduce Mrs. Low, the wife of Dr. George Low."

"Finally, but certainly not least, I would ask the children of our Apollo 14 crew to stand. The accomplishments of your fathers not only provide a sterling example for you but all of the young people of our nation, and we share with you your pride in your fathers' accomplishments."

Low's opening statement also alluded to the success of Apollo 14, and he addressed subsequent funding in his very first sentence.

"It is our privilege this morning, as we begin the hearings on the NASA budget for fiscal year 1972, to bring you a report on the Apollo 14 mission," said Low. "Apollo 14 was America's twenty-fourth manned space flight, the sixth to the Moon, and the third to have landed on the Moon… on this flight, Alan Shepard, Stuart Roosa, and Ed Mitchell demonstrated that man belongs in space, that man can achieve objectives well beyond the capabilities of any machine that has yet to be devised. The astronauts of Apollo 14 have shown us what man can do, and have given us a vision of what man will do in the future."

Shepard spoke first, pronouncing the mission to have been "a total success," and then introduced a brief film and slide show. Roosa began the narration for the film, and the portion that he discussed included the TD&E docking problem.

"As you can see here," Stu said during the TD&E segment, "we are sliding back out, and at this point, like any good fighter pilot, I hit the throttle again, and drove it back…at that point, we again failed to achieve a capture, so we backed out and told Houston. With some procedures they voiced up, we later achieved a hard dock, as you know, and the mission continued."

Mitchell picked up the narration of the film when the separation of the CSM and LM were shown, chronicling the landing and EVAs. Shepard began doing the accompanying voiceover when the ascent stage blasted off from the lunar surface, through the completion of the mission.

Roosa's narration of his portion of the slide presentation accompanied images he had taken from *Kitty Hawk*. He acknowledged the malfunction of the Hycon camera, and noted the area where the S-IVB from his mission had impacted. He also pointed out a geological mystery, perhaps in an effort to provide some intrigue to the legislators who oversaw budgeting for NASA:

"I hesitate to bring this one up, because I don't have the data to support it. This picture was taken quite by accident, along with a series of other photographs. There is a feature right over in this area that the geologists had not seen on any photograph before of the Moon. It is not a ridge, and it is not a rille (lunar groove/canyon), and at this point they don't have a good handle on it. They are rather pleased that they have seen a new feature that they can study and analyze and help tie into the entire picture of the Moon."

Shepard and Mitchell then finished the slide show. Following the slide show, Shepard finished with another positive appraisal of the mission that seemed to cater to the politicians' sensibilities:

"We of Apollo 14 are happy to report to you the accomplishments of *Kitty Hawk* and *Antares*, the contributions that our flight has made to the world of science, the judgments of man that have been demonstrated not only on the Moon and around the Moon, but also on the earth through our support efforts. We want to take this opportunity to thank you for your support for this overwhelming success, and for your enthusiasm, which have helped put this flag here first."

Applause resounded throughout the meeting room.

Miller allowed several questions from members of the committee. One moment that may have been interpreted as awkward occurred when Pennsylvania's James Fulton wanted to know about the mobility of Shepard and Mitchell on the lunar surface.

"Why did you walk the way you did?" asked the Congressman. "Why did you have that sort of a 'Harlem shuffle'?"

"You say a 'Harlem shuffle'?" Shepard replied.

"I don't really think we move like that in central Harlem," Charles Rangel, whose district included that area of New York City, interjected. "Perhaps it is more familiar with where you come from."

Fulton clarified his inquiry, and Shepard noted that the pictures that had been seen were taken "...early in the first EVA. It is a question of adapting to the environment. Towards the end, we found that we were making very rapid progress, very naturally. Primarily I think it's kind of a rolling gait with long strides. There were times when we were just trying to readjust position, and primarily, the mode as you saw there was kind of a hopping maneuver."

Even though America had conquered the Moon, some legislators were still thinking about the Space Race. Joseph Karth of Minnesota asked Roosa about the Soviets' Lunokhod program, without calling it by name, which had sent a robotic rover to the Moon's surface in November of 1970:

"I would like to inquire specifically about your overflight pattern. I am aware of the Russian crawler operations. Did you see any evidence of the Russian crawler operations on the Moon?"

"No, our own vehicle never got near enough to the location of the Russian vehicle," Roosa responded. "Even with the sextant is which I could find the LM, I am not sure that I would have been able to find it anyway, but our orbit was to the south...It was interesting to us that NASA was able to reach agreement with the Soviets for an exchange of lunar samples. Although the Soviet samples are small, they are from an entirely different region of the Moon."

—⁓—

At noon, the three astronauts were introduced to the U.S. House of Representatives, where each gave a brief speech. As mission commander, Shepard was somewhat of M.C. of a different type, as he introduced Mitchell, who gave a brief overview of what he and Shepard had accomplished on the surface. Then, Shepard praised Roosa's lunar photography before turning the microphone over to the CMP, noting, "He did a tremendous job by himself, photographing the lunar surface, and returned with a collection of photographs that will help the cartographers, help the geologists, and will enthuse those who are interested in looking at a strange planet."

Roosa's remarks to the House were as follows:

"You know, of all the thrills of Apollo 14, I do not believe any of them can match the thrill that it is for me to stand in front of this body this morning. I think every American, every citizen of the country, at some time tries his best to visit Washington, D.C. I know I did when I was in high school, and I passed through the galleries and watched the Congress in action, and was extremely thrilled."

"It is very difficult for me to find the words to tell you gentlemen how much I appreciate the opportunity to be standing in this body on this day. I also want to thank all of you who made is possible for Apollo 14 to be the success it was. I look upon Apollo with a great deal of pride and humility—pride in being a crewmember on 14, pride in being associated

"Pad Fuhrer" Guenter Wendt was delighted to receive a "Col. Guenter Klink" German helmet from Shepard, and the von Braun associate reciprocated by presenting the Apollo 14 commander, age 47, with a walking cane. NASA

Apollo 14 blasts off at 4:03 p.m., January 31, 1971. NASA

Responsible for guiding Apollo 14 to the Moon and back to Earth, Roosa donned an eye patch to operate the sextant onboard the CSM. NASA film—scan by Ed Hengeveld.

Stu has a quizzical "I'm-not-so-sure-about-this-packet" look concerning a container of orange liquid (which wasn't Tang). NASA film—scan by Ed Hengeveld.

Kitty Hawk, *as seen from* Antares, *following undocking.* NASA

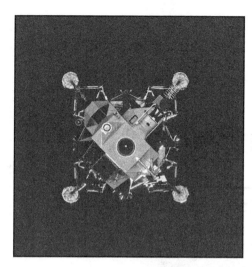

Antares, *as seen from* Kitty Hawk. NASA

February 9, 1971: Clad in protective breathing gear, Roosa, Mitchell, and Shepard wave to the crew members of the USS New Orleans as they disembark from their helicopter that flew them from their spacecraft to the aircraft carrier. NASA

Their quarantine time completed, the Apollo 14 crew re-emerges into the real world on February 26, 1971. Mitchell speaks as the Apollo 14 crew greets their families, NASA employees, and the nation upon their exit from confinement. The Roosa children managed to get right in front of their parents. Shown are, left to right, Shepard, Joan, Chris, Stu, Jack, Allen, Rosemary, Mitchell, and Mitchell's wife Louise. NASA

The Apollo 14 crew briefs the Congressional committee on Science and Astronautics. Seated at the table were, left to right Roosa, Shepard, NASA Acting Director George Low, and Ed Mitchell. Roosa family members are seated behind the foursome. NASA; Scan by J.L. Pickering.

Roosa addresses the U.S. House of Representatives. NASA

One memorable appearance for the crew was on "The Tonight Show," *with Joey Bishop guest hosting for Johnny Carson. Ed McMahon is seen on the left.* NASA

Dewey and Lorine examine the scorched exterior of the Apollo 14 Command Module that their son guided to the Moon and back. Courtesy of Dana Roosa.

Stu and Joan wave to the crowds on during a parade in his honor in Claremore on Friday, March 26, 1971. Photo by Bob Thomas, reprinted from the *Claremore Daily Progress*, March 28, 1971 edition.

Stu and Joan visit with Danny and Wilma and their children, Jeanette, front, and Dana, right.
Courtesy of Dana Roosa.

Spacemen toast to each others' success at the 1971 Paris Air Show. Left to right, Shepard, Pavel Popovich, Mitchell, Vitaly Sevastyanov, Roosa. Courtesy of Dr. Edgar Mitchell.

The Apollo 16 back up crew: Roosa, Fred Haise, Ed Mitchell. NASA

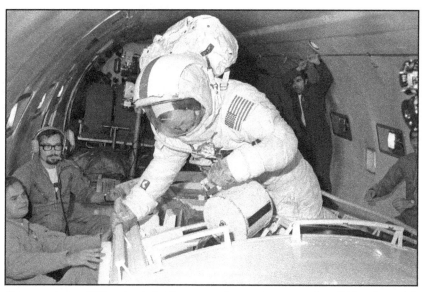

Roosa practices an EVA retrieval of a film cassette of a mapping camera from SIM package while flying aboard an Air Force KC-135 as part of his training as a member of the backup crew for the final Apollo flight. NASA

The infamous "fake mustache" photo shows the Apollo 17 prime, backup, and support crews. Left to right, front, Ron Evans, Gene Cernan, Harrison Schmitt; middle, Roosa, John Young, Charlie Duke; back, Gordon Fullerton, Robert Overmyer, Robert Parker. NASA

Roosa with a Sable Antelope that he took in Mozambique. Courtesy of Bert Klineburger.

Central African Republic ruler Jean-Bédel Bokassa was presented with a rifle by Jim Lovell, Roosa, and Bert Klineburger during one of Roosa's numerous trips to Africa. Courtesy of Bert Klineburger.

Celebrating Stu's birthday in Africa. Seen in the photo are Jim Lovell, Joan, and Brigitte Klineburger. Courtesy of Bert Klineburger.

Stu is shown with Bert Klineburger and a lion that he finally bagged on the 1973 safari. Courtesy of Bert Klineburger.

Klineburger (seen at left) and Roosa (center) encountered a caravan during their safari in the northern desert of Chad in February of 1974. Courtesy of Bert Klineburger.

The Chad desert safari included the opportunity to hunt game such as this Scimitar Oryx. Courtesy of Bert Klineburger.

Stu took part in a hunting trip for members of the Apollo-Soyuz crew and other astronauts. Shown are, left to right, front, Ron Evans, Roosa, Joe Allen; back, Deke Slayton, Vance Brand, cosmonaut Valeri Kubasov, unidentified Native American male, unidentified Native American female, cosmonaut Vladimir Shatalov, cosmonaut Alexei Leonov, Dave Scott. The Native Americans were members of a Shoshone tribe in Wyoming. NASA

School dedication in Claremore, June 12, 1975: North East Elementary School becomes Stuart Roosa Elementary School. Courtesy of Dana Roosa.

Above: Pioneering NASA astronauts pose in front of the Johnson Space Center's Project Management Building on August 21, 1978. Left to right, in front semi-circle near model, Buzz Aldrin, Walt Cunningham, Michael Collins; front row, Alan Shepard, Ed Mitchell, Dick Gordon, Pete Conrad, Ron Evans, Jim Irwin; second row, Wally Schirra, Rusty Schweickart, Bill Anders, Jim Lovell, Dave Scott, Tom Stafford; third row, Gene Cernan, Charlie Duke, Gordon Cooper, Neil Armstrong, Al Worden, Roosa, Bill Pogue. NASA

Roosa was inducted into the Brotherhood of Nicholas, an Italian business society organization, during a visit to that country in 1983. Courtesy of Collection Pizzimenti.

Circa 1990: Hunters at Stan Studer's ranch. Stu and Joan are fourth and fifth from the left. Courtesy of Dana Roosa.

1994: Roosa, Bert Klineburger, and Rosemary with a large turkey taken at Stan Studer's ranch. Courtesy of Bert Klineburger.

Oshkosh '94: During the "Salute to Apollo" festivities, four of the six CMPs from Apollo Lunar landing missions met up with their former geological survey mentor. Left to right, Mike Collins, Dick Gordon, Farouk El-Baz, Roosa, Al Worden. Photo by Donna Bushman/courtesy of E.A.A.

The Roosas' headstone in Arlington National Cemetery. Dan Silva.

with NASA, and pride in being a citizen of this great country. I also feel humble, in association with a project which I like to think personifies the spirit of our forefathers, the spirit that took the American flag from the eastern seaboard to the Pacific coast, and has three times planted it on the surface of the Moon. Thank you very much."

Shepard then gave his own speech, and the Speaker of the House, Carl Albert of Oklahoma, introduced the astronauts' families.

The third facet of the Apollo 14 crew's Capitol Hill appearances was in the Senate at 2 p.m., and was basically a repeat of the presentation by the astronauts to the House, but Shepard's introduction of Roosa following Mitchell's speech was also effusive.

"While we were busy during these two separate excursions to the lunar surface, astronaut Roosa was orbiting the Moon by himself," Shepard said. "He claims that he was working by himself, but I do not know about that! He did a fantastic job of recording—primarily photographically—a tremendous wealth of material which has a great scientific value as well as being pleasing to the eye. He did a tremendous job on the mission. I would like to ask him to say a few words."

Roosa's own speech was similar to his remarks to the House:

"I thank you, Al. It is certainly a thrill for me to be able to address this distinguished body today."

"You know, a CMP, of course, on the mission spends about two days in lunar orbit by himself. But as you come around the Moon, and you see the jewel of the Earth sitting down in the void of blackness, it makes you feel many emotions. One of these is humility. And that is what I feel now as I stand on this podium and address this body, as I think back of the distinguished personalities that have passed through this chamber. It is a tremendous thrill for me as a citizen of this country to sit here. I look upon Apollo 14 as a terrific privilege and opportunity to serve this country."

"I also want to thank each one of you for making the mission possible, and the success of Apollo 14 belongs to each one of you just as it does to me. I take great pride in being part of this mission, I take great pride in being part of the NASA organization. But most of all, I take great pride in being a citizen of the United States."

"I think the space program personifies the spirit of our forefathers that carved this great nation out of a wilderness. I think this spirit is vital for this country. I feel humble to be a part of it, and I thank you very much."

Following Shepard's remarks, the astronauts' families were introduced by Senator Mike Mansfield of Montana, majority leader.

—∿∿—

That evening, a memorable formal banquet in honor of the astronauts was held at the White House, and the Roosa children would figure into a change in policy regarding such events. Normally, younger children did not attend White House soirées of such magnitude, protocol dictating that attendees had to be at least 21 years old.

However, part of the festivities in D.C. included Shepard's promotion to the rank of Admiral, and Smilin' Al wanted his entire family present at the banquet. In a rare move, all of the children of the astronauts were allowed to attend, regardless of their age, and Joan lectured her offspring regarding manners and traditions prior to the event.

Joan had bought Stu a new formal tie and cummerbund, but the latter item didn't fit, so just prior to the event, she took a needle and thread and sewed the cummerbund directly to Stu's pants.

Stu and Joan sat with the Nixons. Joan sat directly beside the President, who pulled out her chair for her when she was seated. She paused for a split-second as she sat, contemplating that the President of the United States was performing a standard social courtesy for a small-town girl from Tupelo.

The Roosa children sat with Tricia Nixon—the boys thought she was gorgeous. The President met the Roosa kids, telling them to have a good time at Camp David.

The Presidential retreat was indeed the next stop for the astronauts and their families, for several days of relaxation. Memories for the Roosas included snowmobile rides, bowling, and screenings of movies like *Tora! Tora! Tora!*, which was still playing in theatres. Popcorn was served in silver bowls.

Another memorable item the family saw at Camp David was the ominous "red phone," to be used in case of a national emergency. It could be linked directly with the Kremlin in Moscow.

The families then went to Chicago, and stayed at the Palmer House Hotel. The Roosas were put up in a penthouse that had more square footage than their home in Houston. The trip to the Windy City also included another formal banquet, a trip to the Ice Capades show, and a ticker-tape parade.

The children then returned to Houston, while the astronauts and their wives journeyed to New York, where the Apollo 14 crew appeared on "The Tonight Show" (Joey Bishop was guest-hosting for Johnny Carson) on March 8, and attended the first Muhammad Ali – Joe Frazier fight the same evening.

Post-flight celebrations and activities in Houston honoring the Apollo 14 crew and their families included attending country and western music shows, as well as Houston Astros baseball games.

One of the most memorable post-flight events for the Roosas was a homecoming celebration presented in Claremore in late March. The Oklahoma town pulled out all the stops to welcome home its very own Moon voyager and his family, and many of Stu's friends from the Claremore High School Class of 1951 were involved in the planning. More than one area newspaper provided plenty of advance promotion.

Friday, March 26th was a long but exciting day for the Roosas and the community where he was raised. Roosa's parents, Danny and his family, and former classmates and teachers were on hand to take part in the festivities. Lorine was proudly wearing the brooch her younger son had given her after it had flown on Apollo 14.

The homecoming began at 9 a.m., as Roosa gave a speech (the first of three during the day) and presented a twenty-minute film on the Apollo 14 mission in the auditorium of his former high school. Stu was particularly impressed with the way the high school program began, with the presentation of colors, a prayer, and the singing of "America," and he told the audience that although he spoken to many schools before and after his flight, Claremore High School was the first that had begun such a program in such a manner, which gave him a tremendous sense of pride in his alma mater. He was presented a plaque by the CHS Student Council president, David Burrows, and in return, gave the school a framed display of a small American flag, an Apollo 14 patch, and a photo taken during the voyage. Both the flag and the patch had flown on the mission.

A press conference followed at 10 a.m., where Roosa compared expenditures of the Soviet economy and the United States' gross national product to support space programs, and noted that more U.S. astronauts were from Oklahoma than any other state, adding that he hoped to be associated with the American space program for many more years.

Oklahoma's lieutenant governor, George Nigh, gave Stu a framed copy of a resolution passed by the State Senate and signed by Governor David Hall that proclaimed March 26, 1971 as "Stuart Roosa Day" throughout the entire state (Ironically, Hall was reportedly unable to attend the event because he was in Houston, touring NASA facilities). Roosa reciprocated with a framed state flag and another patch, both of which had also flown on Apollo 14.

Stu gave similar presentations to Will Rogers Junior High School students at 11 a.m., and to Oklahoma Military Academy cadets and Justus School students at 1 a.m.

A parade through downtown Claremore began at 2 p.m., and drew a crowd estimated at almost 20,000. Stu and Joan rode in a 1957 Ford

Thunderbird convertible, and other dignitaries rode in other '57 T-Birds. High school and college marching bands performed, and drill units from Oklahoma Military Academy participated.

The local military academy also hosted a sold-out banquet that night in the Porter Office Hall on its campus. The dinner was sponsored by the CHS Class of 1951, and Roosa received numerous awards and other memorabilia, including a key to the city from Claremore mayor Jack Marshall, and a scrapbook compiled by his former classmates.

—ᴧᴧᴧ—

The children didn't go on overseas post-flight NASA trips with Stu and Joan, but some of those sojourns were memorable as well. In the ensuing months, the couple would travel to Europe, Africa, and Asia in an effort to generate goodwill and respect for NASA's programs.

The Apollo 14 crew met two Soviet cosmonauts, Pavel Popovich, who had flown on 1962's Vostok 4 mission, and Vitaly Sevastianov, a veteran of Soyuz 9 in 1970, on June 3rd at the 1971 Paris Air Show. The Americans found their Soviet counterparts to be capable, tough and determined pilots, and even the patriotic Roosa was impressed. The five space travelers were interviewed on French television, and toasted to each others' success.

—ᴧᴧᴧ—

Personal/family trips, even after the Apollo 14 mission, weren't necessarily as organized as government-sponsored publicity tours.

After Roosa flew, he and Hartsfield decided to take their families on a vacation together to Acapulco. The plan was to catch a Mexican train in Nuevo Laredo, across the border from Laredo, Texas, ride to Mexico City, then rent a car and drive through the mountains to Acapulco.

The train trip was unique in that Roosa and Hartsfield went searching for beer, as the club car bar had run out of beverages, and they ended up in what Hartsfield termed a "last class" rail car that was hauling people, goats, and chickens. The train also broke down, was repaired, and arrived in Mexico City late.

The families had guaranteed car rental in advance, and had asked for a ten-passenger station wagon, but the Hertz rental facility was closed. A Mexican woman at the train station told them she and her husband had just gotten back from France, noting "We know how it is to be in a country where you don't speak the language, and nobody helps you." She found a nice hotel for the families, and the kitchen opened up and prepared some food for the famished gringos.

The car reservations didn't work out, either—the Roosas got a six-passenger Plymouth and the Hartsfields got a VW "bug." The two families finally made it to Acapulco, where they had a good time, but they took an airline flight back to Mexico City, and had a pleasant return to Laredo by train. Getting to the Moon and back may have ultimately seemed easier.

Apollo 16 and 17 Backup

In another indication that the Apollo program heading to a dead-end, Slayton and Shepard (who was back as the Chief of the Astronaut Office) opted to utilize lunar veterans as backup crews for Apollo 16 and 17, taking a point of view that someone who had already "been there, done that" would be a suitable substitute if a prime crew member was unable to fly.

The prime crew for Apollo 16 consisted of John Young, CDR, Ken Mattingly, CMP, and Charlie Duke, LMP. Backup crew members consisted of Fred Haise, CDR, Ed Mitchell, LMP, and Roosa, who was designated to occupy the center seat if something happened to Mattingly...again. The mission was slated to land at the Descartes formation in the lunar highlands, which Roosa had surveyed from orbit onboard *Kitty Hawk*.

Mitchell: "I was told I had to be on backup if I wanted to fly again, and I would have been scheduled to command (Apollo) 19, but it was one of the ones that was cancelled. And all of the crews had already been selected for Skylab, so I left (NASA) after doing backup on (Apollo) 16. There wouldn't have been anything else until the Space Shuttle, and it was behind schedule."

Stu was delighted to see Charlie picked as the LMP for Apollo 16, but the Dynamic Duo didn't compare Roosa's having been a CMP on Apollo 14 to Duke being an LMP on Apollo 16 *between* the two flights.

"We had helpful conversations about various aspects of the mission" Duke detailed. "I picked his brain about certain phases, along with others like Ed Mitchell and Fred Haise, who were the other members of the backup crew for our flight. I had talked with (Mitchell) a lot *before* he flew on 14, as well as when he was my backup on 16, about his ideas about things like extra-sensory perception and paranormal events. I think he was well 'into' such things by the time he went to the Moon, Back then, I was kind of into UFOs, and I was a fan of *2001: A Space Odyssey*, so there was a little bit of common ground. Ed wanted me to do an experiment on my own flight, but I was so tired I couldn't do it."

—⁓—

Haise recalls that his original backup crew for Apollo 16 would have been the prime crew for one of the cancelled flights (again, the three-mission-backup-to-prime protocol figured into the mission):

"I had actually been training with Bill Pogue and Jerry Carr for about four and a half months. We were going to fly (Apollo) 19, Jerry Carr and I were going to land; Bill Pogue was the CMP. When 18 and 19 were cancelled, Deke moved them into the Skylab program, and pulled in Ed Mitchell and Stu to finish out the backup assignment."

Haise was compelled to stay with the Apollo 16 backup assignment, and got to know Roosa best during their mutual effort:

"We had an experienced crew, since Ed Mitchell, Stu and I had all been to the Moon. We worked very hard. It was a very long training cycle, and there wasn't a problem with the change-out. We knew we were probably not going to go—again—but we weren't slack in our training. We were fully prepared if something had happened at the last minute, as was the situation with (Apollo) 13. Stu was great to work with; he was very diligent and very capable."

Haise also recalled that when the Apollo 16 backup crew was practicing simulations of critical maneuvers such as Trans-Earth Injection, Roosa would scat-sing or hum appropriate dramatic music, as would be heard on a movie soundtrack.

Hank Hartsfield was one of the four support crew members for Apollo 16, and would also serve as a CapCom for the flight. The Alabama native was appreciative of getting the assignment.

"Support crews were third level," he recounted, "but you got to participate in some of the training and simulations."

Roosa's training duties for Apollo 16 *did* have some differences when compared to his Apollo 14 experiences, the primary example of which was an EVA by the CMP on the return portion of the journey, to retrieve a scientific instrument package on the Service Module.

The first deep space EVA had been performed by Apollo 15 CMP Al Worden, who had reported nothing particularly different from what other astronauts had experienced on EVAs while in orbit around the Earth; said spacewalker was usually so busy with the assigned tasks he didn't time to sightsee (or get disoriented). The two moonwalkers on the Apollo 15 mission had been Dave Scott and Jim Irwin.

Mattingly had been assigned a similar spacewalk on Apollo 16, so Roosa had to practice EVAs as well. In practice sessions for such a task, CMPs would don a complete space suit, and would maneuver in the hollow interior of a KC-135 cargo jet that was flying a pattern that would cause temporary weightlessness. While floating, the CMP endeavored to remove the complex instruments from the simulated cylindrical exterior of an Apollo spacecraft.

And Ken Mattingly would finally get his chance to go to the Moon, circling Luna as Young and Duke labored in the Descartes region. Apollo 16 returned safely.

—◁∿▷—

The backup crew assignments for Apollo 17 would have a different and awkward scenario compared to Apollo 16. Originally, the prime crew from Apollo 15 (Scott, Worden, and Irwin) was tapped as backup for the last Apollo mission to the Moon, as another example of NASA's "caboose" use of astronauts who had lunar experience.

However, a controversy erupted regarding the sale of a series of envelopes that had been carried to the Moon by the Apollo 15 crew, some of which had clandestinely been slated to be sold. While such actions were not expressly forbidden by NASA at the time, the so-called "stamp scandal" nevertheless proved embarrassing to the space agency. Apollo 17's original backup crew was unceremoniously removed from their backup role and individually assigned elsewhere. Scott, Worden, and Irwin never flew into space again.

Slayton had to scramble to come up with a backup crew, so Apollo 16's Young and Duke turned right around and became backup crew members for Apollo 17, and Roosa joined them to complete the backup lineup.

Following his backup effort with Apollo 16, Stu had been planning on taking advantage of a post-flight opportunity afforded to astronauts by taking the Advance Management Course, a type of "quickie MBA" (Master of Business Administration) program, at the Harvard Business School, in preparation for a transition to the "real world" of business and finance.

NASA's removal of the Apollo 15 prime crew from their Apollo 17 backup assignment abruptly postponed Roosa's educational option, and he dutifully went through the extensive and requisite spaceflight training yet again.

The prime crew for the last voyage was Gene Cernan, commander, Ron Evans, CMP, and Harrison Schmitt, LMP. Evans and Schmitt were rookies, and Apollo 17's LMP would the first and only Group 4 scientist that went to the Moon. Numerous scientists had lobbied NASA to send one of their own on this last mission, in order to glean as much knowledge as possible from the final voyage, and while the three-mission rotation from backup to prime was applicable to Cernan and Evans, the backup LMP for Apollo 14, Joe Engle, would have to wait until the Space Shuttle program began to ride into space via another craft besides the X-15.

"Volunteering as backups for the later Apollo flights was sort of a dead-end job," Duke summarized, "but you never knew whether you might get a chance to fly again if something happened to a member of the prime crew, so we were excited about it. John Young, Stu, and I volunteered for backup on Apollo 17 knowing that it wouldn't lead anywhere, but it kept us in the program. New guys weren't put into those jobs because the veterans who had already flown would have been able to step right in, if they had been needed. We knew the systems, we enjoyed the training, and we were still excited about what we were doing. The other guys who didn't fly on Apollo had chances on Apollo-Soyuz, Skylab, or the Shuttle, and most of them did fly."

Still, the opportunity of working with each other was something that was cherished by both Roosa and Duke, according to Charlie:

"We got to be really close again when he was doing backup on 16, and when we got to train together on 17. We'd go fishing, and we went hunting down in Vero Beach when we got to be friends with a family named Tripson. There was another guy named Fondren Mitchell who had a *big* ranch west of Vero Beach that was some 30,000 acres; we went quail hunting and deer hunting there several times. Fondren also had a development near Ashville, North Carolina, and Stu and I bought lots up there when he offered us a big discount. Stu and I did a lot of things together; more than training. In those years, we were more like brothers than close friends."

Cernan noted that the experiences of Roosa and Evans as prime and backup CMPs on Apollo 14 meant that their switch in assignments for Apollo 17 made their training go extremely smooth:

"They'd worked together so well on Apollo 14 that it was a 'natural' for Stu to pick up that role in backing up Ron, from an operational point of view, as well as the geology work. They were really compatible."

———⋘⋙———

Stu hadn't forgotten the "Beep-Beep" patch designed by the backup crew of Apollo 14 (of which Cernan and Evans were 2/3 of the membership), and that classic prank may have figured into his possible desire for a bit of payback to the Apollo 17 prime crew.

One personal "gotcha" was aimed at Cernan. Roosa and Duke were jogging on a track behind the simulator building at Cape Kennedy, and encountered a large rattlesnake. The two hunters quickly killed the reptile, beheaded it, and placed the body under Cernan's desk inside the simulator building. Then they pushed his desk chair, which was on casters, a nominal distance from the desk itself.

The two backup astronauts then conspired with a secretary, who informed the Apollo 17 CDR (who was in a simulator) that he had an important phone call.

Cernan exited the "sim" and went to the office, plopped down in his chair, and began rolling towards his desk.

"About halfway there, I saw it," he recounted with a laugh. "They'd coiled that big, ugly snake under my desk with its rattles—there were *sixteen* of them—poking up. It was as big as your forearm, and I *know* my heart stopped. Charlie Duke held it up; he was about six feet tall, and it was as long as he was. I think Stu was probably the instigator of a lot of those kinds of things."

The backup crew for Apollo 17 also decided to do something unusual as a group from their second-string position, opting to wear facial hair throughout training. Ed Mitchell had sported a neatly-trimmed beard when he was on backup with Apollo 16, but this time, Young and Duke grew mustaches, and Roosa affected an even-scruffier look, with a mustache and goatee, and longer hair that was parted down the middle.

"We wanted to be distinctive," Duke recalled with a grin, but he had no recollection about why Roosa's appearance was somewhat like a beatnik or pseudo-hippie.

Even in the waning days of the Apollo program, however, the prime crew had to remain clean-cut and dapper for publicity reasons, and if the Apollo 17 prime crew felt like the backup crew's facial hair was non-traditional, the soon-to-be-final Moon voyagers would execute a reciprocal "gotcha" on Duke, Young and Roosa—a posed shot in front of an LM taken during training shows, as expected, the Apollo 17 prime crew in the front row, the backup crew in the second row, and the support crew (Gordon Fullerton, Robert Overmyer, and Robert Parker) in the third row (Overmyer had also been on the support crew for Apollo 16).

And from left to right in the front, Evans, Cernan, and Schmitt are wearing fake mustaches.

—⁓—

While the Apollo 17 flight was in progress with its prime crew, Congress approved the Space Transportation System (STS)/"Space Shuttle" program.

Roosa and his family did attend the launches of Apollo 16, Apollo 17, and the Apollo-Soyuz mission. The joint venture between the United States and the Soviet Union completed the use of Apollo spacecraft in America's space program, and the crew members of that final mission included veteran Tom Stafford, Deke Slayton (who had recovered from his heart problem and was making his only trip into outer space), and Vance Brand, who would later fly on three Space Shuttle missions.

After Apollo 17 had concluded the Moon program, the only space adventure that beckoned to Roosa, Duke, and other latter day Apollo veterans was a possible Space Shuttle flight, which was some years down the road. The crews for the Skylab space station endurance program had already been named, but Roosa wasn't particularly interested in that program anyway. Likewise, the Apollo-Soyuz project was getting lined up, and that project wouldn't have necessarily appealed to Roosa, either.

Former President Lyndon Johnson, who had fervently championed the American space program in its infancy, died on January 22, 1973. The Manned Space Center in Houston was re-named the Johnson Space Center in his honor.

Roosa, Duke, and others began doing some preliminary research work for the STS, including cockpit layout design, suits, and airlocks. Duke went on to a management position later, doing technical support, and working in an assistant operations position for the manager of the Shuttle program.

Haise took a somewhat different path, switching from the Astronaut Office to NASA's STS project office for three and a half years. It was a bit of dejá vú that harkened back to his work with the development of the LM, and he ultimately became intensely involved in the design of the new STS spacecraft. He later returned to the Astronaut Office, and was at the controls of the *Enterprise*, the prototype/test version of the Shuttle (model designation OV-101), when it separated from its piggyback position on a Boeing 747 jumbo jet over Edwards Air Force Base for its first Approach and Landing Test mission on August 12, 1977. He would command five of the eight flight tests in the Approach and Landing Test program.

Haise never flew into space on a Shuttle, but recalled being assigned to a mission with Jack Lousma to rescue the Skylab orbital laboratory, rendezvousing with the aging space station and pushing it into a higher orbit:

"That would have been a very exciting mission, but sunspot activity had increased, and we would have been delayed because of the (STS) tile problem, and Skylab was allowed to fall into the ocean. So that mission went away, and we still were supposed to fly on a thermal test, but that didn't excite me that much. So I consider my first flight on the *Enterprise* as the highlight of my career."

(The STS had hundreds of tiles on its lower surface to function as an ablative heat shield, and problems had been encountered with some of the tiles being damaged or falling off, creating a potentially hazardous situation during re-entry.)

So unlike some other Apollo veterans, Roosa wasn't particularly enthusiastic about flying on the new Shuttle himself, taking the attitude that since he had been in deep space, doing low earth orbit missions (for the Skylab effort, Apollo-Soyuz, *or* on the STS) would be anticlimactic. While Roosa didn't wax negative about the post-Apollo NASA ventures, it was his perspective that such efforts didn't seem to be as concerted or passionate.

That being said, it needs to be remembered that the probable primary reason the Apollo program might have been more "earnest" was because it was America's entry in a race to the Moon against the Soviet Union. One might speculate as to whether Roosa, an ardent patriot, might have felt differently had the Space Race been ongoing.

But Vance Brand seemed to confirm why Roosa wasn't particularly enthusiastic about later Earth orbital missions:

"I think if you were in the Apollo program, you were considered 'an Apollo guy.' Although Skylab was a wonderful program, a lot of astronauts were more oriented towards going to the Moon."

"Stu and I didn't really discuss Skylab," Charlie Duke said, "but we were happy to see a lot of the guys from the Original Nineteen get a chance to fly. Later, when we were working on the Shuttle, we discussed safety, like the fact that there was no escape system after the first experimental flights, because we'd been in flight safety early in our careers. We also talked about the schedule and the budget—the original plans for the Space Shuttle had been for fifty flights a year. Stu and I knew *while we were in the program* it wasn't going to fly that often."

Roosa even envisioned going back into the regular Air Force as a squadron commander, but was informed that there were numerous pilots who had served in combat missions in Vietnam who were going to get preference for such commands.

———ᵂᵂ———

Much has been made about to what extent Apollo astronauts who journeyed to the Moon—moonwalkers and CMPs alike—were "changed" by that historical experience.

Mitchell has opined that all of the Apollo astronauts—particularly the Lunar Module Pilots who walked on the Moon (in order, Aldrin, Bean, himself, Irwin, Duke, Schmitt) had a life-changing experience, but others feel differently. Mitchell described his experience from what he termed a type of scientific point of view due to his training as an astronomer. Irwin, on the other hand, described it from a religious point of view.

In yet another validation that his "matter-of-fact" personality was still viable (as well as another validation of the differences in the personalities of the Apollo 14 crew), Roosa's point of view was the opposite of Mitchell's. While Stu realized the historical importance of the Apollo program's accomplishments and was proud of his participation, he strongly believed that space travel shouldn't change anyone's personality, and maintained that he didn't have any life-changing experience(s) during the mission.

"My father's attitude was that what you took into space was what you came back with," said Chris. "You didn't go out into space looking for something; you either believed in God before you went, or you didn't."

Duke agreed with Roosa's perspective, which meant Charlie didn't think Mitchell's observation about LMPs applied to his own post-Apollo life. While Dotty and Charlie would each undergo a re-commitment to Christianity, such experiences would happen many years after the Apollo 16 Moon shot.

"It *was* an overwhelming feeling for the majority of us," Duke said of a voyage that only twenty-four people would ever make, "but for me, it was also a flight that had a complex operational plan. It was not a spiritual experience nor a philosophical experience for me, and that's how it was for Stu, as well."

However, Duke also thought, as did other observers, that the voyage of Apollo 14 might have permanently altered Al Shepard's personality, as the Chief Astronaut seemed to be easier to get along with when he reported back to his desk job in Houston.

"He was more like 'one of the guys'—not aloof," Duke remembered. "He could still be a stern boss, but I thought he was more 'approachable'."

—⁓—

Roosa also thought that any so-called influence of being a famous space traveler in attempting to rationalize having extramarital affairs or divorcing a spouse was, to quote Allen (who may have been quoting his father), "a load of crap."

Stu and Joan never fought—at least, not in front of their children—but the whole family was aware of other astronauts' marriages that were breaking up after the husbands had been into space. Nevertheless, there wasn't any kind of discernable post-flight trauma within the Roosa household.

Roosa even had a valid opinion concerning why his marriage to Joan had survived: Many of the astronauts and their wives were from small towns, and had been high school sweethearts; i.e., they'd come of age with each other in a socially-diminutive locale. Accordingly, when the husband had been selected by NASA to be an astronaut, the Houston social scene and the obligations for astronaut wives in such an environment may have swamped many women who simply wanted their husbands to survive in a dangerous career field, and who probably would have been content to be raising their children in as normal of a household as possible.

Figuring in the chronic absences of astronauts from their families, as well as possible (subliminal) feelings by an astronaut's wife that she might have missed out on a fulfilling career for herself, it's not surprising that so many astronaut marriages eventually crumbled.

When Stu and Joan had met, however, they were both already established in their respective careers, and Joan already had a college degree. By having been older and more mature, they were able to acknowledge that they were indeed making a lifetime commitment to each other. Moreover, since Joan had been raised in somewhat of a "society" environment in Tupelo, she had actually enjoyed the Houston social scene.

The marriages of the Dukes and the Hartsfields also endured, and Dotty Duke (who was also a college graduate when she and Charlie met) added a spouse's perspective for the longevity of those marriages:

"I think our marriages survived because we—the Hartsfields, the Roosas, and us—believed in the *commitment* of marriage. I don't know that age had anything to do with it. To me, most of the (astronaut) marriages fell apart because the guys weren't committed; they philandered. But our husbands *had* a commitment, and maybe that's a Southern thing, too."

For the Roosa children, the Apollo 14 flight and the initial post-flight time frame meant a temporary loss of standard identity, as any introductions to someone would include the add-on verbal "tag" that their dad had been to the Moon. Sometimes the Apollo references (that may have resulted in skewed expectations) would seem interminable, even following them into their adult lives, but all four of them handled such fame-by-association well.

"I knew that Daddy had done something spectacular," said Rosemary, "and he wanted us to understand how we were supposed to handle his mission *before* he went, and wanted us to understand *after* he went. He wanted us to travel as a family to (post-mission celebratory) events whenever possible."

Chris: "Later on, there was sometimes an 'assumption' that whatever you succeeded in doing in school, one of the reasons was because your father was an astronaut—winning a part in a play, etc. It was kind of an 'undercurrent'. When I won a track race, it was because I was faster than everyone else, not because my dad was an astronaut."

Hunting Adventures

Before and after the Apollo 14 voyage, Roosa had maintained his friendship with Bert Klineburger, and had been on numerous domestic hunting trips with the safari icon.

The Roosas, often accompanied by Klineburger and his wife Brigitte, went on hunts at Stan Studer's ranch in Texas on a regular basis.

Unique hunting events that Stu and Bert attended included the One Shot Antelope Hunt in Lander, Wyoming, and the Two Shot Goose Hunt, sponsored by Art and Dick Carlsbury, in Lamar, Colorado.

Other astronauts, military heroes, and movie stars participated in those events. Dave Scott recalled one particular One Shot Antelope Hunt where he and Joe Allen, who had been selected as a scientist-astronaut in 1967, were teamed with Roosa. Scott noted that he and Allen were "neophytes," but their team won, thanks to Stu's prowess. Among the losing teams that had to genuflect to the winning team was one led by retired Air Force General Curtis LeMay.

Roosa was also invited to numerous prestigious, hunting-oriented black-tie events, including the annual Weatherby banquet, sponsored by the rifle manufacturer.

"Many of the world's most important hunters were invited," Klineburger recalled, "along with astronauts and movie stars. It was usually held in places like the Beverly Hilton (in Beverly Hills, California), or some other fancy, Los Angeles-area hotel. There was a cocktail party the first night, and the awards presentation dinner was the next night."

A very exclusive (and very private) organization known as the Shikar-Safari Club offered memberships to Joan and Stu.

According to Klineburger, the Shikar-Safari Club, which has slightly over 200 members, is made up of some of the most affluent and active big game hunters in the world. The organization has sponsored game conservation projects across the world, has a non-profit foundation, and offers scholarships.

"Each year they have an auction at their annual meeting," said Klineburger. "Most of the items auctioned are donations from their members, and they have raised as much as one million dollars in one night."

Roosa was the only astronaut ever tapped to be a member of the Shikar-Safari Club.

———

One of the earlier foreign excursions on which Roosa accompanied Klineburger was to Iran, where they met with Prince Abdorezza Pahlavi, the brother of the Shah, and his son. The prince was considered one of the greatest big game hunters in the world, and already had a strong friendship with Klineburger.

The African safaris in which Roosa and Klineburger participated were oriented towards fine hunting and public relations, as well as business projects.

"We were also trying to get permission from certain African heads-of-state to get areas open for hunting, so we could start hunting organizations," Klineburger explained.

Joan often went on African safaris with Stu, as well.

On more than one occasion, Apollo astronaut Jim Lovell accompanied Stu and Bert on African safaris. In negotiations with African heads of state about hunting rights, it always helped the Americans' stance if one or two members of the U.S. party happened to have been to the Moon. Like almost every other informed individual on the planet, African leaders such as Mobutu Sese Seko of Zaire, Francois Tombalbaye of Chad, and Jean-Bédel Bokassa of the Central African Republic (C.A.R.) were fascinated by astronauts.

Roosa, Lovell, and Klineburger were representatives for People-to-People Sports, a program started during the Eisenhower administration to promote goodwill and positive international relations through sports.

"It was a fascinating program," Klineburger recounted. "We'd get donations of sports equipment to distribute in Africa—socks, shoes, baseball bats, tennis rackets, soccer balls."

The threesome, accompanied by other People-to-People Sports officials, including the organization's president, Leonard Milton, and Charles Erwin Wilson, Jr., son of a former president of General Motors, delivered sports equipment to Chad, the C.A.R., and Zaire in 1972, and Klineburger, Roosa, and Lovell used the opportunity (including the astronauts' hero status) to make inroads with those countries' heads of state regarding hunting, presenting Messrs. Tombalbaye, Bokassa, and Mobutu each with a high-quality Weatherby hunting rifle.

In particular, Klineburger was interested in the northern desert area of Chad.

"I had been hunting in the C.A.R. before," recalled Klineburger, "and had really enjoyed the beautiful, wild country. But the southern part of Chad had the same game that the C.A.R. did, and had far superior hunting potential. So we 'worked on' Tombalbaye to get permission to hunt the desert in the northern part of Chad, which had been closed to hunting."

Tombalbaye would ultimately accede to the "pitch" by the Americans, but the desert trek wouldn't happen until 1974.

—∕∕∕—

In his 1999 book, *International Hunter*, Klineburger described a 1973 safari in Mozambique with Roosa and Lovell as "the trip that stands out above all others for me."

Joan Roosa, Marilyn Lovell, and Brigitte Klineburger accompanied their spouses on the journey. The safari would prove to be filled with excitement and success, as well as a "gotcha" worthy of the legendary shenanigans of the astronaut corps.

At the second camp on the trek, plans were made to celebrate Stuart's birthday, and it was announced that Brigitte, who was of German heritage, had volunteered to stay in the camp to make a birthday cake, using an old German recipe.

The Roosas left the camp the next morning, but the Klineburgers remained behind for a few minutes, then set out to find the primary item necessary for Roosa's birthday cake—a large, appropriately-shaped elephant dropping.

Brigitte set about creating a unique-looking item that was globe-shaped, and about ten inches in diameter. The "cake" even had frosting.

It was presented to Roosa that evening after dinner. With the lights lowered, Brigitte brought the "cake" to the table, a large solitary lighted candle protruding from its top.

And Roosa actually cut into the "cake" before realizing what it was. The look on his face was said to be almost indescribable, and the entire safari party bellowed with laughter, including Roosa himself. Brigitte then presented Roosa with a legitimate cake, decorated with a homemade model of an Apollo spacecraft.

Roosa and Lovell both killed elephants on the safari, among other animals, but Stu was itching to bag a lion.

Shortly before the adventure ended, the safari guides managed to attract a lion at night. The large male actually walked up to within ten feet of the rear of the Land Rover, unseen in the darkness. When a spotlight whirled around and illuminated the big cat, Roosa had an opportunity for one shot, and took it, but wasn't sure if he had hit it.

Klineburger recalled that Roosa wanted to pursue what was probably a wounded lion right then, and had to be dissuaded, since the scenario was too dangerous at night.

The lion was tracked the next morning, and the dead animal was found a short distance from where it had been shot.

—⁓—

Not surprisingly, Roosa actively sought to develop his lifelong interest in hunting as one or more business ventures, and it also wasn't surprising that he wanted Bert Klineburger as a business partner. The 1972 People-to-People Sports trip to Chad, the Central African Republic, and Zaire had reinforced that notion.

However, an idea had also germinated between Roosa and Klineburger about a cattle operation in Chad, which would include flow-irrigated land.

"The land and cattle were very cheap," said Klineburger, "and water could be directed from the Chari River."

Klineburger had been considering parting ways with the taxidermy business in Seattle, and the potential cattle project in Chad motivated him to make such a business move.

"Seattle had been good to me, but I felt it was time to move along," he said, "so that's why I was interested in the possible cattle project in Chad. And the possibilities of opening Chad to hunting, and to have a hunting concession in the C.A.R. to go along with the cattle project, looked like a fantastic opportunities."

Roosa and Klineburger would spend a lot of time in Chad working on the project and negotiating with the government. On one trip, Roosa's father Dewey accompanied his son and Klineburger, to learn about the land's irrigation possibilities.

"Dewey came over to use his surveying skills to help figure out how far up the river we would have to go to start the irrigation channels, to get the water to flow to the cattle," Klineburger recalled.

—⁓—

After numerous reminders to Tombalbaye about his promise, Klineburger and Roosa were finally able to hunt the northern desert of Chad in February 1974. The twosome and their hunting party began their trek near the Sudan border in central Chad, in a town named Abéché that Klineburger described in *International Hunter* as appearing to be a set of a movie about the French Foreign Legion, and most of the small clusters of humanity where the safari would stop to rest had indeed been such military outposts in earlier times.

Another stop, Biltine, still had five French army officers stationed there, while another outpost, Arada, was an oasis with an old fort and government building formerly occupied by the French. There was a solitary well to nourish the residents as well as travelers who were passing through.

The hunting party's final occupied settlement stop was at Oum-Chalouba, another old military outpost. The *sous-préfet*, or local governor, warned Klineburger and Roosa against hunting in certain areas, due to bandits. Determined to take advantage of their long-awaited opportunity, the duo decided to push into the desert in spite of the potential dangers, but heeded the *sous-préfet's* admonition about not camping in one place more than one night.

The Chad desert safari would prove to be a unique journey on which the two American hunters bagged unique animals, including scimitar oryx and dama gazelles.

One memorable incident during the northern Chad safari was an encounter with a huge caravan that was crossing the desert. Apprehension meant that Roosa and Klineburger initially kept their rifles at the ready, but the meeting with the camel drivers was cordial. The caravan was taking salt and dried dates to Arada and Abéché, and traded some dates to the hunters for candy and water.

The hunters' route brought them around again to Arada, Biltine, and then Abéché to complete to memorable journey.

As it turned out, the cattle project was abandoned because the American investors that Klineburger and Roosa had lined up wanted to do hunting programs in both countries, and Klineburger felt that it would not be wise to start a safari operation in southern Chad, since the C.A.R. offered better potential.

Roosa would later become a shareholder in Klineburger's C.A.R. safari company, and Klineburger and his wife Brigitte moved to that country for an extended time to start the operation.

—ʌʌ—

In 1975, former Apollo 14 CapCom and Skylab astronaut Bill Pogue, who had accompanied the Roosas, Klineburger, and other People-To-People officials on a five-week trip to Iran, Afghanistan, India, Bhutan, and Nepal.

Among the more memorable events for the goodwill ambassadors was a buzkashi competition in Afghanistan, a team sport that Pogue likened to a gruesome cross between polo and soccer. As the People-To-People contingent watched from a hillside, two teams on horseback battled each other for possession of a decapitated goat carcass.

The ambassadors also visited the giant statutes of Buddha in the Bamiyan Valley, which were estimated to have been built in the Sixth Century. Those icons would be destroyed in early 2001 by the Taliban, the fundamentalist Islamic regime that had taken over Afghanistan.

The group's visit to Nepal included a stay in a jungle environment known as Tiger Tops, where the visitors learned about tiger preservation. The lodging was built on stilts due to the rainy season.

And an unfortunate cultural blunder in Nepal left Roosa frustrated, through no fault of his own.

The Roosas were treated like royalty in Nepal. Joan was informed by locals that since she was married to an astronaut, she herself was a goddess.

However, another Nepalese religious connotation to Roosa's status was awkward. When Roosa spoke at a school, he was asked who he had seen while he was circling the Moon. When he responded that he hadn't seen anyone, his answer seemed to cause a collective feeling of angst among the attendees, and for the astronaut, who was used to speaking publicly about his experiences, it was a rare embarrassing moment.

Stu and Joan would later discover that the spiritual doctrine of many Nepalese included the belief that the souls of departed individuals go to the Moon; i.e., Luna was the "Heaven" of their particular religion. The Roosas hadn't been informed of that religious and cultural facet by any State Department officials. The attendees at Roosa's speech at the school had been seeking to know about their dead relatives and acquaintances, and Roosa had unintentionally punctured their beliefs.

Preparations For Retirement

One post-flight event for the Roosas was unexpected by even their closest friends—in the mid-Seventies, Joan decided to run for the Texas state legislature as a Republican, against an incumbent Democrat. Stu was, of course, still with NASA, and was still in the Air Force at the time.

"It kind of surprised me when she did that," Dotty Duke remembered, "but she was interested in politics. She wasn't a 'women's lib' person, but she believed in equal opportunity for women—she was a strong supporter of women being able to do anything and everything. She was strong-willed, and felt like she could offer something."

Walt Cunningham: "Military people are supposed to be apolitical, and Stu was pretty conservative, but he was okay with her running."

"Mama *did* refer to herself as a feminist," said Rosemary, "and she did believe in equal rights. She got upset later, when the term 'feminist' got 'warped,' and was associated with extreme positions; the term had gotten off of its original meaning or intent. And Daddy thought she could do anything she wanted to do. She didn't want to be 'pigeonholed' as the wife of an astronaut."

Joan's parents had been politically-oriented Democrats, in an era when Republicans were extremely rare in the Deep South, but Joan could apparently see the handwriting on the wall regarding how Republicans and conservative ideals were going to be more compatible with the political points-of-view of Stu, herself, and many Southerners. She'd informed the Barretts years earlier that she was a Republican, which caused some temporary consternation within the family.

For the state legislative race, her slogan was "Vote for Joan Roosa—For All The Right Reasons."

Farouk El-Baz recalled that he campaigned for Joan, and that he "... placed her sticker on every rental car I had."

The idea of a conservative Republican female running for office in such times was still unusual, and went against certain stereotypes, but Joan was an active and aggressive campaigner, and her children eagerly helped out during their mother's effort, stapling signs on phone poles and distributing other campaign materials.

Joan also had a female campaign manager. They traveled in a donated bus, and Joan would speak wherever she had an opportunity. She made a point of *not* mentioning that her husband was an astronaut who had been to the Moon.

The initial reports on the night of the election were encouraging, but the incumbent ultimately won the election by a margin of approximately 1,000 votes. Nevertheless, Joan's efforts as a Republican were somewhat pioneering, and her campaign would inspire more than one of her children to try politics later in life.

——⚡︎⚡⚡—

Alan Shepard had not only shown the way for American space travelers, he had also shrewdly parlayed his experience into highly-successful business ventures and investments, and other astronauts, including Roosa, paid attention to Shepard's accomplishments in the world of commerce. Due to their accomplishments and fame, astronauts—particularly Moon voyagers—always had a head start or inside track regarding being hired as members of corporate boards of directors, etc. Having an astronaut in a prominent position could add to a company's prestige and clout.

Since he wasn't enthusiastic about future orbital missions, Roosa had earlier begun considering possible future career options that he could pursue when he retired from NASA and the Air Force, and after the completion of the Apollo 17 flight, followed through on his previously-cancelled plans to attend Harvard Business School, arriving on the Boston campus in 1973.

While he was there, however, he would occasionally grumble to family and friends about the plethora of "long-haired hippies" that were also enrolled as undergraduates at the legendary institution.

Back in Claremore, North East Elementary School, which had been opened in 1967, was re-named Stuart Roosa Elementary School in a ceremony held on June 12, 1975. The Apollo 14 CMP and family members attended the dedication.

——⚡︎⚡⚡—

Roosa had enough time-in-grade to retire from the Air Force at the rank of Colonel, and chose to do so, retiring from NASA at the same time in 1976.

On Stuart Roosa's final day of active duty, he flew to the four corners of the continental United States in a T-38. Starting at Ellington Air Force Base, he zoomed to the Key West Naval Air Station, Loring Air Force Base in Maine, Fairchild Air Force Base in Washington, and a Naval Air Station in San Diego before heading back to Ellington.

"We went out to Ellington to pick him up," Allen said of his father's last official flight, "and just as we were pulling into Base Operations, we saw a T-38 screaming down the main runway, just a few feet off the ground. It was my dad, buzzing the field one last time."

"And when he landed, he wasn't crying, but he was very emotional."

—⁓—

History shows that Stuart Roosa ended up in an unusual chronological position for an Apollo astronaut: Had the Apollo 18, 19, and 20 missions flown as originally planned, he might have commanded that very last mission.

While a standard/traditional rotation for crews and individuals was in place, such protocol was not set in stone, as exemplified by Shepard's flight. One unofficial rotation precedent had to do with CMPs becoming lunar mission commanders six flights later—Jim Lovell was the CMP on Apollo 8, and was the CDR for the original Apollo 14 mission, which became Apollo 13. Dave Scott had been the CMP on Apollo 9, and had walked on the Moon on the Apollo 15 mission. Likewise, John Young occupied the center seat on the Apollo 10 mission, and commanded the Apollo 16 voyage.

Doing the math shows that Apollo 14 Command Module Pilot Stuart Roosa would have been a frontline contender to be the commander of the Apollo 20 mission.

"Nothing was a 'given,' nothing was guaranteed," opined Gene Cernan, "but there's no question in my mind that (the Apollo 20 CDR) could very well have been Stu Roosa, because he would have been very qualified. I knew him pretty well; he was very capable and very conscientious. The experience he had on 14 as well as his later backup assignments meant that he could have rolled over into that left seat easily.

"But the guys that went to the Moon from Stu's group were some of the luckiest guys in the world," Cernan clarified. "Some of their peers didn't get the chance, and while some of them got to fly on Skylab, I wouldn't have traded Apollo for Skylab, and Stu, Dick Gordon, and Ron (Evans) were among those I talked with who were gratified that they'd had a seat on Apollo. Ask any middle-seat Apollo crew member, and he'll probably tell you that while he would have also liked to have gone on a *later* flight, he was grateful he got to go, and was proud of what he did."

Over time, other names, and what their assigned positions would have been, have been proffered in a murky, "what if" scenario about cancelled

Apollo missions. Mitchell has been cited, of course, along with Fred Haise, and several Original Nineteen members who had never flown on an Apollo mission, including Jack Lousma, Don Lind, Paul Weitz, Gerald Carr, and Bill Pogue. All of them would eventually fly on Skylab and/or the Shuttle, and Lind would wait 19 years—from 1966 to 1985—before flying in space.

Even Pete Conrad's name has been bandied about in the mix of astronauts who might have flown on the three cancelled missions to the Moon.

However, there remains a strong possibility that had those missions been flown, the last astronaut to leave footprints on the Moon might well have been Apollo 20's Stu Roosa, instead of Apollo 17's Gene Cernan.

POST-NASA

Business Ventures, Children's Accomplishments

Roosa's "life after NASA" began, as was the case for some other former astronauts, with business ventures that didn't work out.

Acquiring a job title that was as long as some NASA terms, Roosa became the Corporate Vice-President of International Operations for U.S. Industries, and President of the company's development office in the Middle East. The family was originally slated to live in Beirut, Lebanon, but civil war had broken out. The Roosas then had the choice of living in Cairo or Athens, and opted for the latter.

Roosa's fame as an astronaut did indeed help establish business contacts while the family was living in Greece.

"When he was doing business in the Middle East, the sheer fact that he was an astronaut got him through several 'business doors' that a normal businessman would not have been able to access," said Jack.

However, after a year, Roosa quit, and the family returned to Texas, where Stu joined Kenneth Campbell Investments in Austin. Campbell was a big game hunter, and had first befriended Roosa due to their mutual hunting interests. The investment company's primary facet at the time was commercial real estate development for large scale department stores, and an idea for the development of an electric automobile was also considered, but ultimately went nowhere.

Roosa had noticed the success that Alan Shepard and Charlie Duke had had with distributorships for Coors beer, the unique brew that was made with Rocky Mountain spring water, and was intrigued about the possibility for a distributorship for himself.

Stu and Charlie had actually been Coors fans since their astronaut days. On more than one occasion, while returning from a jaunt to the North American Rockwell's Command Module facility in Downey, California, they had landed their T-38s in El Paso for refueling. The local Coors distributor, a space buff, would bring two cases of beer out to the air facility, and the two grateful astronauts would each stow a case in the baggage pods on their respective aircraft.

Coors beer had a legendary mystique, and by the latter half of the Seventies, was increasing in popularity across the country, to the point of being bootlegged by enthusiasts into states where it wasn't being officially distributed (a massive one-shot bootlegging operation involving a semi-trailer full of Coors formed the basic plot of the 1977 hit movie *Smokey and the Bandit*, starring Burt Reynolds).

Charlie had garnered a distributorship in the San Antonio area in 1975, when territories in the Lone Star State opened up below Interstate 20. Later, Stu and other astronauts sought Coors distributorships in certain areas, all across the country.

"Stu and I both tried to get a Coors beer distributorship," recalled Jim Lovell. "He was successful, and I wasn't."

Roosa and Duke communicated over the years during their respective business ventures. By the time Roosa's effort with Campbell Investments on an electric car fizzled, Duke had sold his beer business and was also working with Campbell, albeit in real estate. When Coors started opening distribution franchises in the rest of the South, Roosa sought Duke's and Shepard's advice; Duke encouraged Roosa to apply. The acquisition of the franchise along the Gulf coast in Mississippi, Alabama, and the Florida Panhandle gave the Roosas a chance to move to Joan's home state.

Gulf Coast Coors opened in Gulfport, Mississippi in 1981. For many years, the distributorship's accounting would be handled by the Oklahoma company headed up by Stu's brother Danny.

"I was really excited for Stu," said Duke. "I thought it would be a great 'fit' for him. Not only did he enjoy a beer, he was a great salesman and was very outgoing. A beer distributor needs to be socially-involved in the community, and Stu and Joan had all of that covered."

Stu's association with Coors would lead to him traveling abroad on business trips regarding other spirits. In September of 1983, he and Joan visited Italy, touring the vineyards of an Italian wine company, and successfully negotiating a distributorship for their products in portions of the U.S.

An Italian newspaper interviewed Stu, who recalled honeymooning in Italy (which, as noted earlier, was actually a TDY assignment soon after the Roosas married), as well as bringing his entire family there in 1976. He also noted seeing that nation from orbit from the Apollo 14 Command Module.

Someone knew of Roosa's interest in hunting, so he was presented with a shotgun engraved with his name, as well as the Apollo 14 patch illustration. He was also awarded an honorary doctorate in the Brotherhood of Nicholas, an Italian business society organization.

216

The Roosas moved into a home on a golf course in Gulfport. Joan was a corporate officer of Gulf Coast Coors, but she also enjoyed her garden club, her bridge club, and other social activities.

―∿―

Of course, Joan and Stu were proud that all three sons became military officers. Chris became an officer in the Marine Reserve, Jack graduated from the Air Force Academy and became a pilot, and Allen went to West Point, and also graduated from Army Ranger School after he was commissioned.

"My father was a patriot first, and an astronaut second," Jack summarized, "His love for this country would, today, make most people blush. When he saw all three of his sons in the military, I don't think he had a more proud moment."

―∿―

The year in Greece had included Chris's last year of high school, and he had worked for Klineburger's safari company in Africa that summer. When the family returned to the States, he began attending the University of Mississippi, later transferring to the University of Texas, He also joined the Marine Reserves, obtaining a commission.

In the late Eighties, Chris began working in the Nation's Capital for the Secretary of Defense, and did advance work for Vice-President George Bush. Some of the earlier assignments he had when he was on active duty with the Marines included Okinawa and Central America.

Chris was deployed to the Middle East during the first Gulf War ("Desert Storm") in 1991. Stu rarely came into the Gulf Coast Coors office during the conflagration, remaining at home to monitor the event on television.

Inspired by his work in Washington, Chris decided to get into politics himself. In a 1988 campaign for Congress, as a Republican, he managed to get Al Shepard, Ed Mitchell, and his father together for a memorable fund-raiser. Chris's effort was unsuccessful, as was a subsequent attempt in 1992. Mitchell recalled that the '88 occasion was the last time he saw Roosa.

And Stu had considered Shepard to be a "commander" even after the Apollo 14 mission. He spoke with Ed Buckbee about his admiration for Shepard when the Apollo 14 commander was inducted into the Astronaut Hall of Fame in 1990. The six surviving Mercury astronauts had helped to found that institution.

"Stu still had a high regard for Shepard," said Buckbee, "and didn't like anybody taking shots at Shepard or making derogatory remarks about him. Shepard was very supportive of his crew, and they stayed in touch."

—⁓—

Jack graduated from the Air Force Academy in 1984, and won his wings in 1985.

Though retired, Stu would still put on his Air Force uniform for special events. One of the most meaningful of those types of occasions was at Jack's pilot school graduation ceremony at Columbus Air Force Base in Mississippi, when he pinned his own pilot wings, which had flown to the Moon, onto the chest of his second son.

"Needless to say, ol' Papa was awfully proud," Roosa would later recall.

After graduating from pilot school, Jack remained at Columbus as an instructor. Later, he cross-trained to F-16s, which he flew for the remainder of his career.

Since both Stu and Jack were career fighter pilots, they often talked about their respective experiences, but most of the time"...he would go into 'receive' mode, and I would go into 'transmit' mode about my adventures," said Jack. "He didn't necessarily share a lot of what he went through; I didn't get a lot of tidbits about his time in the service. He was more of a sounding board for me."

"One of the biggest thrills for me was when I was a first-assignment instructor pilot at Columbus; I was working for the wing commander at the time. I mentioned to him that an Order of Daedalians (a fraternal order of aviators) meeting was coming up, and I had been asked about getting my father to come up and speak. The wing commander thought it was a great idea, and then I asked about getting my father into a formation flight. We checked the regulations, and the best we could come up with was that father and son couldn't fly in the same airplane—the T-38's a two-seater. So they didn't let us in the same plane; I flew with a friend in one airplane, and another friend flew with my father in the other. We took off from Columbus, went north, spent an hour doing acrobatics and formation flying. And don't forget that my father had *so much time* in T-38s from his NASA days; at that point, I had about 1000 hours in 38s, so we both felt very comfortable in that model. And it was such a joy to be able to look from one cockpit to the other, and to see my dad with the visor down, watching what I was doing. I'm sure he felt the same pride and sense of commitment that I did."

When Jack was going through F-16 training at Luke AFB (where his father had also trained), Roosa also gave a talk there, and Jack and his father had the opportunity get into simulators and fly combat missions against each other, "…but that was a little unfair, because I had just finished an intense flying course in the F-16, and he had to 'fly-by-wire.' Nevertheless, I was very impressed with his flying ability, even at that advanced age. He'd never been in that type of cockpit; he was a natural."

Jack and his wife would provide Stu and Joan with the only two grandchildren Stu would ever know.

—∿∿—

And even during their own military days, the Roosa boys kept their father's fame to themselves, and let their own actions speak for themselves. Allen recalled an incident from the time of his pending graduation from West Point, when his longtime friend and roommate discovered who Allen's father was. A captain came by the two seniors' room, asking if Allen's father, who would be attending the graduation ceremony, had any special requirements or requests. Allen said "No, sir," and the officer departed, after which the roommate said "What the hell was that about?"

When Allen explained that his father had been an astronaut and had gone to the Moon, the roommate demanded to know why he'd never been told about Allen's father's history, to which Allen replied, "You never asked."

During his time in the Army, Allen would also receive a set of wings, upon graduating from the Army's elite and rugged Airborne Ranger school. Those, too, were pinned on by his father at a graduation ceremony.

Allen was stationed in Germany from 1988-1992. The Berlin Wall came down during his assignment, and Stu and Joan came to visit during Allen's last year there. They went to Berlin for an astronaut function, then to Holland, being as how Roosa was of Dutch heritage.

Allen found a pile of tulips in a field, and his father abruptly did a backwards "snow angel"/Nestea plunge" into the mound of flowers. The contented look on Stu's face was almost child-like. Life was good.

After his tour in Germany, Allen was assigned to teach ROTC at the University of Tampa. On more than one occasion, Stu would ask his son to escort some friends and/or business acquaintances, including members of the Shikar Safari Club, to a Shuttle launch on the other side of the Florida peninsula.

—∿∿—

One of Roosa's favorite personal accomplishments was teaching Rosemary to fly. She began taking instructions when she was 16, and got her license when she was 18.

"My parents thought I might like to be a commercial airline pilot or a corporate pilot, not a stewardess," Rosemary recalled. "Back then, they were encouraging me to look at non-traditional occupations, but didn't think the military would be the way to go."

While the Roosas were living in Austin, more than one Roosa offspring wanted to learn to fly, out of an aero club located at nearby Bergstrom Air Force Base. Rosemary recalled that for all of his experience, her father still had to get an instructor's license, and his daughter was a quick learner.

Rosemary would later attain a Bachelor's degree in political science from Sophie Newcomb Memorial College in New Orleans, which was a part of Tulane University. She had been accepted at Southern Methodist University in Dallas as well, but Joan was delighted that her daughter ultimately chose to attend a women's college, as she had done herself.

She later worked for Mississippi Congressman Trent Lott, and then went to work for her parents at Gulf Coast Coors in July of 1988. She gave her two weeks' notice to Lott's office during the Congressman's (ultimately successful) campaign for U.S. Senator.

"Daddy loved a challenge," she remembered, "and that included the challenge of Gulf Coast Coors—getting a business off the ground and seeing it succeed. But I think when he asked me to come to work for the company, he had gotten a little bored with the day-to-day operation."

—⁓—

The Roosas maintained a regular religious regimen, even as the children grew up and began to spread their own wings. Even when one of the sons happened to come home to Gulfport for a weekend (and might be heading out to some of the local clubs on a Saturday night), he would be reminded by Joan that they had church the next morning.

Dotty and Charlie Duke each had a religious re-awakening experience after the Apollo 16 flight. For Dotty, a re-commitment to Christianity occurred in October of 1975, while Charlie's spiritual life got back on track in April of 1978. Many persons think their return to being committed Christians was the primary reason Charlie sold his beer distributorship, but he had actually sold the distributorship a month before he made his own choice to re-focus his life on Christ. Duke had gotten out of the beer business due to frustration and boredom rather than any religious influence that might have been germinating, and he equated the chronology of his Coors days to the way the Apollo program had been a dynamic experience, followed by the plodding Shuttle program, which had dampened his enthusiasm. One of his first moves following his re-commitment to Christianity was to set up a prison ministry.

"I knew Stu and Joan were devout Catholics," Duke remembered, "but we didn't discuss (religion) much before our flights. After I became a believer, they were living in Gulfport, and we had a lot of deep discussions about our faith...and he *was* a man of faith. Sometimes those discussions went on late into the evening. Catholicism and Protestantism still have the same Jesus; it's just a different way of worshipping."

Stu would also call Duke at times with specific prayer requests, and they would often pray together over the phone. Of course, the two pilots continued to talk flying as well. When the Dukes drove from Texas to Atlanta, they would often stay with Roosas in Gulfport. Dotty recalled that Joan's culinary skills remained undiminished over the years:

"She was always a great cook, and when we'd go through Gulfport, she'd make a gourmet dinner, a lot of times with shrimp, or crab. She and Stu were very generous and hospitable, and there were times when we went fishing out in the Gulf.

The Roosas also remained close to the Hartsfields, as well as Walt Cunningham and his wife Dot. The Hartsfields and Cunninghams would also visit the Roosas in Gulfport, as would Roosa's old rockhound friend Farouk El-Baz.

El-Baz and his wife Pat considered one visit with Stu and Joan to have been a highlight of a lifetime, as the Roosas took their visitors on an extended trip to New Orleans.

—⁓—

Stu and other family members participated in the filming of a 1989 film on the Apollo program titled *The Other Side Of The Moon*. The well-made documentary proffered the comments of eight Apollo astronauts on their experiences during their respective space voyages, as well as how their lives had evolved after returning to Earth. In alphabetical order, the astronauts were Buzz Aldrin, Alan Bean, Pete Conrad, Jim Irwin, Ed Mitchell, Stu Roosa, Rusty Schweickart, and Al Worden. One segment also presented some observations by Russian cosmonaut Aleksandr Aleksandrov, in an ABC News television appearance with Schweickart.

All of the Apollo astronauts put forth their recollections and opinions in a straightforward manner, and most of them waxed philosophical at various points in their respective remarks. Their viewpoints regarding their post-Apollo days were eloquent, as each space veteran sought to validate why he had chosen certain paths in life following his departure from NASA.

Some facets of some of the profiles were, perhaps, expected. Irwin, a born-again Christian, was shown in eastern Turkey near Mt. Ararat, searching for Noah's Ark; Worden discussed why he had opted to write a book of poetry (*Hello, Earth—Greetings From Endeavour*); Mitchell offered details about his epiphany (although that term was not used) on the homeward voyage of Apollo 14.

Roosa had plenty to say about his solo orbits around Luna, citing the intense darkness when there was no sunlight and/or Earthlight. The Apollo 14 CMP also opened up about his training for the possibility of returning to Earth by himself. Stu hinted, however, that he would have attempted to rescue the LM crew if they had managed to blast off from the surface, explaining that it would have been a last resort for a CMP, and that while the crew didn't discuss such a morbid scenario much, the remote possibility still existed.

Most of the astronauts discussed the gradual subsiding of the accolades, parades, honors, etc., that many of them had experienced, and the need to get on with a different facet of life and a different career.

Roosa admitted to a "letdown," contradicting, to some extent, his usual public attitude. He opined that every astronaut had such feelings, noting that "...some tried to ignore it, some tried to laugh it off...I *did* sense this feeling of 'Now that I've been to the top of the mountain, where do I go from here?,' and I resolved that I could go on and accomplish other goals. At the age of 37, (I was) certainly too young to stop trying, stop working and stop seeking new goals."

Some of Roosa's segments were somewhat unique, as they also offered commentary from three generations of Roosas, including Joan, Dewey, and Jack (who was now an Air Force pilot himself, and was shown being greeted by his father when he landed at the Gulfport Air National Guard airfield in a T-38).

Dewey recalled the Wright brothers' first flight, and remembered his own first flight in airplane in Texas.

"They were charging two dollars for the flight," the elder Roosa said with a chuckle. "Lindbergh flew the Atlantic, and I could never forget that. It was in May, 1927."

He appeared to get emotional when he recalled watching the Apollo 14 launch with his son onboard, describing what it was like with "...your 'very own' laying up there, 360 feet up before blastoff."

Joan discussed the travails of being, for all intents and purposes, a single mom during the week until the astronaut husbands came home on Friday night to broken appliances and other standard family problems.

Mrs. Roosa also opined with a laugh that the term "Original Wives" might have first referred to the spouses of Mercury astronauts, but now it could applied to those women who had actually stayed married to astronauts.

("I don't really want to delve into all of that," said Ed Mitchell, when asked about the divorce rate among astronauts. "We weren't trained to be quasi-celebrities, and some of us didn't handle it very well.")

Jack recalled being inspired to be a pilot himself when he was around eight or nine years old, and watched his father take off in a T-38 from Patrick Air Force Base near the Kennedy Space Center "...on a pitch-black night, and I watched the light disappear into the clouds. It looked exciting and challenging, and I said to myself 'I think that's what I want to do.'"

Gulf Coast Coors was profiled in the documentary, with Stu proudly pointing out that his company had expanded into the distribution of wine coolers and other beverages besides Coors beer.

—∿∿∿—

Ron Evans, the Original Nineteen astronaut with whom Stu had traded prime and backup CMP assignments on Apollo 14 and Apollo 17, died of a heart attack on April 7, 1990.

Stu's parents had eventually ended their nomadic travels with a trailer, and had returned to Oklahoma. They lived in a mobile home in Oologah before finally moving into Claremore. Dewey Roosa died on September 3, 1990, at the age of 91. His widow, Lorine, passed away on July 8, 1993 at the age of 84.

—∿∿∿—

Stu still gave a myriad of speeches each year, and had developed an eloquent speaking style, probably because he was much more comfortable with audiences, and he always enjoyed sharing his experiences. As always, his patriotism would shine through in such appearances, as he would note that there were six American flags that had been planted on the Moon, and that no other country in the world could make such a claim. He never dwelt on why he never walked on the Moon; he emphasized that he was just proud to have gone.

"I was amazed at Daddy's speeches," said Rosemary, who would occasionally accompany her father to speaking engagements. "He would never write formal notes about what he was going to do, and no two speeches were ever alike. I learned something new whenever he spoke. He never had a 'canned' speech."

However, even after his retirement from NASA and the Air Force, Roosa still had to answer the inevitable questions Apollo CMPs would get from space enthusiasts and others about the "so-close-yet-so-far" notion of having been in orbit around the Moon, but having never walked on it. One response of his would be that CMPs who orbited the Moon solo were actually in a more exclusive club than moonwalkers, and such an assignment—soloing—was what pilots loved doing.

There was also a similar inquiry along the lines of "Do you feel like you missed something because you were almost there, but didn't get to walk on the Moon?" Roosa's standard reply would be that first of all, it was very competitive to get selected for a mission at all, so every Apollo astronaut who had flown felt lucky to have been picked. Roosa emphasized that before he flew, he had no personal preference as to what his job would be on his first mission, which would turn out to be his *only* mission—he would just be thrilled to be selected. His normal answer was "You don't worry about what seat you're sitting in on your first mission; you're just thankful that you got the opportunity to go into space."

And Roosa believed in that premise. Most of the astronauts realized that the program was not going to go on forever, and there had, of course, already been mission cancellations by the time Apollo 14 launched.

Roosa even had to answer quasi-philosophical questions along the lines of whether or not the human race was the only intelligent species in the galaxy or Universe. His typical response would be a statistical reference to the billions of galaxies in existence, and the stereotypical billions or trillions of stars in each galaxy, which meant (to him) that humans weren't alone in the cosmos.

—◁◁◁—

Over the years, Stu also would still occasionally refer to the "could-it-have-happened" scenario of having commanded the Apollo 20 mission, albeit in a usually-private and wisecracking manner. However, his outward/public attitude reflected more of a sense of lament about the termination of the Apollo program before its original schedule had been fully completed, rather than whether or not he might have gone on another mission, just as had been the collective attitude around the Astronaut Office in the early Seventies.

Charlie Duke probably spoke for the entire Apollo astronaut corps when he opined that the cancellation of the last three missions had been "a big mistake…a tragedy. They had the hardware; everything was in place. All they had to do was pay the operational costs. I think the reason NASA stopped Apollo was political more than anything else. There's no question that we were all disappointed."

Stu had been reminded of what he considered to be the premature end of the Apollo saga in an unusual location during the Christmas season of 1976, when his family went to Egypt. The Roosas stayed at the Nile Hilton and visited the Pyramids, then flew to Luxor to tour the burial sites of Pharaohs, as well as other ancient sites.

"We were touring the Valley of the Kings area with a guide," Allen recalled, "and one fascinating item was an obelisk that was incomplete. It had been engraved from the top down, with all kinds of symbols, and for whatever reason, the construction had just stopped."

Years later, Roosa would liken the Apollo program to the obelisk at Luxor, comparing the ancient Egyptian dynasties to the United States as the most advanced nations/civilizations of their respective times. Roosa's perspective was that America had gotten to the point to where it could go to the Moon as a matter of routine, but had abruptly stopped, just like the artisans who had been constructing the Egyptian obelisk. Just as modern-day historians speculate as to why the obelisk wasn't completed, future historians might wonder why the Apollo program wasn't completed.

More than one of the Roosa children echoed the sentiments of Charlie Duke and other astronauts about the Apollo program being terminated before its originally-scheduled completion.

"He never said 'I didn't get my ride,'" said Allen, referring to the fact that his father didn't walk on the Moon. "I never heard him complain, and there was no 'sour grapes.' He knew he was lucky to have gotten a flight, but he thought that to have stopped the program the way it happened made no sense."

"My father was disappointed that the (Apollo) space program had been discontinued at its particular stopping point," Chris echoed. "He would talk about all of the advances in technology—computers, heart monitors—that the space program had contributed to, and he wished that people could be made aware of all of the significant breakthroughs that had been made."

Roosa would impart the same perspective to writer Andy Chaikin, when Chaikin was interviewing the Apollo 14 CMP for his book *A Man on the Moon*, which was the primary source for the HBO mini-series *From the Earth to the Moon*.

Chaikin would recall that Stu was "...wistful, not melancholy" about the Apollo program having come to a halt when it did, and in a memorable analogy, which was probably inspired by the obelisk in Egypt, Roosa compared the trio of Saturn V assemblies on display at the Johnson Space Center, the Kennedy Space Center, and the U.S. Space & Rocket Center in Huntsville "...to toppled monuments from an extinct civilization," Chaikin said.

And while Roosa tended to remain publicly reticent concerning his personal perspective on whether he would have returned to the Moon on one of the Apollo missions that had been cancelled, he would occasionally refer to the leftover Saturn V on its side at the Kennedy Space Center as

"Apollo 20" or "my rocket," in asides to family members or close friends. NASA records indicate that the three remaining Moon rocket displays are actually made up from various stages designated for various missions or as test models, but Roosa was sometimes privately proprietary about the one in Florida.

———ᴡᴡ———

Roosa attended more than one reunion for former astronauts over the years. In 1978, many of the veteran space travelers, including all three crew members of Apollo 14, met at the Johnson Space Center, and the following year, an event was staged in Las Vegas to note the tenth anniversary of the Apollo 11 moon landing, followed by a party hosted at former President Richard Nixon's home in San Clemente, California.

"We went to the Dunes Hotel in Las Vegas, played golf, and had a great time," Al Worden said of the Vegas get-together, but the Apollo 15 CMP did not go to the San Clemente event.

In the late Eighties, Stu joined the Association of Space Explorers (ASE), an organization of astronauts from all nations, the idea for which had been developed in the early Eighties by his old socio-political opposite, Rusty Schweickart, and several Soviet cosmonauts and space officials.

The organization had gotten off to an awkward start, through no fault of its own, according to Ed Mitchell, as visits to the U.S. by Soviet cosmonauts and other cultural exchanges were banned by President Ronald Reagan following the shooting down of a South Korean airliner by a Soviet fighter plane in September of 1983.

But it was actually a 1990 incident that is the most vivid recollection of Schweickart's concerning Roosa.

"My major memory of Stu which stands out is that we were *very* far apart politically" Schweickart remembered, "and when I was organizing and running the ASE, he was certain I was a 'Commie-pinko turncoat.' He attended his first ASE Congress in Riyadh, Saudi Arabia, in 1990, somewhat with the intent of 'ripping it up'."

"Instead, in a very emotional and touching moment, Stu stated publicly that he was blown away by what we were doing, and while reserving the right to strongly disagree with me, he gave me full credit for getting this amazing organization up and running. It was a very powerful moment, and I always admired Stu after that, for not only admitting that he had misjudged what I had done with ASE, but he admitted it very publicly, and became one of our most loyal and active members."

In mid-1991, Stu, Joan and Rosemary went to the Soviet Union, as did other astronauts, to commemorate the 30th anniversary of the flight of

Yuri Gagarin. They visited the cosmonauts' training center at Star City near Moscow, as well as the Baikonur Cosmodrome launch facilities in Kazakhstan. They did not, however, visit the usual tourist sights in Moscow proper. The Soviet Union was beginning to collapse, and there were safety concerns around the capital of the U.S.S.R. The gigantic nemesis of the United States would implode later the same year, and numerous new democracies sprang from the ideological rubble.

Decline, Departure

1994: Jack had last seen his father sometime in 1992, due to a deployment in Germany. When that assignment was completed in 1994, he went directly to Fighter Weapons School at Nellis Air Force Base in Nevada. The young F-16 pilot received some photos of his father around that time, and was struck by how frail he looked.

In April, Roosa gave a speech in San Antonio, and both Joan and Rosemary accompanied him. An opportunity came up to go on a turkey shoot at the Stan Studer Ranch with the Roosas' old friend Bert Klineburger, and while the hunt was successful, Klineburger was concerned about his friend's wellbeing.

"Joan and Rosemary both shot turkeys," he recalled. "You could look at Stu's face; he just didn't look healthy."

Allen was stationed in Tampa, teaching ROTC, and attended an event at the Kennedy Space Center in summer of 1994 with his parents.

"I noticed he didn't look too good," Allen recalled.

Rosemary, who worked with her parents daily, also began to notice a decline in her father's health.

A reunion of Apollo astronauts at the Experimental Aircraft Association (EAA) Annual Convention and Fly-In in Oshkosh, Wisconsin in July of 1994 would be the last time many space veterans would see Stu Roosa.

Marilyn and Jim Lovell invited Joan and Stu to attend the event with them. The Lovells now resided in the Chicago area, and the Roosas flew into the Windy City, then the foursome flew to Oshkosh in Lovell's private plane.

EAA official Dick Knapinski was a media/public relations specialist at the time, having joined the organization in 1992. He recalled that the original idea was that the EAA wanted to commemorate the 25th anniversary of the Apollo 11 Moon landing. There had been previous events at early Fly-Ins honoring astronauts, but the "Salute to Apollo" in 1994 had at least one crew member from every manned Apollo mission,

7 through 17, including the complete crew of Apollo 8 and Apollo 11. Roosa was the only Apollo 14 crew member to attend, but he and Charlie Duke hung out with each other, perusing displays and riding the shuttle bus together.

A large evening program was hosted by David Hartman of ABC's "Good Morning, America" television show, and other smaller forums were held.

Other NASA veterans who weren't astronauts also attended, including Farouk El-Baz, and Knapinski noted that flight controller Gene Kranz was also at the event.

Opinions varied as to Roosa's appearance.

"I don't recall that he looked frail; he seemed like the same ol' Stu to me," said Walt Cunningham. Charlie Duke had the same opinion of Roosa at Oshkosh.

Farouk El-Baz recalled that he had been advised of the event by Andy Chaikin.

"I decided to go because I had not seen the guys in many years," El-Baz remembered. "It was a good gathering from all points of view. Stu had begun to look frail then, but was still quite lively. We spoke about the good old days, and bemoaned NASA's regressive path."

The geologist would be photographed with four Apollo CMPs—Michael Collins, Dick Gordon, Roosa, and Al Worden.

The next month, Stu, Joan, and Rosemary went to Russia again, on behalf of the Association of Space Explorers. This time, they were ultimately able to visit Moscow. Roosa and his daughter stood in the very middle of Red Square, perusing a panorama of historic buildings that included the Kremlin, St. Basil's Cathedral, and the gigantic GUM department store.

"After seeing this, I sure would have hated to have blown it up," he said softly, almost as if he was speaking to himself. Most likely, he was referencing his nuclear delivery assignment when he had been with the 510th Fighter Squadron in the mid-Fifties.

"I didn't really understand what he was talking about at the moment," Rosemary remembered, "but I could tell that the impact and the feelings he was experiencing were profound."

And one night while on the same trip, Stu seemed to be in an unusual mood, wanting to recall facets of his Apollo days that he usually didn't discuss.

"We were flying out to Siberia," said Rosemary, "and I could tell Daddy was wanting to talk about the (Apollo 1) fire with me—the feelings he had afterwards. But I could also tell it was painful, so I stopped him. Later, I wished I had not done that."

Each of the Roosa children had memories of their father's last days.

Stu, Joan, and Rosemary drove to the D.C. area to Chris's residence for Thanksgiving, and Stu complained of a stomach ache en route. They made plans to swing by a park that had already been decorated with Christmas lights on the return trip.

He started feeling worse the day before Thanksgiving. Chris didn't have his own doctor but had a health management organization (HMO) managed care plan. He finally took his father to Northern Virginia Community Hospital, where he himself had gone once when he had the flu. Tests were run, and the diagnosis quickly came back as pancreatitis, the deadly inflammation of the pancreas.

Chris recalled what had happened to his father as analogous to an aircraft accident—"a sequence of small events that led to a catastrophic failure. We were basically told 'Get him into a hospital *now*.'"

Roosa was transferred to Fairfax General Hospital.

"I hadn't noticed that Stu had any kind of problems at all," said Charlie Duke, "so I was really stunned when Chris called on the day Stu was admitted, and said 'Daddy's in the hospital, and he's really sick.' Stu's parents had lived long lives, and I'd told him he had some great genes. Chris asked us to start praying, and we prayed hard."

"I don't think we realized the severity of pancreatitis," Rosemary said, "and I would go sit and talk with him for several hours, but somebody had to tend to the business of Gulf Coast Coors. I told him we had payroll coming up, so I flew home to take care of company business. When that decision was made, he was sitting up in a chair, and was talking. Just before I flew back to Mississippi, one of the doctors had asked him 'When you get out of here, can you come speak at my child's school?'"

Rosemary would stay in Gulfport for about a week, but the family reports regarding her father's condition began to get increasingly ominous.

"I got a first call from Chris that Dad was sick," Allen recalled. "Then he called again, saying that I needed to grab a suit, because it looked like Dad wasn't going to survive."

Jack was participating at Fighter Weapons School at Nellis AFB, Nevada, and remembered his last conversation with his father:

"Fighter Weapons School is an incredibly intense five and a half months. You literally live on the cutting edge of packaged training—very long days, a lot of pressure-filled flights. I got a call after Thanksgiving Day that he was doing poorly, but we conversed on the phone. I could tell that he was medicated, because he was talking more rapidly than he normally did. We talked a lot about flying since I was going through Weapons School at the time, and my dad was a passionate aviator, so he always got a charge out of flying. I don't want to sound egotistical, but he was very proud of the fact that I was a fighter pilot like he was. To keep his mind off of what was going on, we talked a lot about that. My dad was never one to complain about his own health. If he was in pain, you'd never know it. If he understood the seriousness of his final illness, he never communicated it to me, but he was always like that."

Roosa was placed into an induced coma soon afterwards, and Rosemary returned to Washington. Joan was struggling with her husband being in such a helpless condition.

Jack flew into D.C. when Roosa was transferred to Fairfax General Hospital, but Stu was unconscious the entire time, and Jack returned to Nellis. It appeared that Roosa's body functions were beginning to shut down, and pneumonia was creeping in. His children began conversing about post-mortem contingency plans, if such plans were needed.

"There was no sense in me just sitting there, day by day," Jack recalled, "and I thought it would be practical for me to go back to Nellis."

Late at night on December 11th, Rosemary was talking tenderly to her comatose father, even though Roosa couldn't respond in a demonstrable way.

"I had a feeling that he was not going to make it much longer," Rosemary recalled, "and I wanted to 'let him go,' so to speak."

"So I told him, 'Daddy, your daughter loves you very much.' At that point a tear welled up in his eye, and that's when I knew he heard me."

"I flew back (to Nellis) on a Friday," said Jack, "and did some mission planning on Sunday for Monday. I got a call at about 4:30 a.m. that my dad was gone. I was supposed to be lead in a large exercise, and managed to get out of it."

—⁓—

Stuart Allen Roosa, Colonel, USAF (Retired) breathed his last at dawn on December 12, 1994. Logistics were immediately implemented to bury the Moon pilot with full military honors in Arlington National Cemetery, just across the Potomac River from Washington, on December 16th.

Chris used some of his D.C. connections to arrange a "Missing Man" flyover by Air Force fighter jets. Ed Mitchell recalls that such a procedure was standard protocol for deceased astronauts, and the Arlington ceremony meant that air traffic in and around the nearby Washington National Airport would be shut down for several minutes to allow a straight-in approach by the fighter squadron.

The Missing Man formation was to be comprised of F-15 Eagle aircraft. Jack, who had flown Missing Man formations himself, called the F-15 squadron the night before, identified himself as an F-16 pilot, and thanked the duty officer in advance for the effort.

The forecast for December 16th looked lousy—a low ceiling and typical dreary weather for that time of year in D.C. appeared to be in the offing.

Standing on Chris's back porch the night before the funeral, Allen looked up at the sky and said of the ominous forecast, "Well, Dad's up there now, and he's got a hot line to the Man, and if He wants to make it happen, it'll happen."

The next morning, the sun rose through clear blue skies in the D.C. area.

The service was a Catholic funeral mass, and was held in the Post Chapel at Fort Myer, next to the Arlington cemetery. The honor guard performed its duties with impeccable precision as it brought the casket into the chapel. Roosa's funeral happened to be the first full-military-honors funeral, complete with a horse-drawn caisson, that Charlie Duke had ever attended.

Each of the Roosa children had a part of the funeral. Chris gave his father a military salute, and Jack read the classic flying paean "High Flight." Allen gave some remarks, as did Rosemary. Al Shepard and Ed Mitchell spoke, and Charlie Duke read the Scripture. Attendees included Stu's brother Danny and his family, Hank Hartsfield, Marilyn and Jim Lovell, Gene Cernan, Al Worden, Farouk El-Baz, and Neil Armstrong. Representatives from NASA, the office of Secretary of the Air Force was in attendance. Congressman Jim Sensenbrenner, Republican of Wisconsin, represented the Congressional Committee on Science and Technology (Sensenbrenner served on the Sub-committee on Science and Aeronautics).

The caisson took the casket to a site not far from the Tomb of the Unknown Soldier. The ceremony at the gravesite included the expected 21-gun salute and the Missing Man flyover.

"Much of the funeral was a blur," Chris said succinctly. Joan held up well during the ceremony.

Perhaps surprisingly, the Missing Man formation wasn't what "got" to Jack, emotionally. Instead, it was the playing of "Taps," which is universal at all military funerals, but his experience at the Air Force Academy had given him special reason to revere "Taps" even more.

"The Academy had an annual ceremony," he detailed. "The entire cadet wing—some 2500 people—would form up, and there would be a roll call of Academy graduates who had died the previous year. At the end of the ceremony, 'Taps' would be played. It was emotional then, so hearing it at Dad's funeral really hit home. It gets to me even now."

A post-funeral reception was held in the bar of the Officer's Club at Fort Myer, which is the base of operations for Arlington's honor guards and burial teams.

While it is an Army installation, Fort Myer is also important in aviation history. In 1908, the post had been the first location of the flight of an airplane at a military installation, when Orville Wright took an early airplane aloft on several demonstration flights.

"My parents met in an Officer's Club bar," said Chris, "and we sent him off from an Officer's Club bar."

———

"His death was a surprise to all of us," said Gene Cernan. "It stunned me; I'd seen him at Oshkosh, and it seemed like it was just a few weeks or months later that we were burying him at Arlington."

Charlie Duke agreed with the opinion of the Roosa children that he and Stu were best friends.

"We were close from '64 until he died," Duke would remember wistfully over a decade and a half after Roosa had crossed the way. "We enjoyed doing things together outdoors like hunting, and we shared the same values. But we also respected each other professionally, and were pleased with the success of each other's careers."

———

Some months after Stu's death, Jack was in a movie theater watching *Mr. Holland's Opus*, a film about a school orchestra conductor, starring Richard Dreyfuss. There was a funeral scene about one of the instructor's pupils that had been killed in Vietnam, and the former student was buried with full military honors at Arlington National Cemetery, and the ceremony included a 21-gun salute and the playing of "Taps."

And the haunting, plaintive trumpet melody caused Jack to become overwhelmed, yet again.

Aftermath

The headstone for Stuart Roosa's grave at Arlington National Cemetery included an illustration of a complete Apollo/Saturn V vehicle. The gravesite is close to some of the most-walked paths through the cemetery, and the eye-catching image of the massive rocket makes it likely that hundreds of visitors per day see it.

Joan never remarried following Stu's death, and didn't particularly have any suitors. She and Rosemary traveled extensively together. One particular facet of their mother-daughter travel experiences was Joan's insistence that she did not want to be in Gulfport during the Christmas holiday season, as Christmas of 1994 had been too hard on her, so they were usually gone during that time of the year.

She would begin to experience her own health problems, such as high blood pressure and tachycardia, and would be seen in a wheelchair at some public events. Hospitalized on more than occasion for something that doctors thought might have been terminal, Joan would rebound, and she and Rosemary would go on another trip.

Looking back on his father's experiences as well as his own military adventures, Chris compared one of his 1991 Desert Storm combat sights to the launch of Apollo 14 two decades earlier, recalling, "I've seen two things in my life that I don't think they'll ever be able to convey realistically on TV. One is a Saturn launch—I've also seen Shuttle launches but even those are hard to 'relate to' on a small screen. In both launches, the intensity of the flame was so bright, it almost hurt your eyes."

"The other thing was the burning oil fields in Kuwait (in the 1991 Gulf War). It was unimaginable how huge that was."

Chris continued his government work in D.C., and would be deployed with the Marines again, following the September 11, 2001 terrorism conflagration. He would have numerous assignments to Iraq and Afghanistan. Among his duties were operations of remotely-piloted aircraft, and when possible, he would update his friends and family from his station via e-mail newsletter.

Jack put in a full 20 years in the Air Force, and retired in 2004, taking a job with the Raytheon Corporation in Tucson, Arizona. One of his primary projects for a number of years was an upgrade version of the venerable Sidewinder air-to-air missile.

Allen was discharged from the Army in 1995, and went to work with Gulf Coast Coors. In 1998, the company was sold, and he relocated to the Orlando area, where he works for another beverage distributor, and has gotten involved in local politics. One of his political associates is Paul Mitchell, adopted son of Ed Mitchell.

Rosemary was appointed as president of Gulf Coast Coors by her mother soon after Stu's death. She later attended Harvard Business School, taking the Owner/President Management program, which began on January 31, 1997, the 26th anniversary of the launch of Apollo 14.

After the beer distributorship was sold, Rosemary enrolled in a Master's program at William Carey University (located near Stu and Joan's house) in Industrial & Organizational Psychology. She graduated on May 23, 2004, her mother's 70th birthday, and in 2005, began teaching various psychology courses at a satellite campus of Tulane in Biloxi, known as the Tulane University School of Continuing Studies.

She also began planning on chronicling and tracking down the "Moon trees" and their subsequent generations, in memory of her father.

She had saved the breast feathers and tail feathers of the tom turkey that she shot near San Antonio in April of 1994, on the final hunt that her father had done with Bert Klineburger, and gave those items to a Biloxi taxidermist to be mounted, along with other hunting trophies of hers, in July of 2005. The next month, Hurricane Katrina did serious damage to the taxidermist's business, and all of Rosemary's items, including the turkey breast feathers and tail feathers, were lost.

―――

Leukemia claimed the life of Alan Shepard on July 21, 1998, and a NASA memorial service was held at the Johnson Space Center on August 1st. Shepard's wife Louise died just over a month later, on August 25th.

The Shepards were cremated, and their family held a service to scatter their ashes into a cove of the Pacific Ocean, near their home in Pebble Beach, California on November 18th. Chris Roosa attended the family ceremony, as did Ed Buckbee, who had formed a strong friendship with Shepard in their post-Apollo years. In 1982, Buckbee had founded the renowed Space Camp in Huntsville as a motivational tool for young science and technology students.

A flight of Navy F-18 fighters performed a Missing Man formation, after which two Navy Sea Hawk helicopters dispersed the ashes of the Shepards (one from each aircraft).

Joan and all four children assembled at Arlington National Cemetery again on February 9, 2005, the thirty-fourth anniversary of the Apollo 14 splashdown, to plant a second-generation Moon tree, a sycamore. The event honored not only Stuart Roosa, but all deceased astronauts, including the crews of Apollo 1 and the *Challenger* and *Columbia* Space Shuttles.

The ceremony included remarks from Christopher as the family representative, NASA Administrator Sean O'Keefe, and NASA Associate Administrator William Readdy. Other facets of the event include a flyover by an Air Force fighter squadron, an honor guard, and an Air Force band. The tree was planted near the Tomb of the Unknown Soldier, and was just up the hill from Roosa's grave.

In 2004, NASA had begun an "Ambassadors of Exploration" program that presented early American astronauts with a small Moon rock encased in acrylic, to be displayed at an institution of the astronauts' choice. Examples were also presented to the families of deceased astronauts, and on February 9, 2006—a year to the day after the planting of the sycamore at Arlington National Cemetery—Roosa family members presented Stu's posthumous Ambassadors of Exploration award to the Astronaut Hall of Fame in Titusville, Florida.

Joan was in a wheelchair, but smiled brightly as family members posed for photos with officials from NASA and the Astronaut Hall of Fame in front of the *Kitty Hawk* Command Module, which was on display at that facility at the time (it was later transferred to the Apollo-Saturn V Center display building at the nearby Kennedy Space Center).

Al Worden was at the presentation ceremony, and recalled: "When Stu's moon rock went to the Astronaut Hall of Fame down at the Cape, I made a point of being there to honor him, and to see Joan and the rest of his family. By then, I felt like I'd known Joan all my life."

Chris and Rosemary attended the christening of the USNS *Alan Shepard* (T-AKE 3), a dry cargo/ammunitions ship (described in Navy jargon as a "combat logistics force vessel"), in San Diego on December 6, 2006. It is in the *Lewis and Clark* class of "underway replenishment ships," and is 689 feet long, has a 106-foot beam, and displaces 42,000 tons.

Also in attendance at the christening were Shepard family members, Apollo astronauts Gene Cernan and Bill Anders, and Ed Buckbee.

Chris recalled that at the christening, Anders told him that he respected how the Roosa kids had all turned out to be decent adults.

Roosa's friend Farouk El-Baz had become the recipient of perhaps an even-more-unique honor regarding a vessel's moniker (albeit in the entertainment field). The executive producer of the television series *Star Trek: The Next Generation*, Rick Berman, had been a sound technician for a film crew that had profiled El-Baz during the Apollo program, and many years later, Berman named one of the shuttle craft seen in the series the *El-Baz*.

Joan's health continued to decline, and she passed away on October 30, 2007. The Roosas' marriage had been based on simple and permanent dedication to each other, and Chris noted that she had had been involved with "the astronaut career" as much as her husband had been.

"She went through it with him," the oldest Roosa son observed.

Joan was buried in Arlington on top of her husband's casket, and the headstone was updated.

Danny Roosa died in March of 2008.

—∿∿—

January 29, 2011: One Baby Boomer who had an apparent predilection for alliteration in his manner of speech pronounced the event to have been "supper in the shadow of a Saturn V."

The Apollo 14 40th Anniversary Soirée was sponsored by the Astronaut Scholarship Foundation, a non-profit organization founded in 1984 as the Mercury Seven Foundation by the six surviving Mercury astronauts, Gus Grissom's widow Betty, flight surgeon Dr. William Douglas, and Orlando businessman Henri Landwirth. Other astronauts from later programs eventually came onboard, and the name change occurred in 1995. To date, the ASF has awarded nearly $3 million in scholarships to deserving students. Apollo 15 CMP Al Worden had been serving as the organization's chairman of the Board of Directors since 2005 when the benefit to honor Ed Mitchell and the memories of Al Shepard and Stu Roosa was scheduled.

Attendance was limited to fifty ticket-purchasers. In addition to Mitchell, veteran astronauts who attended the event were, in alphabetical order, Neil Armstrong, Alan Bean, Gene Cernan, Walt Cunningham, Fred Haise, Bruce McCandless, Rusty Schweickart, Dave Scott, Tom Stafford, and Al Worden.

The attendees appeared to be mostly affluent Baby Boomers, almost all male, and the relatively small size of the private function added to its exclusivity, intimacy, and meaningfulness.

The evening began with a champagne reception at a resort in Cape Canaveral. Worden was an exuberant host, offering an upbeat opening statement before turning the microphone over to Laura Shepard Churchley and Rosemary Roosa, who led a toast to their departed fathers. The two daughters of the deceased members of the Apollo 14 crew had spent an extended time communicating with each other to prepare for the event, and both of their statements were heartfelt and touching. Rosemary popped a cork on a bottle of champagne, proclaiming that she was launching it to the Moon, and the room was filled with laughter and applause.

Astronauts and family members then boarded a bus for the Apollo-Saturn V Center on the Kennedy Space Center complex, and were followed by a second bus bearing the paying guests.

Before the second bus left the resort, however, what may have struck some Boomers as a definitive example of synchronicity occurred—or maybe it was just bizarre timing—as actor Adam West, the title character in television's "Batman" series in the mid-'60s, strode through the lobby as the attendees were waiting to board. Prior to his role as the Caped Crusader on TV, West had starred in a 1964 movie titled *Robinson Crusoe on Mars*, which has been pronounced by many sci-fi buffs to have been a cult classic.

Several hundred feet long, the Apollo-Saturn V Center houses the giant rocket that Stu Roosa had privately proclaimed to have been his, along with other exhibits of other equipment and memorabilia from the glory days of the Space Race, including a section of a moon rock that visitors can touch.

A recent addition to the facility is the Apollo Treasures Gallery, which opened in 2009. Included in the collection of artifacts is the Apollo 14 Command Module, and Alan Shepard's space suit from that mission.

The approximately 100 participants had the huge facilities to themselves for the banquet. More casual schmoozing went on among astronauts, family members and guests. All of the veteran spacemen seemed to be enjoying themselves. A silent auction was conducted to raise more funds for the ASF, and the featured item was a 4 X 6-inch American flag that had flown to the Moon inside Ed Mitchell's Personal Preference Kit.

One intriguing sight was that of Armstrong and Scott conversing briefly with each other for an extended time. No would-be hangers-on bothered the two moonwalkers, who had survived one of America's earlier space crises in March of 1966, onboard Gemini VIII, which had tumbled out of control due to a thruster malfunction while practicing primeval docking maneuvers in orbit.

Tables were set up under the S-II second stage, with an astronaut designated to sit at almost every table, although Armstrong and Mitchell sat next to each other at the center table.

Following dinner, the group assembled in the Apollo Treasures Gallery for the evening's program, which was hosted by CNN News correspondent John Zarella. Special guests, such as retired Shuttle astronaut Bob Springer, and Kennedy Space Center Director Robert Cabana, a veteran of four Shuttle flights, were introduced, and Worden introduced a brief video presentation that described the purpose and works of the Astronaut Scholarship Foundation, after which Zarella called on several veteran astronauts to give brief remarks. Standing at a lectern in front of the scorched, cone-shaped Apollo 14 Command Module, each spacefarer presented recollections about that mission and its crew members.

In particular, Neil Armstrong's short speech was impressive and eloquent. The first human being to set foot on another world spoke in layman's terms for the benefit of the attendees, without coming across as more intellectual, as Armstrong exuded the impression that he was talking *with* the attendees instead of talking *to* them. He stressed the importance of the Apollo 14 mission as the first to the lunar highlands, and after noting the diverse backgrounds of the crew, pointed out that Messrs. Shepard, Roosa and Mitchell meshed together, as a crew, "like the gears of a fine Swiss watch." Armstrong carried the timepiece analogy a step further, noting that Swiss watches are known for precision, and precision was a key component of the success of the Apollo 14 mission.

Ed Mitchell was pronounced by Zarella to be "the man of the hour," and the Apollo 14 LMP's remarks closed out the presentation. In a clear voice that sounded both confident and humble, Mitchell proudly acknowledged the accomplishments of the three Apollo 14 crew members that had gone to the Moon forty years earlier in the vehicle that was on display immediately behind him. He also sang the praises of the Astronaut Scholarship Foundation and its efforts to assist students who had the potential to contribute to the ongoing evolution of technology.

It was a commendable way to wrap up the program, and following dessert, the two buses took the attendees back to the resort in Cape Canaveral, leaving many of the individuals who had come to the event with some magnificent memories of a once-in-a-lifetime occasion.

—∿∿—

Al Worden is philosophical about America's earliest space programs and the passing of many of its participants, as the history of the ambitious, cutting-edge days of Mercury, Gemini, and Apollo become relegated to books and television documentaries. He noted that for all of the competitive "scrambling for a space flight" among astronauts in Houston during the Space Race, perhaps the fact that even astronauts are mortal seems to have given the space veterans a different type of camaraderie in their sunset years that didn't exist during the Sixties and the first half of the Seventies.

"Members of my peer group have started going," the Apollo 15 CMP reflected. "I think there's a sense of realism about it, and I've actually seen more of a 'coming together'—of surviving astronauts—just in the last few years."

Asked if the Roosa children should be told why they should be proud of their father, Worden replied, "It's more like 'I *know* you're proud of your dad, because he was a self-made man. He got himself through college, was a fire jumper, got into the Air Force, test pilot school, the Apollo program. Those weren't easy things to do; you had to be pretty capable. Most of us in test pilot school would have been very happy just to test airplanes, but we had a chance to go into space. So I know you're already very proud of him. NASA was proud of him too, and so was America. He was one of the very best.'"

—∿∿—

The advent of the internet has brought space history enthusiasts across the planet closer together, and some sites have even discussed the "what if" scenarios of cancelled Apollo missions. What's more, "reproductions" of a curious embroidered patch appeared in the marketplace, and later, on internet auction sites such as eBay. It has no official or legitimate history, and is most likely the "wishful thinking" creation of a space buff.

It's a so-called "Apollo 20" mission patch, and has an image of two astronauts riding on a Lunar Roving Vehicle (LRV), a battery-powered, four-wheeled "Moon buggy" that was utilized on the Apollo 15, 16, and 17 missions.

The "Apollo 20" mission patch bears the surnames of Stuart Roosa, Don Lind, and Jack Lousma.

OUTRO

E-mail from an undisclosed location in Iraq

5 February 2009

This evening, I had an emotional moment: I was sitting in a compound that had a bar. The bar is called the "HVT Bar" - short for "High Value Target." It was a tough day at work and I was drinking a beer. The TV was on and I happened to glance up and see the Armed Forces Network doing a short blurb, "On this day in history...." Though the mute button was on, I could see various scenes from the Korean War in 1951, the flooding in mid-America in 1954, and other similar events of historic note. Suddenly I saw familiar footage: the Apollo 14 flight in 1971. The review closed with Alan Shepard hitting the golf ball on the Moon. It got me thinking of my father. With all the work here, I hadn't been paying attention to the dates. This time, 38 years ago, my father was circling the Moon.

I finished my beer and headed back to my POD. The days here are long and I needed to get some sleep before work the next day. As I walked out, I noticed the Moon was directly over my head. With a thin layer of clouds, the light created a circle around the moon. I started to imagine in what phase the Moon might have been at that time, 38 years ago.

It is hard to believe he has been dead for over fourteen years. I wondered what he would think of me today. I know as a parent he would be nervous of me being in a war zone, just as he was during Desert Storm. I know he would have been proud of me for being in a war zone, just as he was during Desert Storm.

I think everyone who has lost a parent ponders these same questions: "Would they've been proud?" "Would they've thought I was doing the right thing?" "What would he think of my life?" I just know that I miss him and I love him very much. Looking at the Moon brought a tear to my eye. I may not know what I will accomplish in life, but I can only wish to have the same magnitude of impact as he did. He was an amazing man.

On a different note, I am just over half way through this tour. While the days are long, I feel a sense of accomplishment at the end of each day. The weather has been very nice and enjoyable. We still have random incoming rockets and mortars, but overall the situation is good. The elections in Iraq went smoothly. Not like when I was here before with suicide bombers, VEIDS, violence, and mass abstention from the polls. There is still some concern regarding what will happen when results are released. We will wait and see.

Best regards,
Christopher

AFTERWORD AND ACKNOWLEDGMENTS

Believe it or not, this project began with a conversation with a rock star. No name-dropping intended, but here's the actual chronology:

STYX guitarist Tommy Shaw and I grew up in Montgomery, Alabama (he's three years younger than me), and while my so-called musical aspirations in the Sixties were those of the stereotypical teenager who bashed away on a cheap-and-barely-in-tune guitar, most of the musicians around town—amateurs *and* pros—knew Tommy was capable of becoming a participant in the proverbial "big time," and he proceeded to do exactly that.

Several decades later, I had established what seemed to be a decent rapport with Tommy and other STYX members, having done numerous interviews with them for *Vintage Guitar Magazine*, and I also had a courteous and professional relationship with STYX's management and road crew. Each year, I would try to get to at least one of their concerts in my area, where I'd show up early, get the appropriate press passes, and distribute copies of the magazine backstage to bands members, guitar technicians, and other tour personnel prior to the show.

Such was the scenario in the spring of 2003 when the Missus and I went to hear the band at the Grand Casino in Gulfport, Mississippi. STYX was out on tour promoting a new album called *Cyclorama*, and the afternoon prior to the concert, several members of the band and road crew, including Shaw, had visited Marines at a nearby military installation, the event having been set up by a U.S. Marine Corps officer named Christopher Roosa (although I didn't know the name of that individual at the time).

As expected, the veteran rockers put on a professional and enjoyable show that night.

A few years later, my family heard Apollo 15 Command Module Pilot Al Worden speak at the Kennedy Space Center's "Astronaut Encounter" presentation hall; we were there as average tourists, and I was, of course, fascinated—this guy was one of the 24 people who had made the most ambitious voyage of exploration ever attempted.

I'd recently read Andrew Smith's *MOONDUST: In Search Of The Men Who Fell To Earth*, and had enjoyed the way he tried to figure in the "human factor" of the moonwalkers' personalities.

And after hearing Worden's presentation, a light bulb flickered on in my noggin.

It had always seemed to me that the Apollo Command Module Pilots were the "forgotten" members of the Moon program, since they had to remain in orbit while their two fellow crew members walked on the surface of the hostile, alien world that the human species has revered ever since it gazed skyward.

But the half-dozen CMPs on Apollos 11, 12, 14, 15, 16, and 17 had been the most isolated human beings in history. The point could be made that Apollo 10 CMP John Young was isolated as well, but on that flight, the LM didn't land on the Moon, but remained in lunar orbit; i.e., Young wasn't on the far side of the Moon, out of communication with Earth, while his fellow crewmen was on the lunar surface on the near side, as was the case for the CMPs for the landing missions.

And following the historic first Moon landing in July of 1969, Ian Anderson of Jethro Tull even wrote a song about such abject solitude, "For Michael Collins, Jeffrey, and Me," which appeared on the band's third album, *Benefit*. The song speculated about the "left behind" and/ or "loneliness" aspects of what the Apollo 11 CMP might have been experiencing (and curiously, Anderson's son-in-law, Andrew Lincoln, would portray Collins several decades later in a British docudrama about the Apollo 11 saga).

Worden's talk at KSC prompted me to do my own speculating, about the viability of a collection of extended profiles of Apollo Command Module Pilots. While I had enjoyed Smith's "quest" approach in his profiles of moonwalkers in *Moondust*, I resolved that anything I might attempt about a somewhat-similar subject would be straightforward, and would be written in third person, instead of taking a first-person/"personal journalism" approach. I could always comment about the space program—past, present, or future—in my newspaper column.

More than one individual with whom I broached the idea of an Apollo CMP book thought it was a decent idea, averring that their part in the history of space travel had been perhaps overlooked.

"Yeah," said a bookstore owner, "I always sorta wondered about those guys; you never really knew much about them."

"So close, yet so far," said another acquaintance, confirming a stereotypical statement/point of view of a lot of folks about CMPs.

And I happened to mention my idea to Tommy Shaw, who not only opined that "Back then, the astronauts were about as 'rock star' as it got," but cited his friendship with Col. Roosa as well. I asked the guitarist to be an intermediary regarding an introduction to the oldest son of the Apollo 14 CMP, and Shaw followed through.

As it turned out, however, the proposed book of CMP profiles had more than one flat tire before it even attempted to get cranked up—two of the six potential subjects, Roosa and Evans, were deceased, and more than one of the remaining CMPs apparently wasn't interested in participating. Michael Collins had written his own memoir in the mid-Seventies without a ghost writer (and many space enthusiasts have considered *Carrying The Fire* to be one of the better personal histories of the Apollo program). Another CMP was reportedly working on his own book. Accordingly, my original concept never got underway.

But for some reason, I continued to do some research regarding Stuart Roosa, and the more I delved into his past, the more intriguing it became. Here was a guy who had taken a decidedly different path to an Apollo spacecraft, and ultimately, the decision was made to concentrate on his story alone. I'd ghosted an autobiography before, but Roosa was deceased, so it would mean tracking down as many friends, relatives, former NASA astronauts and Apollo program officials as possible. I would also be soliciting the assistance of other space enthusiasts, historians, curators, and authors, some of whom lived in other countries.

And the vast majority of people I contacted eagerly agreed to help out. "Stu was one of the good guys," one former Apollo astronaut said succinctly, when I first approached him.

One interesting (and much-appreciated-by-me) response to my inquiry was that of Apollo 12 LMP Alan Bean, who advised that he couldn't offer me any personal input because he did not have any involvement with Roosa in mutual training programs or flights, but he gave me contact information for several other potential sources who came through.

Accordingly, my heartfelt thanks goes out to the following individuals, in alphabetical order, for their input and assistance:

James Allen, Ian Anderson, Neil Armstrong, Cathy Beals, Alan Bean, Al Boucher, Vance Brand, Ed Buckbee, Eugene Cernan, Andy Chaikin, John Charles, Walt Cunningham, Jimmie Dollard, Charlie Duke, Dotty Duke, Farouk El-Baz, Lucy Farrow, Donna Lantow Fettig, Francis French, Colin Fries, Stephen Garber, Fred Haise, Hank Hartsfield, Ed Hengeveld, Jeff Hill, Bob Jacobs, Claire Johnson, Shelly Kelly, Bert Klineburger, Dick Knapinski, Karen Kornegay, Jim Landreth, Linn LeBlanc, Jim Lovell, Richard McColman, Dorothy McKeever, Bob McKinley, Edgar Mitchell, Charley Moseley, Luigi Pizzimenti, Kim Poor, Sally Poor, Pat Reeder, Laura Rochon, Allen Roosa,

Christopher Roosa, Dana Roosa, Jack Roosa, Rosemary Roosa, Jennifer Ross-Nazzal, Todd Sampsel, Harrison Schmitt, Rusty Schweickart, Dave Scott, Tommy Shaw, Chuck Sheley, Dan Silva, Bert Ulrich, Otha Vaughan Jr., Bruce Watson, Clarence Wheatley, Karen Williams, David Woods, Al Worden.

I hope to goodness I haven't left anyone out, and in particular, I need to thank Mr. French, the Director of Education for the San Diego Air and Space Museum, for his tireless direction and encouragement. Francis and I bounced ideas, questions, comments and suggestions off of each other via e-mail on an almost-daily basis for many months, and as busy as he was with his own museum and literary projects, he always took time to respond promptly to my inquiries or correct any facet where I was headed down the wrong path, chronology-wise and/or accuracy-wise. His detailed replies were earnest and straightforward, simply because he wanted to see the Stu Roosa story finally imparted in print. He also conducted an important interview regarding Roosa with Al Worden (and French is an Englishter, by the way).

The time, travel, and expense it took to research this book would probably have been considered worth it to almost any space history buff/penguin like me (but I had to sell a few guitars to finance some of the trips to places like San Diego and south Florida). Some of the interviews with key astronauts were conducted in their respective residences, and not only were they hospitable, they seemed to "open up" once I made it obvious that I'd done my homework in advance. One wonders how many of their neighbors know of their accomplishments.

And on one occasion during the work-in-progress phase, I updated Francis French about who I'd visited and what I'd accomplished, and he rightly opined that the veteran astronauts would usually give an interviewer as much time as needed if the interviewer demonstrated that he/she had done a lot of preparatory research and knew what he/she was talking about, and that was indeed the way most of my on-the-record conversations developed. One Apollo veteran had originally said he could talk with me for two hours, but opted to keep the conversation going for yet another hour, because he was enjoying the dialogue, and he felt my inquiries were appropriate.

One image that was memorable, for reasons I can't fully explain, happened at a resort where several astronauts were appearing at a memorabilia/art show. One evening, while I was walking back to my room after dinner, I spotted an Apollo veteran walking along a breezeway; he was carrying a small plastic container from his own room and was looking for the ice dispenser machine.

And that sight struck me as somewhat ironic. He wasn't disoriented or befuddled; the man had been to the Moon, and had returned safely, and was now, like millions of average tourists or guests at a hotel or motel, simply looking to get a bowl of ice for his own room.

The "average guy" scene just seemed to be unique, and it also seemed to validate how these heroes from the Space Race were now, as noted in the final chapter of this book (as well as the final chapter of *The Right Stuff*), being relegated to nearly-forgotten historical status while they're still alive. In contemporary American society, more citizens seem to be concerned with monitoring the lurid exploits of celebrities (past and present) rather than appreciating what science, technology, and the individuals associated with such cutting-edge career fields accomplished in the past, and what their modern counterparts are accomplishing these days...and that's not only depressing, it's scary.

My love and thanks go out, once again, to Gail and Elizabeth for their patience and understanding. Thanks also to Pop, Caroline, and Mr. Robert.

Glenn Mackey, Col., USAF (Ret.) deserves a tip of the guitar headstock for another much-appreciated pre-submission editing effort. Special thanks to Alan Greenwood and Kim Price for ongoing writing opportunities.

I'd also like to acknowledge Hartley Peavey's continued encouragement and support, and here's yet another "read between the lines" salute to the Messrs. Spilman for encouraging me to become a full-time writer.

One final experience regarding this biography occurred just as it was about to go to the publisher: I had attended the Astronaut Scholarship Foundation's Apollo 14 40th Anniversary Soirée on January 29, 2011, and a few weeks later, I received a professionally-assembled packet from the organization that contained a photo CD, a DVD of the program, and an 8 X 10 color photo of Ed Mitchell and me posing in front of *Kitty Hawk* (all attendees got such a photo op).

A portion of the interior of the Command Module can be seen through the hatch, which is sealed with a piece of clear Plexiglas. Directly behind Mitchell and me, the middle seat of the CM is visible.

That seat was assigned to Stu Roosa during the Apollo 14 mission.

Call it karma, synchronicity, or whatever, but noticing that unique juxtaposition gave me a slight case of the willies.

—Willie G. Moseley
March 2011

246

BIBLIOGRAPHY AND REFERENCES

Buckbee, Ed, with Wally Schirra. *The Real Space Cowboys*. Burlington. Ontario, Canada: Apogee Books, 2005.

Cernan, Eugene, with Don Davis. *The Last Man On The Moon*. New York: St. Martin's Press, 1999.

Chaikin, Andrew. *A Man On The Moon*. 4th ed. New York: Penguin Group (USA) Inc., 2007.

Chaikin, Andrew, with Victoria Kohl. *Voices From The Moon*. New York: Viking Studio, 2009.

Collins, Michael. *Carrying The Fire: An Astronaut's Journeys*. New York: Farrar, Straus & Giroux, 1974.

Cunningham, Walter, with Mickey Herskowitz. *The All-American Boys*. New York: Mcmillan, 1977.

French, Francis, and Colin Burgess. *Into That Silent Sea: Trailblazers Of The Space Era, 1961-1965*. Lincoln, Nebraska: University of Nebraska Press 2007.

French, Francis, and Colin Burgess. *In The Shadow Of The Moon: A Challenging Journey To Tranquility, 1965-1969*. Lincoln, Nebraska: University of Nebraska Press, 2007.

Irwin, James B., with William A. Emerson, Jr. *To Rule the Night*. Philadelphia: Holman (Lippincott), 1973.

Jones, Lloyd S. *U.S. Fighters*. Fallbrook, California: Aero Publishers, Inc., 1975.

Klineburger, Bert, *International Hunter, 1945-1999: Hunting's Greatest Era*. Long Beach, California: Sportsmen on Film, Inc. 1999.

Kranz, Gene. *Failure Is Not An Option: Mission Control From Mercury To Apollo 13 And Beyond*. New York: Simon & Schuster, 2000.

Lovell, Jim, and Jeffrey Kluger. *Apollo 13*. New York: Houghton Mifflin, 2000.

Pogue, William R. *But for the Grace of God: An Autobiography of an Aviator and Astronaut*. Rogers, Arkansas: Soar with Eagles, 2011.

Schirra, Walter M., Jr., with Richard N. Billings. *Schirra's Space*. Boston: Quinlan, 1988.

Shepard, Alan, and Deke Slayton (with Jay Barbree and Howard Benedict). *Moon Shot*. Atlanta: Turner Publishing Inc., 1994.

Slayton, Donald K., with Michael Cassutt. *Deke! U.S. Manned Space From Mercury To The Shuttle*. New York: Forge, 1994.

Smith, Andrew. *Moondust: In Search Of The Men Who Fell To Earth*. New York: Harper-Collins, 2005.

Watkins, Billy. *Apollo Moon Missions: The Unsung Heroes*. Westport, Connecticut. Praeger, 2006.

Wolfe, Tom. *The Right Stuff*. New York: Farrar, Strauss & Giroux, 1979.

Woods, W. David. *How Apollo Flew To The Moon*. Berlin/Heidelberg/New York: Praxis Publishing, 2008.

Worden, Al, with Francis French. *Falling To Earth: An Apollo 15 Astronaut's Journey To The Moon*. Washington, D.C.: Smithsonian Books, 2011.

—⁓—

Apollo 14: The NASA Mission Reports (Robert Godwin, editor). Burlington. Ontario, Canada: Apogee Books, 2000.

Apollo 14 Onboard Voice Transcription (NASA document)

Apollo 14 Air/Ground Transcript Index (NASA document)

—⁓—

Periodical articles

"Apollo Streaks For Splashdown After Smashing Lunar Success." *The Atlanta Journal,* February 9, 1971.

"Astronaut Fulfills Dream, Returns Triumphantly." *The Rogers County Observer*, March 25, 1971

Becker, Lyle. "Mankind's Highest Adventure Is Exploration, Roosa Says." *The Claremore Daily Progress,* March 26, 1971.

Becker, Lyle. "Roosas Go To Houston." *The Claremore Daily Progress*, March 28, 1971.

Gann, Ernest K. "The Magnificent Apollos." *Flying*, September 1970.

"He May Describe Moon In A Philosophical Way." *Today*, January 31, 1971.

"He's Best Trained To Take Pilot's Seat." *Today*, January 31, 1971.

LaMont, Sanders. "Apollo 14: "We're Ready." *Today*, January 31, 1971.

LaMont, Sanders. "Veteran Pilot Dominates Every Bird He Commands." *Today*, January 31, 1971.

Larkin, Larry. "Roosa Feels 'Right At Home'." *The Claremore Daily Progress*, March 26, 1971.

"Last Apollo Astronaut Trains At Ellyson." *Gosport*, June 2, 1967.

"Moonwalk Plans Still Up In Air." *Orlando Evening Star*, February 1, 1971.

"Roosa Is Coming Home." *The Claremore Daily Progress*, March 25, 1971.

"Stuart Returns For Homecoming." *The Rogers County Observer*, March 25, 1971.

The Congressional Record—House. March 2, 1971.

The Congressional Record—Senate. March 2, 1971.

The Congressional Record—Hearings Before The Committee On Science And Astronautics, U.S. House of Representatives. March 2, 1971.

———

Video

The Right Stuff, Ladd Company, 1983.

For All Mankind, Apollo Associates/FAM Productions, 1989.

The Other Side Of The Moon, Lemle Pictures, 1990.

From The Earth To The Moon, Home Box Office, 1998.

"ABC News," January, 1971.

"CBS Evening News," January 1971.

"NBC Nightly News," January, 1971.

ABOUT THE AUTHOR

A self-described "child of the Space Race," author/columnist/lecturer Willie G. Moseley came of age in Montgomery, Alabama during the original Civil Rights Movement. And while he paid attention to the historical changes that were unfolding in the Deep South in the Sixties (and would write about such occurrences decades later), he was, like millions of other people around the globe, fascinated by the primeval efforts of the human species to journey into outer space, and paid close attention to the events that were taking place on the Atlantic coast of Florida and somewhere inside the Soviet Union.

Moseley is the Senior Writer for *Vintage Guitar Magazine*. He began writing for that periodical in 1989, and in the ensuing decades, has interviewed hundreds of guitar players and builders. He also presently serves as News Editor/columnist/photographer for *The Tallassee Tribune*. He has been collecting guitars (with a current emphasis on basses and custom-made instruments) since 1972.

Willie resides in central Alabama with his wife Gail, daughter Elizabeth, and their pet Schnauzhund, "Josie."

This is his eighth book.

INDEX

253

255

Printed in the USA
CPSIA information can be obtained
at www.ICGtesting.com
BVHW040539170823
668633BV00002B/10